THE ANALYSIS OF BEHAVIOR

A Program for Self-Instruction

THE ANALYSIS
OF BEHAVIOR

JAMES G. HOLLAND and B. F. SKINNER

Harvard University

McGRAW-HILL *Book Company, Inc.*   1961
New York   Toronto   London

Library of Congress Catalog Card Number: 61-11128

ISBN 07-029565-4
202122232425 HDBP 765

TO THE INSTRUCTOR

Edward Thorndike and Arthur Gates in their *Elementary Principles of Education*, published in 1929, wrote, "If, by a miracle of mechanical ingenuity, a book could be so arranged that only to him who had done what was directed on page one would page two become visible, and so on, much that now requires personal instruction could be managed by print." The present volume is perhaps the beginning of the fulfillment of this dream. Nothing miraculous was required. A simple type of teaching machine achieves the result by taking the student through a carefully prepared sequence of steps (generally items to be completed) so designed that he usually takes each step successfully. Early steps in the sequence prepare him for later, more advanced material.

Simple as this may seem, efforts to produce effective teaching machines were for a long time unsuccessful. Patents go back well into the nineteenth century. The wish of Thorndike and Gates was not fulfilled in their day, even though Sidney Pressey saw the need for instrumentation. What was lacking in early efforts was a set of techniques for analyzing and controlling behavior. Such techniques have gradually emerged from an experimental analysis of behavior and from its extension to the verbal field. What appears to be a revolution in education, beginning only six years ago, is now under way as scholars prepare programs in areas ranging from beginning arithmetic to calculus, from modern behaviorism to the Old Testament, from spelling and English grammar to many modern languages, from biology and physics to medical-school courses, and in hundreds of fields of industrial education.

Machine programs share with the individual tutor many advantages over other techniques of teaching: (1) Each student advances at his own rate, the fast learner moving ahead rapidly while the slower learner moves at a speed convenient for him. (2) The student moves on to advanced material only after he has thoroughly mastered earlier stages. (3) Because of this gradual progression and with the help of certain techniques of hinting and prompting, the student is almost always right. (4) The student is continuously active and receives immediate confirmation of his success. (5) Items are so constructed that the student must comprehend the critical point in order to supply the answer. (6) "Concept" is represented in the program by many examples and syntactical arrangements, in an effort to maximize generalization to other situations. (7) A record of students' responses furnishes the programmer with valuable information for future revisions. [The present program has been thoroughly revised twice, and minor changes have been made from time to time. The number of errors made by students was halved (reduced to about 10 per cent) as a result of the first revision.]

Earlier versions of this material have been widely used as models for programming other subject matter. The authors would like to believe that it has been helpful not only as a model but in teaching some elementary aspects of the science from which this type of programming emerged. This program is offered, however, mainly as a teaching instrument to be used in an introductory course in psychology emphasizing the analysis of behavior. The material has been thoroughly tested on more than seven hundred undergraduates at Harvard and Radcliffe, and the authors have profited from comments by many psychologists who have used the material in other institutions.

TO THE STUDENT

With this book the student should be able to instruct himself in that substantial part of psychology which deals with the analysis of behavior—in particular the explicit prediction and control of the behavior of people. The practical importance of such a science scarcely needs to be pointed out, but understanding and effective use of the science require fairly detailed knowledge. This program is designed to present the basic terms and principles of the science. It is also designed to reveal the inadequacy of popular explanations of behavior and to prepare the student for rapidly expanding extensions into such diverse fields as social behavior and psychopharmacology, space flight and child care, education and psychotherapy. This book is itself one application of the science.

How to Use the Book

The material was designed for use in a teaching machine. The teaching machine presents each item automatically. The student writes his response on a strip of paper revealed through a window in the machine. He then operates the machine to make his written response inaccessible, though visible, and to uncover the correct response for comparison.

Where machines are not available, a programmed textbook such as this may be used. The correct response to each item appears on the following page, along with the next item in the sequence. Read each item, write your response on a separate sheet of paper, and then turn the page to see whether your answer is correct. If it is incorrect, mark an "x" beside it. Then read and answer the next question, and turn the page again to check your answer.

Writing out the answer is essential. It is also essential to write it *before* looking at the correct answer. When the student, though well-intentioned, glances ahead without first putting down an answer of his own, he commits himself to only a vague and poorly formulated guess. This is not effective and in the long run makes the total task more difficult.

It is important to do each item in its proper turn. The sequence has been carefully designed, and occasional apparent repetitions or redundancies are there for good reason. Do not skip. If you have undue difficulty with a set, repeat it before going on to the next. A good rule is to repeat any set in which you answer more than 10 per cent of the items incorrectly. Avoid careless answers. If you begin to make mistakes because you are tired or not looking at the material carefully, take a break. If you are not able to work on the material for a period of several days, it may be advisable to review the last set completed.

The review sets will help you to find your weaknesses. When you miss an item in a review set, jot down the set number given in the answer space and review that set after you have completed the review set.

Conventions

Observe the following conventions:

1. The number of words needed to complete an item is indicated by the number of blanks. Thus "___" indicates a one-word response, whereas "__ __" indicates a two-word response. When asterisks (* * *) are used in place of blanks, fill in as many words as you think necessary to respond to the item.

2. The abbreviation TT calls for a technical term. When it is used, a nontechnical word is incorrect.

3. There are often several reasonably equivalent responses, and it would be a waste of time to list them all. This is particularly true when the response is nontechnical. Use reasonable judgment in deciding whether your response is synonymous with the printed form. Score it correct if it is.

JAMES G. HOLLAND

B. F. SKINNER

ACKNOWLEDGMENTS

Unlike conventional textbooks, this program omits detailed citations of data within the textual material itself. This is because the program includes only material which the student is taught. We are nonetheless indebted to the many scientists who have contributed to this analysis of behavior. Quantitative data have been used from the following sources:

Anliker, J., and Mayer, J. Operant conditioning technique for studying feeding patterns in normal and obese mice. *J. appl. Psychol.*, 1956, *8*, 667–670. (Set 28.)

Azrin, N. H. Effects of punishment intensity. *J. exp. Anal. Behav.*, 1960, *3*, 123–142. (Set 40.)

Brady, J. V. Assessment of drug effects on emotional behavior. *Science*, 1956, *123*, 1033–1034. (Set 35.)

Ferster, C. B., and Skinner, B. F. *Schedules of reinforcement.* New York: Appleton-Century-Crofts, Inc., 1957. (Sets 18, 19.)

Guttman, N. The pigeon and the spectrum and other perplexities. *Psychol. Rep.*, 1956, *2*, 449–460. (Set 22.)

Morse, W. H. An analysis of responding in the presence of a stimulus. Unpublished Ph.D. dissertation, Harvard Univer., 1955. (Set 21.)

Morse, W. H., and Herrnstein, R. J. Unpublished data. (Sets 19, 34.)

Sidman, M. Avoidance conditioning with brief shock and no exteroceptive warning signal. *Science*, 1953, *118*, 157–158. (Set 34.)

Sidman, M. By-products of aversive control. *J. exp. Anal. Behav.*, 1958, *1*, 276. (Set 35.)

Skinner, B. F. *The behavior of organisms.* New York: Appleton-Century-Crofts, Inc., 1938. (Sets 13, 26, 38.)

Pavlov, I. P. *Conditioned reflexes.* London: Oxford University Press, 1946. (Set 4.)

We are indebted to the students of Harvard's course entitled "Natural Sciences 114, Human Behavior," who gave valuable data which made possible the development of this program, and to the many persons who aided in supervision of the self-instruction room, tabulation of data, and typing of material. Particularly outstanding has been the diligent assistance of Beverly Meeker, Stella Kramer, and Dorothy Schneider.

CONTENTS

THE ANALYSIS OF BEHAVIOR

stimulus (tap on the knee)	Technically speaking, a reflex involves an eliciting stimulus in a process called elicitation. A stimulus _____ a response.
1-7	1-8
threshold	The fraction of a second which elapses between "brushing the eye" and "blink" is the _____ of the reflex.
1-15	1-16
threshold	The greater the concentration of onion juice (stimulus), the _____ the *magnitude* of the response.
1-23	1-24
elicit	In the pupillary reflex, a very bright flash of light elicits a response of greater _____ than a weak flash of light.
1-31	1-32
latency	A solution of lemon juice will not elicit salivation if the stimulus is _____ the threshold.
1-39	1-40
(1) magnitude (2) latency	Presentation of a stimulus is the "cause" of a response. The two form a(n) _____.
1-47	1-48

A doctor taps your knee (patellar tendon) with a rubber hammer to test your _____.

1-1

---

elicits

1-8

To avoid unwanted nuances of meaning in popular words, we do not say that a stimulus "triggers," "stimulates," or "causes" a response, but that it _____ a response.

1-9

---

latency

1-16

In the patellar-tendon reflex, a forceful tap elicits a strong kick; a tap barely above the threshold elicits a weak kick. Magnitude of response thus depends on the intensity of the _____.

1-17

---

greater
(higher,
larger)

1-24

Onion juice elicits the secretion of tears by the lachrymal gland. This causal sequence of events is a(n) _____.

1-25

---

magnitude
(intensity)

1-32

A response and its eliciting stimulus comprise a(n) _____.

1-33

---

below
(less than,
sub-)

1-40

The latency of a reflex is the (1) _____ between on-set of (2) _____ and _____.

1-41

---

reflex

1-48

The layman frequently explains behavior as the operation of "mind" or "free will." He seldom does this for reflex behavior, however, because the _____ is an adequate explanation of the response.

1-49

reflexes (reflex) 1-1	If your reflexes are normal, your leg _____ to the tap on the knee with a slight kick (the so-called knee jerk). 1-2
elicits 1-9	In a reflex, the stimulus and the elicited response occur in a given temporal order; first the (1) _____, then the (2) _____. 1-10
stimulus (tap) 1-17	The magnitude of a response corresponds to (is a function of) the _____ of the stimulus which elicits it. 1-18
reflex (lachrymal reflex) 1-25	When speaking technically, instead of saying onion juice "stimulates" tears; we say onion juice "_____" tears. 1-26
reflex 1-33	In a warm room, your sweat glands rapidly excrete sweat. The response is (1) _____; the stimulus is (2) _____; and the two together form a(n) (3) _____. 1-34
1) time (interval) 2) stimulus (and) response 1-41	A very hot surface brought into contact with the hand, elicits arm flexion with a(n) _____ latency than a less hot surface. 1-42
stimulus 1-49	Because the stimulus is sufficient in accounting for the reflex response, there * * * a need to explain reflex behavior with concepts of "mind" or "free will." 1-50

responds (reacts)	In the knee jerk or patellar-tendon reflex, the kick of the leg is the _____ to the tap on the knee.
1-2	1-3

(1) stimulus (2) response	A kick of the leg is _____ by a tap on the patellar tendon.
1-10	1-11

intensity (magnitude, strength)	A reflex consists of *both* a(n) (1) _____ and a(n) (2) _____, occurring in that order. The term "reflex" (3) * * * synonymous with the single term "response."
1-18	1-19

elicits	A child touching a hot surface withdraws his hand quickly. The word "quickly" suggests that the response has a short _____.
1-26	1-27

) sweating xcretion of sweat)) heat emperature, armth)) reflex	The softest touch on the surface of the eye needed to elicit a blink, marks the _____ of the stimulus.
1-34	1-35

shorter (smaller)	A very hot room causes (1) _____ sweating than a merely warm room (i.e., the response has a(n) (2) _____ magnitude).
1-42	1-43

is not	Latency is the _____ between the onset of an energy change and the onset of a response which it elicits.
1-50	1-51

response (reaction) 1-3	The stimulating *object* used by the doctor to elicit a knee jerk is a(n) ____. 1-4
elicited 1-11	The time which elapses between the onset of the stimulus and the onset of the response is called the *latency.* Thus the time between tap and kick is the ____ of the knee-jerk reflex. 1-12
(1) stimulus (2) response (3) is not 1-19	When a person is startled by a loud noise, his sudden movement is his (1) ____ to the noise which has acted as a (2) ____. The two together are called a(n) (3) ____. 1-20
latency 1-27	In withdrawing the hand from a hot surface, arm movement is a(n) (1) ____ which is elicited by a painful (2) ____ to the hand. 1-28
threshold 1-35	A cat held upside down and dropped will land on its feet. In this "righting reflex," acceleration due to gravity is the main ____ for righting. 1-36

(1) more
    (greater)
(2) greater
    (larger)
 	
1-43
	The greater the concentration of onion vapor reaching the surface of the eye, the (1) ____ the magnitude of the response, and the (2) ____ the latency.
	
	1-44

time (interval, period) 1-51	The (1) ____ of a stimulus is the intensity which is barely sufficient to (2) ____ a(n) (3) ____. 1-52

hammer (mallet) 1-4	The *stimulus* which elicits a knee jerk is the ____ delivered by the so-called stimulus object or hammer. 1-5
latency 1-12	The weakest stimulus sufficient to elicit a response marks the *threshold* of the reflex. A tap on the knee will not elicit a kick if it is below the ____. 1-13
(1) response (2) stimulus (3) reflex 1-20	If a sip of very weak lemonade does not cause salivation, the stimulus is said to be below the ____. 1-21
(1) response (2) stimulus 1-28	In the hand-withdrawal reflex, the stimulus must be intense enough to exceed the ____ or no response will occur. 1-29
stimulus 1-36	In any (1) ____, there is a stimulus which (2) ____ the response. 1-37

(1) greater
 (2) shorter
    (less,
    smaller)
 	
 1-44
	The greater the concentration of lemon juice sipped, the (1) ____ the flow of saliva, and the (2) ____ the interval of time between onsets of stimulus and response.
	
	 1-45

(1) threshold (2) elicit (3) response 1-52	In a reflex, a(n) (1) ____ always precedes a(n) (2) ____. 1-53

tap (blow)	In the knee-jerk reflex, we call the rubber hammer the (1) _____ _____ and the tap or blow, the (2) _____.
1-5	1-6
threshold	If you blink when something brushes your eye, the _____ is a response.
1-13	1-14
threshold	In the salivary reflex, the (1) _____ (food) precedes the response (secretion of saliva) by an interval of time called the (2) _____.
1-21	1-22
threshold	A light flashed into the eye elicits constriction of the pupil. This sequence is called the pupillary _____.
1-29	1-30
(1) reflex (2) elicits	Sticking a finger in your throat may (1) _____ vomiting. (2) _____ is the response. The (3) _____ is tactual (touch).
1-37	1-38
(1) greater (2) shorter (smaller)	A very bright light flashed into the eye elicits a pupillary response with a short _____.
1-45	1-46
(1) stimulus (2) response	In a reflex, the magnitude of response varies with the _____ of the stimulus.
1-53	1-54

(1) stimulus
    object
(2) stimulus
 	
       1-6
	An event is explained when its cause is identified. The "cause" or explanation of the knee jerk is, technically, the _____ which elicits it.
	
	                                         1-7
	                           ← To p. 1

blink
 	
       1-14
	A puff of air striking the eye will elicit a blink only if the force exerted by the air exceeds the _____ value.
	
	                                       1-15
	                           ← To p. 1

(1) stimulus
(2) latency
 	
       1-22
	If an actress uses onion juice on her handkerchief to elicit tears during an emotional scene, she must use enough to exceed the _____.
	
	                                       1-23
	                           ← To p. 1

reflex
 	
       1-30
	In the pupillary reflex, a flash of light is said to _____ the response.
	
	                                       1-31
	                           ← To p. 1

(1) elicit
(2) Vomiting
(3) stimulus
 	
       1-38
	If vomiting began 0.1 second after the onset of the stimulus, the reflex had a(n) _____ of 0.1 second.
	
	                                       1-39
	                           ← To p. 1

latency
 	
       1-46
	The more intense the stimulus, the greater the (1) _____ of the response, and the shorter the (2) _____ of the reflex.
	
	                                       1-47
	                           ← To p. 1

intensity (magnitude) 1-54	**End of Set**

Page 8

cannot

2-4

On the *first* occasion when a young child simply hears the word "candy," his mouth * * * water.

2-5

---

conditioning

2-9

Technically speaking, when the word "candy" is repeatedly paired with eating candy, _____ takes place.

2-10

---

nconditioned

2-14

After conditioning, the word "candy" is a conditioned stimulus which elicits salivation. In this case, salivating is the (1) _____ response in a(n) (2) _____ reflex.

2-15

---

xtinguished

2-19

A conditioned reflex is extinguished when the conditioned stimulus is repeatedly presented * * * the unconditioned stimulus.

2-20

---

nconditioned
flex

2-24

In this unconditioned hand-withdrawal reflex, heat is the _____-ed _____.

2-25

---

tinction

2-29

In reflex behavior, the process by which a new stimulus comes to elicit a response is called (1) _____. A process by which a stimulus loses the power to elicit a response is called (2) _____.

2-30

▷

In a reflex, a sufficient explanation of the response is a description of the preceding _____ .

2-1

---

will not

2-5

No learning (or conditioning) is necessary in order that candy in the mouth elicit salivation, but the word "candy" will make a child's mouth water only after some _____ has taken place.

2-6

---

conditioning

2-10

After conditioning, the word "candy" alone will elicit salivation in a conditioned reflex. The word "candy" is a learned or _____ stimulus.

2-11

---

(1) conditioned
(2) conditioned

2-15

Candy in the mouth is an unconditioned stimulus which elicits salivation. In this case, salivating is the (1) _____ response in a(n) (2) _____ reflex.

2-16

---

without
(in the
absence of)

2-20

In extinction, the word "candy" is repeatedly presented * * * the unconditioned stimulus.

2-21

---

uncondition (-ed)
stimulus

2-25

In the unconditioned hand-withdrawal reflex, the movement of the arm is the _____ _____ .

2-26

stimulus 2-1	When food in the mouth elicits the secretion of saliva, the whole series of events is called a(n) ____. 2-2
conditioning (learning, experience) 2-6	When a child has often had candy in his mouth after hearing the word "candy," the word alone may cause ____. 2-7
conditioned 2-11	The word "candy" is a learned or (1) ____ stimulus. Candy in the mouth is an *un*learned or (2) ____ stimulus. 2-12
1) unconditioned 2) unconditioned 2-16	After conditioning, the word "candy" will ____ the response of salivating. (TT) 2-17
without 2-21	In conditioning, the word "candy" is repeatedly presented * * * the unconditioned stimulus. 2-22
unconditioned response 2-26	If a bell sounds 30 seconds before a hot object touches the hand (and the procedure is repeated several times), ____ will take place. 2-27

reflex (salivary reflex) 2-2	Candy put in the mouth of a child for the first time _____ salivation. 2-3
salivation (the response) 2-7	If the child is to learn to salivate to the word "candy," "candy" and eating candy must occur nearly _____. 2-8
1) conditioned 2) unconditioned 2-12	Salivation elicited by the word "candy" is a conditioned response, whereas salivation elicited by candy in the mouth is a(n) _____ response. 2-13
elicit 2-17	Conditioned stimuli presented repeatedly but not paired with unconditioned stimuli cease to elicit the response. If the word "candy" is often repeated without pairing with candy in the mouth, it * * * elicit(s) salivation. 2-18
with (just before, at the same time as) 2-22	The process by which a conditioned stimulus loses its power to elicit the conditioned response is called *extinction*. When the word "candy" is presented alone, the conditioned reflex undergoes _____. 2-23
conditioning 2-27	After conditioning, the bell will elicit movement of the arm. The conditioned stimulus is the _____. 2-28

(1) S^Ds (stimuli) (2) incompatible Set 51 **53-3**	When a person cannot recall some previously punished behavior, we say he has _____ it. **53-4** ← To p. 333

(1) (controll-)ed
 (2) reinforcing
     or
 (3) aversive
   (EITHER ORDER)
 Set 47   **53-8**
	In the laboratory, it (1) * * * possible to isolate simple functional relations; but in interpreting most events outside of the laboratory, we must be alert to the possibility of (2) _____ effects in complex situations.
	 53-9
	 ← To p. 333

(1) respondent (reflex) (2) operant Set 46 **53-13**	The goal of a science of behavior is to be able to (1) _____, (2) _____, and (3) _____ the behavior of living organisms. **53-14** ← To p. 333
counter- aggression Set 51 **53-18**	When we admit, even to ourselves, only the least punishable reasons for our behavior, we are _____. **53-19** ← To p. 333
is not Set 45 **53-23**	We sometimes speak of cause and effect. A cause is a(n) (1) _____ variable, and an effect is a(n) (2) _____ variable. The relation is a(n) (3) _____ _____ or a(n) (4) _____. **53-24** ← To p. 333

elicits 2-3	Since the young child salivates the very first time candy is put in his mouth, we _____ (can or cannot?) attribute this reflex to learning. **2-4** ← To p.9
simultaneously (together) 2-8	The technical term for one kind of learning is conditioning. The word "candy" comes to elicit salivation after _____. **2-9** ← To p.9
unconditioned 2-13	Salivation elicited by candy in the mouth is a(n) _____ response. **2-14** ← To p.9
ceases to (no longer, does not) 2-18	When the conditioned stimulus can no longer elicit the response, the conditioned reflex is said to have been extinguished. If the word "candy" is repeatedly presented alone, the conditioned salivary reflex is _____. **2-19** ← To p.9
extinction 2-23	When a man's hand is touched by a hot surface or receives an electric shock, the hand is immediately withdrawn. Since this reflex was not established by previous conditioning, it is a(n) _____ _____. **2-24** ← To p.9
bell 2-28	If the bell sounds many times without being paired with contact with a hot object, _____ will take place. **2-29** ← To p.9

(1) algebraic
    summation
(2) oscillation

Set 44   **53-2**

Reaction formation may be interpreted as behavior which removes (1) _____ which make the punishable behavior more probable; it may also be interpreted as behavior which is (2) * * * with punishable behavior.

53-3

---

many
(multiple, more than one)

Set 44   **53-7**

In self-control, the (1) controll-_____ response usually has both (2) _____ and (3) _____ consequences.

53-8

---

(1) decreased
    (lowered,
    reduced)
(2) frequently (more
    frequently, often)

Set 50   **53-12**

Sneezing which clears the upper respiratory passages is (1) _____ behavior. However, the "imitative" sneezing by the little boy who "only does it to annoy" is (2) _____ behavior.

53-13

---

(1) non-punishing
    audience
(2) extinguished

Set 52   **53-17**

A man who strikes his adversary shows _____ .

53-18

---

(1) withdrawal
    symptoms
(2) aversive stimuli
    (aversive
    conditions)
            53-22

Set 50

To eliminate undesired behavior, such as a dog's scratching a door, it * * * necessary to use aversive control.

53-23

---

(1) multiple
    (several,
    different)
(2) multiple
    (several,
    different)   **53-27**
Set 44

End of Set

(A) The conditioned reflex was discovered by Pavlov, a Russian physiologist.

(B) A dog is placed in a special room, free of extraneous stimuli.

(C) Under anesthesia, a small opening has been made in the dog's cheek and the duct of a salivary gland brought to the surface where it remains after healing. A tube fastened to the cheek leads to the next room where the experimenter can count the drops of saliva secreted.

(D) In a typical experiment, a tone is sounded several times. After an early slight disturbance has passed, the dog does not salivate in response to the tone. The tone is called a *neutral stimulus* because it is ineffective in eliciting salivation.

(E) When food powder is dropped nearby, the dog eats the powder and salivation occurs. Food powder in the dog's mouth is an *unconditioned stimulus,* and the salivation it elicits an *unconditioned response.*

(F) The sequence of food-in-mouth and salivation is called an *unconditioned reflex.*

(G) Next, a new stimulus, a tone (neutral stimulus), is presented either simultaneously with the food (unconditioned stimulus) or just before the food.

(H) The two stimuli are presented together, or paired, this way many times.

(I) When the tone is then presented alone, it elicits salivation.

(J) *Conditioning* is said to have taken place. The tone is no longer a neutral stimulus, it is a *conditioned stimulus.*

(K) In this *conditioned reflex,* salivation is the *conditioned response,* and the tone the *conditioned stimulus.*

(L) If the tone is now repeatedly presented but no longer paired with food, it loses its power to elicit salivation. The conditioned reflex is said to have been *extinguished.* The process is called *extinction.*

The letters in parentheses in the accompanying set refer to the letters above.

independent (and a) dependent variable Set 42 **53-1**	When a dog stands "not too close and not too far" from a strange object, its behavior shows (1) ____ ____. When it approaches, jumps back, approaches, jumps back, approaches, etc., it shows (2) ____. **53-2**
(1) conditioned (2) incompatible with Set 48 **53-6**	A word which "expresses multiple meanings" is controlled by * * * stimuli. **53-7**
transference Set 52 **53-11**	The effects of conditioned aversive stimuli are (1) ____ by drinking alcohol. This is shown when behavior which automatically generates aversive stimuli occurs (2) * * * under alcohol. **53-12**
isolate (analyze, study) Set 43 **53-16**	A therapist frequently tries to change his patient's behavior by acting as a(n) (1) * * * and thereby the aversive properties generated by previously punished behavior can become (2) ____. **53-17**
stimulus generalization Set 52 **53-21**	A man is said to be addicted to a drug if withholding the drug produces (1) ____ ____ which furnish (2) ____ ____. **53-22**
multiple (several) Set 43 **53-26**	A single event may have (1) ____ effects on behavior, and (2) ____ events may have a common effect. **53-27**

Set 3

PART I Reflex Behavior

Conditioned Reflexes (continued)

See exhibit on preceding page

Estimated time: 15 minutes

Turn to next page and begin ▶

neutral stimulus 3-4	In (E), the food powder is an unconditioned stimulus in the sense that conditioning * * * necessary to make it an eliciting stimulus. 3-5
together (nearly simultaneously) 3-9	If, instead of the procedure described in (G), the tone had *followed* the food, the conditions required for _____ would not have been present. 3-10
not be (be not, is not) 3-14	In (J), conditioning is said to have taken place because a previously neutral stimulus is now capable of _____ salivation. 3-15
conditioned 3-19	The conditioned response, salivation, is elicited by the conditioned stimulus, a tone. The tone and the salivation elicited comprise a(n) _____ salivary _____. 3-20
(1) conditioning (2) extinction 3-24	In Pavlov's famous experiments on conditioning, _____ was the unconditioned response. 3-25

In a functional relation, there is an observed systematic relation between a(n) * * * and a(n) * * *.

53-1

---

(1) does not
   (cannot)
(2) is not

Set 49   53-5

Inadequate self-knowledge may result because we have not yet been (1) _____ to notice some aspect of our behavior, or because we engage in behavior which is (2) * * * noticing this behavior.

53-6

) reinforcement
  (conditioning)
*) aversive stimuli
  (conditioned
  aversive stimuli)

Set 47   53-10

In psychotherapy, a patient often manifests strong love or hate toward his therapist. This is sometimes called _____.

53-11

---

activation
syndrome

Set 51   53-15

By using simple organisms with controlled histories in simple environments, we hold many variables constant in order to _____ one effective variable at a time.

53-16

---

(1) respondent
(2) operant

Set 46   53-20

Transference during psychotherapy can be interpreted as an example of _____ _____.

53-21

---

(1) controlling
(2) controlled

Set 47   53-25

A single aversive stimulus used in punishment elicits respondents, conditions other stimuli to elicit these respondents, and makes possible the conditioning of avoidance behavior. The single aversive stimulus has _____ effects.

53-26

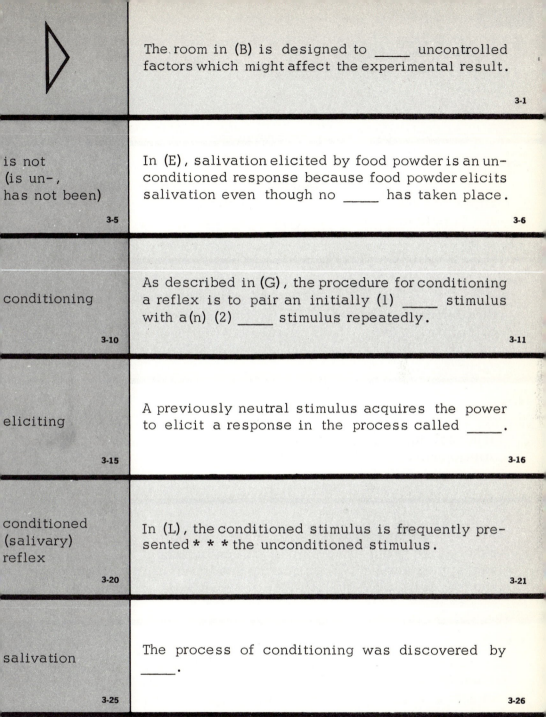

The room in (B) is designed to _____ uncontrolled factors which might affect the experimental result.

3-1

---

is not
(is un-,
has not been)

3-5

In (E), salivation elicited by food powder is an un-conditioned response because food powder elicits salivation even though no _____ has taken place.

3-6

---

conditioning

3-10

As described in (G), the procedure for conditioning a reflex is to pair an initially (1) _____ stimulus with a(n) (2) _____ stimulus repeatedly.

3-11

---

eliciting

3-15

A previously neutral stimulus acquires the power to elicit a response in the process called _____.

3-16

---

conditioned
(salivary)
reflex

3-20

In (L), the conditioned stimulus is frequently pre-sented * * * the unconditioned stimulus.

3-21

---

salivation

3-25

The process of conditioning was discovered by _____.

3-26

---

repressed

Set 48   53-4

In rationalization, a person (1) "* * * tell the whole truth" even to himself. Rationalization (2) * * * the same as lying.

53-5

---

(1) is
(2) multiple
    (many,
    various)
Set 43   53-9

In so-called self-control, the controlling response is established through (1) _____. Usually this takes place through the reduction of the (2) * * * associated with the controlled response.

53-10

---

edict, control,
nd) interpret
NY ORDER)

Set 42   53-14

The bodily malfunctions called "psychosomatic" result from prolonged elicitation of the responses characteristic of the * * *.

53-15

---

rationalizing

Set 49   53-19

By tickling his throat with a feather, a man can regurgitate poisonous food. The controlled response is a(n) (1) _____ (TT) and the controlling response is a(n) (2) _____. (TT)

53-20

---

(1) independent
(2) dependent
(3) functional
    relation
(4) law
Set 42   53-24

In self-control, the (1) _____ response affects variables in such a way as to change the probability of the (2) _____ response.

53-25

---

eliminate (remove, avoid, control) 3-1	(C) is used to obtain a measurement of the _____ of the response. 3-2
conditioning 3-6	In (F), the unconditioned reflex has (1) _____ components; an unconditioned (2) _____ and an unconditioned (3) _____ 3-7
(1) neutral (2) unconditioned (EITHER ORDER) 3-11	In (G), little or no conditioning would have occurred if the tone had preceded the food by more than a few seconds. The interval between the stimulus-to-be-conditioned and the unconditioned stimulus must be rather _____. 3-12
conditioning 3-16	In (K), the tone is called a *conditioned* stimulus because it elicits the response only after some _____ has taken place. 3-17
without (in the absence of) 3-21	In (L), the conditioned reflex has been extinguished in the sense that the stimulus has frequently been presented without being _____ with the unconditioned stimulus and has, therefore, lost its ability to elicit the response. 3-22
Pavlov 3-26	A stimulus able to elicit a response without previous conditioning is called a(n) (1) _____ _____; a stimulus able to elicit a response only after conditioning is called a(n) (2) _____ _____. 3-27

punish

52-3

A person may be unable to remember past punished behavior if a reduction in the conditioned aversive stimuli generated by covert forms of this behavior has reinforced behavior (1) _____ with it. This phenomenon is called (2) _____.

52-4

← To p. 328

extinction

52-8

Early in psychotherapy, the patient cannot recall aversive situations. He is said to _____ memories of them.

52-9

← To p. 328

punished

52-13

A patient "blocks" or shows "resistance" when he suddenly (1) _____ talking because he is about to emit (2) _____ verbal behavior.

52-14

← To p. 328

is

52-18

One possibility is that the responses which appear to be the recalling of childhood experiences are, in part, conditioned by the therapist's attentive interest in such responses. The therapist may accidentally _____ descriptions of a particular kind of experience.

52-19

← To p. 328

stimulus generalization

52-23

A patient may manifest strong "love" or "hate" toward his therapist. In so far as this is due to the therapist resembling a parent, sibling, or other person, it is an example of generalization. It is sometimes called _____.

52-24

← To p. 328

(1) non-punishing audience
(2) environment (world)
(3) body (physiology)

52-28

End of Set

magnitude (amount) 3-2	In (D), "neutral stimulus" means a tone which * * * effect on salivation before conditioning. 3-3
(1) two (2) stimulus (3) response 3-7	When a response is elicited by a stimulus without previous conditioning, the sequence is called a(n) _____ _____. 3-8
short (brief) 3-12	An important aspect of the conditioning procedure is the _____ between presentation of the initially neutral stimulus and of the unconditioned stimulus. 3-13
conditioning 3-17	Before conditioning, the tone was a(n) (1) _____ stimulus; after conditioning, the tone has become a(n) (2) _____ stimulus. 3-18
paired (presented) 3-22	In the extinction process, the _____ _____ is presented alone. 3-23
1) unconditioned stimulus 2) conditioned stimulus 3-27	A response elicited by a conditioned stimulus is a(n) (1) _____ _____; a response elicited by an unconditioned stimulus is a(n) (2) _____ _____. 3-28

conditioned aversive 52-2	Most listeners _____ verbal responses which they describe as immoral, unjust, etc. 52-3
(non-)punishing 52-7	As a non-punishing audience, the therapist arranges conditions under which the stimuli generated by talking about punished behavior lose their aversive properties through _____. 52-8
extinguished 52-12	The patient may suddenly stop talking and show signs of anxiety (that is, he may "block" or show "resistance"). This probably occurs when a response is about to occur which has been severely _____ and, therefore, strongly repressed.　52-13
reinforce 52-17	Many responses became repressed in very early childhood. When these are recalled by the patient, the accuracy of his account * * * difficult to check. 52-18
generalization 52-22	Strong emotional behavior may be evoked by a therapist if he resembles in any way people with respect to whom these emotions have been conditioned. This is sometimes called transference. It illustrates _____ _____.　52-23
changing (manipulating, controlling) 52-27	A therapist frequently tries to change his patient's behavior by acting as a(n) (1) * * * . He may also change the (2) _____ in which the patient is to live, and he may change the person's (3) _____ as with drugs, surgery, or shock treatment.　52-28

has no 3-3	Since the tone has no effect on salivation before conditioning, it is a(n) * * *. 3-4 ← To p. 15
unconditioned reflex 3-8	According to (G), conditioning will occur only if the two stimuli occur * * * in time. 3-9 ← To p. 15
time (interval, temporal relation) 3-13	The presence of a conditioned reflex is occasionally tested as in (I). It is essential that the unconditioned stimulus, food, * * * presented on these test trials. 3-14 ← To p. 15
(1) neutral (2) conditioned 3-18	A tone elicits salivation as a(n) _____ response. 3-19 ← To p. 15
conditioned stimulus 3-23	A new neutral stimulus is able to elicit a response after (1) _____ has taken place. It ceases to do so after (2) _____ has taken place. 3-24 ← To p. 15
) conditioned response) unconditioned response 3-28	To condition a reflex, a neutral stimulus is (1) _____ with a(n) (2) _____ _____. 3-29 ← To p. 15

punish 52-1	If a child is severely punished for sex play, stimuli associated with the behavior become ____ ____ stimuli. 52-2
punishment (aversive stimuli) 52-6	The psychoanalyst may listen to the "free associations" of his patient for hours and never show displeasure or shock at anything the patient says. The therapist is acting as a non-____ audience. 52-7
non-punishing 52-11	As more and more punishable behavior is emitted and not punished, conditioned aversive stimuli are ____. 52-12
repressed 52-16	The therapist may show particular interest when his patient speaks of emotional experiences. This is likely to ____ (TT) talking to the therapist about emotional experiences. 52-17
generalization 52-21	We may immediately like or dislike a stranger because he resembles someone we have known. This is stimulus ____. 52-22
change (manipulate, control, alter) 52-26	Some therapists may use drugs, electroconvulsive shock, or surgery. These therapists attempt to change behavior by ____ the body. 52-27

EXPERIMENT 1.

Pavlov placed a dog in a standard experimental situation. On repeated *conditioning* trials a tone was sounded for 5 seconds, and approximately 2 seconds later the dog was given powdered food. This pairing of tone and food powder was repeated, with trials spaced from 5 to 35 minutes apart at random intervals, for fifty trials. Trials 1, 10, 20, 30, 40, and 50 were *test* trials, that is, the tone was sounded for 30 seconds and *no* food powder was given.

I Trial Number (tone alone)	II Drops of Saliva	III Time Between Onset of Tone and Salivation (in seconds)
1	0	—
10	6	18
20	20	9
30	60	2
40	62	1
50	59	2

EXPERIMENT 2. (Do not read Experiment 2 until instructed to do so.)

A dog had been conditioned to salivate to a metronome beating at 104 ticks per minute. Several interspersed test trials (metronome ticking for 30 seconds but not followed by food powder) provided approximately 10 drops of saliva on each trial. The ticking metronome was then presented on every trial for 30 seconds without being paired with food powder. (Sufficient time was allowed between trials to avoid appreciable fatigue.) The results for this series of consecutive trials without food are presented on the following table.

I Trial Number	II Drops of Saliva	III Time Between Onset of Metronome and Salivation (in seconds)
1	10	3
2	7	7
3	8	5
4	5	4
5	7	5
6	4	9
7	3	13
8	0	—
9	0	—

015400

▷

If a person publicly says he hates his father, many persons are "shocked" or otherwise _____ (TT) his response.

52-1

---

cannot
(do not)

52-5

If incompletely repressed punished behavior is emitted, it will again be followed by _____ if the same or a similar punishing audience is present.

52-6

---

little

52-10

As free association continues, the patient may say punishable things or act in punishable ways (e.g., exhibit strong emotions). To extinguish responses to the aversive stimuli generated by this behavior, the therapist remains a(n) _____ audience.

52-11

---

extinguished
resistance

52-15

When the patient shows resistance, the therapist may use the various procedures designed to induce the patient to emit the behavior which continues to be _____ and which causes resistance.

52-16

---

reinforce
(condition)

52-20

Emitting the same response to two different but similar stimuli, only one of which was present during earlier reinforcement, is an example of stimulus _____.

52-21

---

conditioned
aversive
stimuli

52-25

In addition to providing a non-punishing audience, the therapist may recommend changing jobs, getting a divorce, etc. He is attempting to _____ environmental contingencies.

52-26

Set 4

---

followed by
(paired with,
presented 2
seconds before)

4-4

On Trial 10 (a "test" trial), the tone * * * followed by food powder.

4-5

---

(1) tone
(2) conditioned
    response

4-9

Experiment 1. The magnitudes of the conditioned response are found in Column _____.

4-10

---

conditioned
response

4-14

If the experiment had continued to Trial 60, the magnitude of the conditioned response would probably be in the vicinity of _____ drops. (IN ROUND NUMBERS)

4-15

---

minimum

4-19

Experiment 1. Conclusion: As the number of pairings of the conditioned and unconditioned stimuli increases, the latency of the conditioned reflex (1) _____ and the magnitude of the conditioned response (2) _____ until both reach a limit.

4-20

---

conditioned

4-24

When a conditioned stimulus is repeatedly presented alone, the magnitude of the conditioned response (1) _____ and the latency of the conditioned reflex (2) _____.

4-25

---

(1) conditioning
(2) extinction

4-29

End of Set

Set 52

Psychotherapy

Estimated time: 11 minutes   **Turn to next page and begin** ▶

) incompatible
) repression

52-4

Since repressed behavior is not often emitted, the conditioned aversive stimuli * * * undergo extinction.

52-5

---

repress

52-9

From the patient's point of view, the therapist is at first much like any other audience. The patient therefore emits very _____ punishable behavior.

52-10

---

(1) stops
(2) punishable
   (repressed)

52-14

When repressed behavior is emitted, in therapy, conditioned aversive stimuli may be (1) _____ ; but when a particularly punishable response is about to occur, the patient may "block" or show (2) _____ (i.e., be unable to continue to recall experiences).

52-15

---

reinforce

52-19

A therapist who has a theory that incestuous tendencies are the basis of many neuroses may show special interest in any emotional reference to parents, children, or siblings and thereby inadvertently _____ that class of verbal responses.

52-20

---

transference

52-24

Many different forms of psychotherapy have in common, the creation of a non-punishing audience which extinguishes _____ _____ _____ generated by the early stages of behavior which have been punished.

52-25

In Experiment 1, the food powder is a(n) ____ ____ for salivation.

4-1

---

was not
(is not)

4-5

On Trial 10, the initially ____ ____ is presented alone.

4-6

II

4-10

Experiment 1. Column III lists the ____ of the conditioned reflex. (TT)

4-11

---

60 (59-62)

4-15

In the early conditioning trials, while magnitudes of the conditioned responses are increasing, the latencies of the conditioned reflex are ____.

4-16

---

(1) decreases
(2) increases

4-20

READ EXPERIMENT 2 AND REFER TO IT AS NEEDED.
Experiment 2. The technical term for the data in Column II is the (1) ____ of the conditioned response and for Column III, the (2) ____.

4-21

---

(1) decreases
   (declines)
(2) increases

4-25

Experiment 2. After repeated presentations of the conditioned stimulus alone, the ____ ____ no longer occurs. (TT)

4-26

---

does not
(will not,
fails to)

51-3

When ordinary conversation generates conditioned aversive stimuli, withdrawing is _____ by a reduction in these stimuli.

51-4

← To p. 323

---

avoidance

51-8

Overthrowing a harsh dictator is similar to slapping a mosquito in that both are forms of _____-aggression.

51-9

← To p. 323

---

counter-
aggression

51-13

A criticizes B. B criticizes A in return (counter-aggression). A in defending himself stops criticizing B. B's criticism of A has received _____ reinforcement.

51-14

← To p. 323

---

has little
(has no, loses)

51-18

Many so-called "psychosomatic" disorders are bodily malfunctions resulting from prolonged elicitation of the responses characteristic of the * * *.

51-19

← To p. 323

---

reaction
formation

51-23

While preoccupied with fighting a certain type of sinful behavior, a person is * * * likely to emit that type of behavior.

51-24

← To p. 323

) incompatible
) S^D s (stimuli)

51-28

In a play, a young man is persecuted as a homosexual by a college coach who is eventually shown to be a latent homosexual. The coach's persecution of the young man may illustrate * * *.

51-29

← To p. 323

unconditioned stimulus 4-1	Experiment 1. Technically speaking, Column II reports the _____ of the response in each test trial. 4-2
neutral stimulus 4-6	Experiment 1. Column II shows that on Trial 10 there were (1) _____ drops of saliva. This is evidence that the tone is already a(n) (2) _____ _____ . 4-7
latencies (–y) 4-11	The magnitude of the conditioned response _____ appreciably as the number of conditioning trials increases until about Trial 30. 4-12
decreasing (becoming shorter) 4-16	On Trials 30, 40, and 50, the latency of the conditioned response remains essentially constant, fluctuating slightly between _____ and _____ seconds. 4-17
(1) magnitude (2) latency 4-21	Experiment 2. Before these data were collected, _____ had already taken place. 4-22
conditioned response 4-26	Experiment 2. When the conditioned stimulus is repeatedly presented alone, the conditioned reflex undergoes _____ . (TT) 4-27

avoidance 51-2	We sometimes describe someone as "withdrawn" if he * * * take an active part in social interactions. 51-3
avoid 51-7	Spraying a room to kill mosquitoes might be called a form of counteraggression. Aversive stimuli are prevented by attacking the organism which may generate them. In that case, counteraggression is an example of _____ behavior. 51-8
aggressively (aggressive) 51-12	A person who, when criticized, criticizes in return shows _____. 51-13
is 51-17	An individual in a state of anxiety * * * interest in sex, food, art, etc. 51-18
withdrawal symptoms 51-22	In so-called "reaction formation," a person engages in behavior which is incompatible with or otherwise displaces or weakens behavior which has both aversive and reinforcing consequences. The action of a former libertine in crusading against sin may exemplify _____ _____. 51-23
(1) eliminates (avoids) (2) reduces (decreases, lowers) 51-27	Reaction formation may be interpreted both as behavior which is (1) * * * with punishable behavior, and as behavior which removes (2) _____ which make the punishable behavior more probable. 51-28

magnitude 4-2	Experiment 1. The zero in Column II for Trial 1 is evidence that the tone is a(n) _____ _____ on this trial. 4-3
(1) six (2) conditioned stimulus 4-7	Between Trials 1 and 10, the neutral stimulus must have begun to elicit salivation. It was becoming a(n) _____ stimulus. 4-8
increases 4-12	On Trials 30, 40, and 50, the magnitude of the conditioned response remains essentially constant, fluctuating slightly between a low of (1) _____ and a high of (2) _____ drops. 4-13
1 (and) 2 4-17	If the experiment had continued to Trial 60, the best guess is that the latency would have remained between _____ and _____ seconds. 4-18
conditioning 4-22	Experiment 2. The 10 drops of saliva recorded for Trial 1 in the table demonstrate that the tick of the metronome is a(n) _____ _____. 4-23
extinction 4-27	As the number of trials in which a conditioned stimulus is presented alone increases, the latency of a conditioned reflex (1) _____, and the magnitude of a conditioned response (2) _____ until (3) _____ is complete. 4-28

interpreted 51-1	We interpret a neurotic symptom when we say that the hermit's behavior is a form of _____ in that it reduces aversive stimuli administered by society. 51-2
reinforced (conditioned) 51-6	A man sprays a room to kill mosquitoes in order to _____ getting stung. 51-7
(1) positive (2) negative 51-11	The aggressive person, though often reinforced, generates conditions in which others are reinforced for acting _____ toward him. 51-12
incompatible 51-16	Extensive use of aversive control results in a chronic (i.e., more or less continuous) activation syndrome with the result that the normal functioning of the body * * * continuously disrupted. 51-17
reinforced 51-21	Reduction in the aversive stimulation of "guilt" may contribute to the early use of alcohol or other drugs, but after frequent use, the drug continues to be taken because of the * * * which otherwise occur. 51-22
(1) not likely (2) stimuli (S^Ds) 51-26	A person may control his own tendency to drink by righteously boycotting magazines which publish liquor ads. In so doing, he (1) _____ S^Ds for his own drinking and (2) _____ the probability that he will engage in behavior from which he receives aversive stimuli. 51-27
aversive (punishing) 51-31	**End of Set**

neutral stimulus	On Trials 2 through 9, the tone is * * * food.
4-3	4-4 ← To p. 21
conditioned	Experiment 1. On Trials 10, 20, 30, 40, and 50, the (1) * * * is a conditioned stimulus eliciting salivation; on these trials, salivation is termed the (2) * * *.
4-8	4-9 ← To p. 21
(1) 59 (2) 62	After Trial 30, there is no further appreciable increase in magnitude of the ____ ____. (TT)
4-13	4-14 ← To p. 21
1 (and) 2	When the response magnitude has reached a maximum, the latency has essentially reached a(n) ____.
4-18	4-19 ← To p. 21
conditioned stimulus	Experiment 2. When the data in the table were collected, only the ____ stimulus was presented.
4-23	4-24 ← To p. 21
(1) increases (2) decreases (3) extinction	Experiment 1 follows the course of the (1) ____ process, and Experiment 2 follows the course of the (2) ____ process.
4-28	4-29 ← To p. 21

> Even though conditions may be too complex for precise control or prediction, a variety of everyday behaviors can to some extent be _____ in terms of their possible causes.
>
> 51-1

---

more

51-5

One who gives up a belief in hell escapes from the aversive stimuli of a "fear of damnation," and skeptical behavior is thereby _____.

51-6

---

counter-
aggression
(aggression)

51-10

An aggressive person is often reinforced when he coerces others, either to produce (1) _____ reinforcers or to cease using (2) _____ reinforcers.

51-11

---

activation
syndrome

51-15

The activation syndrome may be useful when extreme exertion is required, but the responses are often _____ with the normal, relaxed functioning of the body.

51-16

---

aversive

51-20

In a person who has been punished severely, any return of the resulting repressed behavior will generate conditioned aversive stimuli often called "guilt." Drinking alcohol may be _____ (TT) by a reduction in these aversive stimuli.

51-21

---

stimuli (S^Ds)

51-25

In reaction formation, a person controls a tendency to drink by campaigning for prohibition with great zeal. While so doing, he is (1) * * * to drink and if his campaign succeeds, he will have eliminated (2) _____ for drinking.

51-26

---

avoids

51-30

In general, many types of behavior which in their extreme forms characterize neurosis are conditioned as unfortunate by-products of _____ contingencies.

51-31

unconditioned
response

5-8

A person can sometimes be "cured" of drinking al-
coholic beverages by adding to beverages a chem-
ical which elicits vomiting. After conditioning,
liquor is a(n) _____ _____ for vomiting.

5-9

---

extinguished

5-17

When the tone elicits salivation, *salivating* is then
a(n) _____ _____.

5-18

---

same (painful)

5-26

Blood pressure is increased by a painful or "frightening" stimulus. In "fear," there is a(n) _____ in
blood pressure.

5-27

---

conditioned
responses

5-35

If you are punished for telling lies, stimuli generated by lying may become _____ stimuli for responses similar to those in fear and anxiety.

5-36

---

extinction

5-44

A child who stutters may be laughed at by other
children or scolded by a thoughtless adult. Hearing oneself stutter then becomes a(n) _____ stimulus
which elicits anxiety.

5-45

---

(1) conditioned
    stimuli
(2) conditioned
    responses

5-53

One way to avoid undesirable conditioned responses is to condition an incompatible response to
the same stimulus. A funny picturebook in a dentist's office may elicit responses _____ with fear.

5-54

reinforced

51-4

Military desertion is prevented mainly by making the consequences of desertion * * * aversive than the consequences of serving.

51-5

---

counter

51-9

The harsh dictator puts down a revolt if he can. In doing so, he shows _____ against revolutionaries.

51-10

---

negative

51-14

Aversive stimuli are not only a condition for the reinforcement of escape and avoidance behavior; they elicit a group of respondents comprising the

_____ _____.

51-15

---

activation syndrome

51-19

Alcohol, morphine, cocaine, and certain other drugs reduce the effects of _____ stimuli.

51-20

---

less (not)

51-24

In reaction formation, a person who has stopped smoking may insist that others around him not smoke. This is self-control through the elimination of _____ which increase the probability that he himself will smoke.

51-25

---

reaction formation

51-29

The extremely restrained behavior of the meticulous or "inhibited" person may be the result of aversive control. The meticulous person _____ the consequences of certain kinds of punishable behavior.

51-30

An object brushing the eye is a(n) (1) _____ stimulus which will (2) _____ the unconditioned response of blinking.

5-1

---

conditioned
stimulus

5-9

In Pavlov's experiment, a tone did not normally elicit salivation when first presented. The tone was a(n) _____ _____ prior to conditioning.

5-10

---

conditioned
response

5-18

Electric shock, sudden loud noises, and other painful or "frightening" stimuli elicit perspiration. The very "frightened" person may break out in a "cold _____."

5-19

---

rise (increase)

5-27

Many different reflexes are observed in "fear" or "anger." In emotional states, many responses are _____ by a common stimulus.

5-28

---

conditioned

5-36

Stimuli for responses which occur in fear or anxiety are paired with lying when it is punished. Lying generates stimuli which acquire the power to elicit the conditioned responses which occur in _____.

5-37

---

conditioned

5-45

When the previously scolded stutterer is no longer scolded, his anxiety * * *.

5-46

---

incompatible

5-54

The dentist's office provides conditioned stimuli for fear. This office can also come to provide conditioned and unconditioned _____ for more favorable emotional responses.

5-55

(1) aversive (2) emotional (anxious, sorrowful) 50-3	When a truck driver keeps himself from falling asleep and running off the road by drinking strong coffee, his coffee drinking exemplifies _____ behavior. 50-4 ← To p. 318
increased (greater, heightened) 50-8	Obscene and blasphemous verbal responses are common in the behavior of intoxicated people. Under the influence of alcohol, a man is more likely to engage in forms of behavior commonly _____ (TT) by society. 50-9 ← To p. 318
1) negative (-ly) 2) positive (-ly) 50-13	A man who frequently engages in positively reinforced behavior is commonly said to have a habit. Thus, a man who watches television a great deal is said to have the television _____. 50-14 ← To p. 318
withdrawal symptoms 50-18	A drug is called habit-forming not because it is so highly reinforcing that it is repeatedly used, but because its withdrawal after continued use generates (1) _____ _____ which, as (2) _____ _____ function as negative reinforcers for taking the drug. 50-19 ← To p. 318
cannot (would not) 50-23	In giving up tobacco, some people space their smoking, allowing longer and longer periods between cigarettes. This is effective in avoiding extreme * * * (but is usually a poor technique for other reasons). 50-24 ← To p. 318

) unconditioned) elicit 5-1	A neutral stimulus repeatedly paired with an un- conditioned stimulus is soon able to elicit the re- sponse alone. _____ has occurred. 5-2
neutral stimulus 5-10	The unconditioned stimulus, food, will elicit sal- ivation. Salivation is then called the _____ _____. 5-11
sweat 5-19	A rise in temperature is a(n) (1) _____ stimulus for increase in perspiration; similarly, a painful stim- ulus is a(n) (2) _____ stimulus for perspiration. 5-20
elicited 5-28	Many reflexes occur together in a(n) _____ state. 5-29
fear (anxiety) 5-37	The "lie detector" records some of the reflex re- sponses which occur in fear (e.g., galvanic skin response, breathing pattern). In "detecting a lie," the instrument measures responses which became _____ through the pairing of lying and punishment. 5-38
is extinguished (decreases, ceases) 5-46	When the stutterer is no longer scolded, but en- couraged to talk frequently, the reflexes involved in the state of anxiety are _____. (TT) 5-47
stimuli 5-55	The "tear-jerker" movie makes use of stimuli pre- viously _____ to elicit crying and other emotional responses typical of states of sadness. 5-56

018775

positive 50-2	"Drowning one's sorrow" refers to the use of alcohol to escape from the (1) _____ properties of a(n) (2) _____ state. 50-3
would (will, does) 50-7	If caffeine and alcohol have opposite effects (i.e., are antagonists) and if alcohol decreases anxiety, one might interpret the "jitters" and wakefulness caused by coffee as due in part to _____ control exerted by aversive stimuli. 50-8
frequently (more frequently, often) 50-12	Alcohol decreases the aversive stimulation characteristic of anxiety. Drinking is therefore said to be (1) _____-ly reinforced. Taking a drug which produces a state of well-being above the normal (*euphoria*) is (2) _____-ly reinforced. 50-13
aversive stimuli (negative reinforcers) 50-17	Many habitual breakfast-coffee drinkers get a headache if they do not have coffee for breakfast on a given morning. These coffee drinkers have * * * (TT) when the morning coffee is skipped. 50-18
is not 50-22	Taking alcohol or morphine for the *first time* may be followed by a state of euphoria and by escape from ordinary aversive stimuli. From these facts alone, however, we * * * be sure that these drugs lead to addiction. 50-23
(1) withdrawal symptoms (2) addict 50-27	**End of Set**

Conditioning	If a bell often rings a fraction of a second before something brushes the eye, the bell may become a(n) (1) _____ _____; in other words, the bell may (2) _____ a blink.
5-2	5-3

unconditioned response	When tone and food are repeatedly paired, _____ of a salivary reflex takes place.
5-11	5-12

) unconditioned) unconditioned	A special instrument (a galvanometer) is used to measure the electrical resistance of the skin. Perspiration lowers the resistance of the skin. This can be recorded by a(n) _____.
5-20	5-21

emotional (e.g., state of fear, etc.)	A painful stimulus will (1) _____ the set of responses involved in "fear" and "anger." The painful stimulus is the (2) _____ _____ in this set of reflexes.
5-29	5-30

conditioned	Would the "lie detector" be successful with a person from a culture which never punishes lying?
5-38	5-39

extinguished	Any form of physical energy which is sufficient to cause a given bit of behavior without previous conditioning is called a(n) _____ _____.
5-47	5-48

conditioned	When a young child's fear of furry animals is eliminated by bringing him gradually more and more into contact with harmless furry animals, his fear is said to be _____. (TT)
5-56	5-57

negative 50-1	The "good flavor of coffee," unlike "getting a lift," is a stimulus property which is a(n) _____ reinforcer for drinking coffee. 50-2
have 50-6	From the use of black coffee to keep an intoxicated man awake, one would (correctly) predict that an injection of caffeine sulphate, a drug found in coffee, * * * reverse the process of "passing out" from too much alcohol. 50-7
(1) aversive stimuli (2) is (may be) 50-11	That alcohol reduces the effect of conditioned aversive stimuli is shown when behavior which automatically generates aversive stimuli occurs * * * under alcohol. 50-12
withdrawal 50-16	Withdrawal symptoms furnish _____ _____ which exert powerful control over the behavior of drug-taking. 50-17
addiction 50-21	The "television habit" produces no true withdrawal symptoms. Therefore, it * * * an addiction in this sense. 50-22
are not 50-26	"I can take it or leave it alone" asserts that "leaving it alone" produces no overpowering (1) * * * and that the speaker is not a(n) (2) _____. 50-27

(1) conditioned stimulus (2) elicit 5-3	After conditioning, the bell alone will elicit a blink. The blink is a(n) _____ _____ which is similar to (but not quite identical with) the blink elicited by brushing the eye. 5-4
conditioning 5-12	During conditioning, the neutral stimulus (tone) acquires the power to (1) _____ salivation. Salivation elicited by the tone is called a(n) (2) _____ _____. 5-13
galvanometer 5-21	A sudden drop in the electrical skin resistance is called a *galvanic skin response* (GSR). When a painful stimulus produces this effect, it is an unconditioned _____ _____ response. 5-22
1) elicit 2) unconditioned stimulus 5-30	The emotional states of "fear" and "anger" are marked by many reflexes (e.g., sweating, contraction of blood vessels, erection of hair or "goose flesh"). Many responses are elicited by the conditions which generate _____ states. 5-31
No 5-39	Hearing vulgar words may elicit a weak galvanic skin response, etc. This suggests that these words are conditioned _____ for some of the reflex responses involved in fear or anxiety. 5-40
unconditioned stimulus 5-48	The process by which a conditioned stimulus loses the ability to elicit a response is called _____. 5-49
extinguished 5-57	A young child is afraid of furry animals. Furry animals are brought closer during each meal. While enjoying food (an unconditioned stimulus), responses are conditioned which are _____ with fear. 5-58

| | A man who drinks a cup of coffee "to get a lift" reduces the aversive properties of fatigue, of "being low," etc., and coffee drinking is reinforced by a(n) _____ reinforcer. |
| | 50-1 |

| aversive stimuli (conditioned aversive stimuli) 50-5 | Drinking strong, black coffee to keep from falling asleep after drinking too much alcohol suggests that the drugs, alcohol and caffeine, * * * opposing or antagonistic effects on behavior. 50-6 |

| decrease (reduction) 50-10 | Alcoholism may be due in part to the effect of this drug in decreasing the effects of (1) _____ _____. Alcoholism is a form of "neurosis" which (2) * * * the result of severe punishment or other avoidance contingencies. 50-11 |

| reinforced 50-15 | The aversive effects of withholding a drug after the drug has been repeatedly taken are called withdrawal symptoms. Further use of a drug is reinforcing in part by the avoidance of, or escape from, such _____ symptoms. 50-16 |

| escape (relief) 50-20 | A coffee drinker who gets a headache if he misses his morning coffee is suffering from a(n) _____ to caffeine. 50-21 |

| withdrawal symptoms 50-25 | The reinforcing effects of caffeine, alcohol, and morphine in producing euphoria * * * dependent on addiction. 50-26 |

conditioned response 5-4	In the conditioned eye-blink reflex just described, the ringing bell becomes the ____ ____. 5-5
(1) elicit (2) conditioned response 5-13	For conditioning to occur, the tone must either coincide with the presentation of food or * * * it by a very short interval. 5-14
galvanic skin (response) 5-22	A painful stimulus elicits a GSR. This sequence of events (the stimulus and its response) is called the galvanic skin ____. 5-23
emotional 5-31	A child hurt by the dentist will be afraid when returning to the dentist's office at a later date. Through conditioning, the dentist's office has come to provide many ____ ____ for the reflex behavior in fear. 5-32
stimuli 5-40	When a newspaper identifies the race of a person committing a particularly odious crime, the race label can become a(n) ____ ____ which will elicit the emotional responses aroused by other parts of the crime report. 5-41
extinction 5-49	After conditioning, the response elicited by a previously neutral stimulus is the ____ ____. 5-50
incompatible 5-58	In an experiment, people learned to "like" modern music by hearing it while they ate. The music became the (1) ____ ____, and the food was the (2) ____ ____, for reflex responses characterizing "pleasure." 5-59

Set 50

Drug Addiction

Estimated time: 11 minutes

Turn to next page and begin ▶

---

avoidance

50-4

Alcohol is often said to reduce feelings of guilt. Technically speaking, it reduces the effect of _____ _____ generated by previously punished behavior.

50-5

---

punished

50-9

Laboratory animals, which normally refuse alcohol, drink alcohol under conditions in which reinforced behavior is also punished. They may then emit the punished behavior, suggesting a(n) _____ in the effectiveness of aversive stimuli.

50-10

---

habit

50-14

To say that a man has the "morphine habit" means more than that he frequently takes the drug. After repeated use, discontinuing morphine generates an extremely aversive condition.   Further use of the drug will be strongly _____ by escape from this condition.

50-15

---

(1) withdrawal
    symptoms
(2) aversive
    stimuli

50-19

A man is said to be *addicted* to a drug if withholding the drug produces withdrawal symptoms. The addict's behavior of taking a drug is strongly reinforced by _____ from the withdrawal symptoms.

50-20

---

withdrawal
symptoms

50-24

A "chain smoker" avoids * * * by allowing no time for them to appear.

50-25

---

conditioned stimulus	If the bell is sounded many times when nothing brushes the eye, the conditioned eye-blink reflex will be _____. (TT)
5-5	5-6

precede	After a sufficient number of pairings of tone and food, the tone becomes a(n) (1) _____ _____ which will (2) _____ salivation.
5-14	5-15

reflex	Conditions which give rise to the so-called emotions of fear, anger, and anxiety produce a(n) _____ in the electrical resistance of the skin.
5-23	5-24

conditioned stimuli	If the dentist's behavior continues to provide unconditioned stimuli for fear reflexes, the child's conditioned fear of the dentist's office will not become _____. (TT)
5-32	5-33

conditioned stimulus	A favorable predisposition to a political candidate might be conditioned by serving a free lunch at a political rally. The food is a(n) _____ _____ used to condition many "favorable" reflex responses.
5-41	5-42

conditioned response	A stimulus which has acquired the ability to evoke a reflex response is the (1) _____ _____; the response it evokes is the (2) _____ _____.
5-50	5-51

(1) conditioned stimulus (2) unconditioned stimulus	**End of Set**
5-59	

← To p. 313

(1) conditioned
(2) unconditioned

49-3

We may punish a child for eating before others are served; yet eating is not usually punished. Thus, it (1) * * * always the *form* of behavior which makes it punishable but rather the (2) _____ (TT) under which it occurred.

49-4
← To p. 313

---

do not (cannot)

49-8

To say that we hurt someone with a careless remark unconsciously means that we do not notice a consequence of the behavior because of which it may be _____.

49-9
← To p. 313

---

has (results in)

49-13

We readily report that we have spanked a child "for his own good" because striking a child is *not* _____ under such conditions.

49-14
← To p. 313

---

likely (more likely)

49-18

When we criticize a friend in anger, we may feel guilty when we are no longer angry because responses which hurt friends have been _____.

49-19
← To p. 313

---

himself

49-23

In lying, a person recognizes the punishable reason for his behavior. Therefore, rationalization (1) * * * to be considered lying in this sense because the person (2) * * * "tell the whole truth" even to himself.

49-24
← To p. 313

---

forgiveness

49-28

If you are *actually not* angry when a person has insulted you because you know he is maladjusted, then you * * * be rationalizing if you reported that reason for not returning his aggression.

49-29
← To p. 313

---

extinguished 5-6	(1) _____, the Russian physiologist, discovered the process called (2) _____. 5-7
(1) conditioned stimulus (2) elicit 5-15	If the conditioned stimulus (tone) is presented a great many times *without* food, the tone eventually _____ to elicit salivation. 5-16
drop (decrease) (acceptable: change) 5-24	A previously neutral stimulus repeatedly paired with a painful stimulus will acquire the power to elicit a GSR through _____. 5-25
extinguished 5-33	Words like "bad" and "wrong" are frequently heard just before punishment. These words come to elicit responses characteristic of fear or anxiety. They become _____ stimuli. 5-34
unconditioned stimulus 5-42	During the free lunch at a political rally, the candidate's name may become a(n) (1) _____ _____ which evokes favorable emotional responses similar to those evoked by the (2) _____ _____. 5-43

(1) conditioned
    stimulus
(2) conditioned
    response
 	
5-51
	We now have reason to believe that much of the apparently "spontaneous" flow of saliva when no food is in the mouth is caused by unnoticed _____ _____.
	
	5-52

conditioned 49-2	"Doing something else" avoids the (1) _____ aversive stimuli generated by a frequently punished response, as well as the possibly (2) _____ aversive stimuli of punishment. <div align="right">49-3</div>
punished 49-7	We may not realize that we are spanking a child because he made us angry rather than to correct his behavior. Thus, we * * * notice that our behavior is emitted for punishable reasons. <div align="right">49-8</div>
aversive 49-12	Striking the first blow is frequently punished; striking in self-defense is condoned. The same form of behavior * * * different consequences depending upon the circumstances. <div align="right">49-13</div>

(1) punished
    (criticized)
(2) reinforced
    (condoned)
49-17
	A man who is late for work is * * * to say that he stayed in bed because he needed rest rather than because he was lazy.
	
	<div align="right">49-18</div>

rationalization 49-22	In rationalization, a person "believes" (tells himself) that his behavior was a function of variables with respect to which he is least likely to be punished. In rationalization, he deceives _____ as well as others. <div align="right">49-23</div>
has (has both) 49-27	Not striking a person who has just hurt you is reinforced as forgiveness or punished as cowardice, depending upon the circumstances. You might be rationalizing your behavior if you described it as _____. <div align="right">49-28</div>

(1) Pavlov (2) conditioning 5-7	Chemical irritants in the stomach elicit vomiting. Vomiting is, then, a(n) _____ _____. 5-8 ← To p. 26
ceases (fails, loses the power) 5-16	When the conditioned stimulus loses its power to elicit salivation because of repeated presentation without the unconditioned stimulus, the conditioned reflex is said to be _____. 5-17 ← To p. 26
conditioning 5-25	A painful stimulus may also elicit changes in the breathing pattern: "catching the breath," and then deeper inhalation of air. This respiratory change and the GSR are, thus, two responses to the _____ unconditioned stimulus. 5-26 ← To p. 26
conditioned 5-34	Words like "bad" and "wrong" elicit (1) _____ _____ similar to the unconditioned responses elicited by painful stimuli. 5-35 ← To p. 26
) conditioned stimulus) unconditioned stimulus (food) 5-43	A process through which we can eliminate conditioned responses is called _____. 5-44 ← To p. 26
conditioned stimuli 5-52	Words like "love" and "hate" are (1) _____ _____ which writers may use to elicit emotional (2) _____ _____. 5-53 ← To p. 26

aversive (negatively reinforcing) 49-1	Previously punished behavior generates _____ aversive stimuli. 49-2
aversive 49-6	Society punishes the unjust. Unfairly administering punishment is itself sometimes _____ by others. 49-7
contingent (dependent) 49-11	It is easier for a man to notice and describe unpunished reasons for his own behavior because they are less _____ than punished reasons. 49-12
probable (likely) 49-16	Staying in bed late is often (1) _____ as laziness or indolence. It is often (2) _____ as wise self-therapy when one needs a rest. 49-17
rational(-izes) 49-21	You may admit, even to yourself, only the least punished reasons for a given response. This type of defective self-description is called _____. 49-22
punished 49-26	A man can rationalize his own conduct only if the behavior * * * punishable and non-punishable aspects. 49-27

Read exhibit now and refer to it as needed.

Types of Response Mechanisms

1. Contractions of *striated* or striped muscles (so called because of their appearance under a microscope) move parts of the skeletal frame, as well as certain "flaps" of tissue such as the tongue, eyelid, and vocal cords.

2. Contractions of *smooth* muscles generally change the dimensions of various internal organs.

3. *Glands* secrete fluids into ducts or directly into the blood stream.

Some behavior is criticized or otherwise punished by society, that is, it is frequently followed by _____ stimuli.

49-1

---

emitted
(made)

49-5

If a man "does not notice" that he is engaging in behavior which is often punished, he avoids _____ stimuli generated by the behavior.

49-6

---

(1) punishable
(2) do not

49-10

When a response is a function of two variables, punishment may be _____ upon its relation to only one of them.

49-11

2

49-15

If a man can avoid reporting a punishable reason by reporting a non-punishable reason for his behavior, it is * * * that the non-punishable reason will be reported.

49-16

---

less

49-20

Emphasizing the non-punishable aspects of one's own behavior is called rationalization. Thus, one _____ -izes the behavior of striking a friend by saying, "I did it for his own good."

49-21

---

punished

49-25

Behavior which does not need to be, and in fact cannot be, rationalized is behavior which has never been _____.

49-26

Set 6

PART I Reflex Behavior

Response Mechanisms

See exhibit on preceding page

Estimated time: 12 minutes

Turn to next page and begin ▶

smooth
muscles

6-4

In vomiting, the _____ muscles of the stomach wall contract vigorously, thus forcibly ejecting the contents of the stomach.

6-5

---

glands
(gland)

6-9

Blushing and blanching result when _____ muscles change the diameters of small blood vessels near the skin.

6-10

---

(1) smooth
(2) glands

6-14

The pupil of the eye is the opening through the iris. Like other muscles controlling the diameters of organs, the iris contains _____ muscle.

6-15

---

smooth
muscles
(and) glands

6-19

Smooth muscles contract in which *three* of the following? (USE LETTERS) (a) vomiting, (b) running, (c) turning the head, (d) stomach cramps, (e) sweating, (f) reaching, (g) blushing, (h) eyes watering.

6-20

---

(1) glands
(2) smooth
       muscles
(3) elicited

6-24

Responses of smooth muscles and glands are elicited by appropriate (1) _____. They are response mechanisms in the stimulus-response relations termed (2) _____. (TTs)

6-25

Set 49

Rationalization

Estimated time: 11 minutes

Turn to next page and begin ▶

) is not
) S^Ds (stimuli,
  circumstances)

49-4

Sometimes, as in a verbal slip, we may not notice that we have _____ a response which is often punished.

49-5

---

punished

49-9

In talking to others, we usually do not talk about our own (1) _____ behavior; similarly in thinking ("talking to ourselves"), we often (2) * * * think about our own punishable behavior.

49-10

---

punished
(aversive)

49-14

If a response is punished when controlled by Variable 1 and not punished when controlled by Variable 2, Variable _____ will more probably be recognized and reported.

49-15

---

punished

49-19

If we report that our friend has benefited from our criticism, it is _____ punishing to report having criticized him.

49-20

---

(1) is not
(2) does not
    (cannot)

49-24

Claiming that bumping a rival on the dance floor was an "accident" is attributing the behavior to reasons for which bumping is not usually _____.

49-25

---

would not

49-29

When we admit only the least punishable reasons for our behavior, we are (1) _____. This is one of several forms of (2) * * * self-knowledge.

49-30

Contraction of _____ muscles moves parts of the skeletal frame.

6-1

---

smooth

6-5

Muscle fibers from the stomach appear _____ when viewed under a microscope.

6-6

---

smooth

6-10

Name the type of response mechanism (or organ) active in (1) walking, (2) stomach contraction, (3) salivation.

6-11

---

smooth

6-15

Tears which wash away irritants from the surface of the eye are provided by _____.

6-16

---

a, d, g

6-20

Which type of response mechanism is usually involved in the organism's action upon the *external* environment?

6-21

---

(1) stimuli
(2) reflexes

6-25

Most of the behavior which acts upon the external environment is not elicited by stimuli in the form of simple reflexes. That is to say, eliciting stimuli are *not* the principal "causes" of the responses executed by _____ muscle.

6-26

s^Ds (stimuli) 48-3	In a "description," verbal behavior is under the control of appropriate S^Ds. Even in describing our own behavior, the behavior to be described must provide _____ for some verbal response. 48-4 ← To p. 308
reinforce 48-8	The child who once cried when his stomach hurt later whines, "It hurts." Crying (1) * * * reinforced after a certain age, but a (similar) response, whining, (2) * * * reinforced (provided the child is not too old to whine). 48-9 ← To p. 308
s^Ds (stimuli) 48-13	A man may fail to notice even rather advanced medical symptoms which presumably produce strong stimuli. Possibly these symptoms have never come to function as S^Ds because the man has not been adequately _____ for reporting them. 48-14 ← To p. 308
incompatible with 48-18	I may not remember where I parked my car because appropriate self-observing behavior has not been (1) _____ or because I was preoccupied with some (2) _____ covert behavior at the time. 48-19 ← To p. 308
reinforced 48-23	Repressed responses have (1) _____ consequences which provide conditions under which incompatible behavior is reinforced; but they have also probably had (2) _____ consequences which, alone, would make the response likely to occur. 48-24 ← To p. 308
incompatible (avoidance) 48-28	We interpret repression as the effect of incompatible behavior which avoids the (1) _____ consequences of the behavior the psychoanalyst would call (2) _____. 48-29 ← To p. 308
repression 48-33	**End of Set**

striated (striped, skeletal) 6-1	In the arm-flexion reflex, the response is executed by the contraction of ____ ____. 6-2
smooth (unstriped) 6-6	Smooth muscles change the (1) ____ of various (2) ____ organs. 6-7
(1) striated muscles (2) smooth muscles (3) glands 6-11	Reaching and throwing involve (1) ____ muscles. Nodding the head, making facial expressions, and talking involve (2) ____ muscles. 6-12
glands 6-16	A response may be the action of ____ ____, ____ ____, or ____. 6-17
striated muscles 6-21	The types of response mechanisms principally active in maintaining the "internal economy" of the organism are ____ ____ and ____. 6-22
striated 6-26	In some cases, as in the flexion reflex, responses by striated muscles (1) * * * elicited by stimuli, but most responses of striated muscles (2) * * * under the control of eliciting stimuli. 6-27

did not (was not able to) 48-2	We cannot describe someone's behavior if we did not notice it. That is, we can describe another's behavior only if that behavior provided _____ controlling some response. 48-3
s^{D}s (stimuli) 48-7	As the child grows older, parents (and others) usually cease to reinforce crying and begin to _____ such verbal behavior as "It hurts." 48-8
shaped (differentiated, conditioned) 48-12	Some patients report very slight painful symptoms to their doctor. In their history of reinforcement, even weak painful stimuli have served as _____ for this verbal behavior. 48-13
incompatible with 48-17	The "absent-minded" scholar cannot describe as much of his overt behavior as others because of covert verbal behavior which is * .* * noticing or "thinking about" what he is doing. 48-18
) aversive (conditioned aversive)) reduction (termination, elimination) 48-22	We do not even think about severely punished behavior when we "repress" it. Doing, saying, or thinking something else is _____ by a reduction in conditioned aversive stimuli. 48-23
repress (-ed) 48-27	A laboratory analysis suggests that repressing is simply engaging in _____ behavior reinforced by the reduction of aversive stimuli generated by recalling an experience. 48-28
incompatible 48-32	Inadequate self-knowledge may occur when the unreportable behavior generates conditions under which incompatible behavior is reinforced. This incompatible behavior is the main "force" or "agent" in _____. 48-33

striated muscles (striped, skeletal) 6-2	Muscle fibers in the arms appear to be _____ when viewed under a microscope. 6-3
(1) dimensions (2) internal 6-7	Not all responses involve muscles. Sweating is the action of _____. 6-8
(1) striated (2) striated 6-12	Chewing food involves (1) _____ muscles. In swallowing, after food passes from the oral cavity, it is moved through the esophagus or gullet principally by (2) _____ muscles. 6-13
smooth muscles, striated muscles, (or) glands (ANY ORDER) 6-17	Most of our interaction with the external environment involves gross or subtle movements of our skeletal frame. In other words, action upon the environment most directly involves _____ muscles. 6-18
smooth muscles (and) glands 6-22	Name the response mechanism in the following: walking to the dinner table and chewing food (1) _____; moistening food with saliva (2) _____; passing food into stomach (3) _____; and providing the stomach with digestive juices (4) _____. 6-23
(1) are (2) are not 6-27	Action upon the environment involves (1) _____ muscles and usually does not fit the pattern of the simple (2) _____. 6-28

conditioned (reinforced, learned) 48-1	A person with an adequate verbal repertoire may not be able to describe a past event if he * ẍ * verbalize it, at least covertly, at the time. 48-2
reinforces (conditions) 48-6	When crying in response to a painful stimulus has been reinforced, crying may become a verbal response emitted in the presence of other somewhat similar ____. 48-7
successive approximations 48-11	When pain is reported in an unusually high pitch, a completely "natural" voice in reporting pain has apparently not yet been completely ____ by the verbal community. 48-12
incompatible with 48-16	A person doing one thing and "thinking about" something else may later be unable to describe what he was doing because covert verbal behavior is * * * noticing what he was doing. 48-17
reinforced 48-21	Severely punished behavior generates stimuli which have become (1) * * * stimuli. Behavior which avoids (is incompatible with) the punished behavior is reinforced through the (2) ____ of these stimuli. 48-22
repression 48-26	We may not be able to recall an early childhood experience. Under some conditions a psychoanalyst would say we have ____-ed it. 48-27
conditioned 48-31	Inadequate self-knowledge may result if we engage in behavior * * * with noticing some aspect of our other behavior. 48-32

striated
(striped)

Contraction of _____ _____ changes diameters of blood vessels.

6-3

6-4
← To p. 36

---

glands

Salivation is the action of the salivary _____.

6-8

6-9
← To p. 36

---

(1) striated
(2) smooth

Movements of the stomach and intestines in digestion involve (1) _____ muscles. Digestive juices are provided by (2) _____.

6-13

6-14
← To p. 36

---

striated

The internal economy of the body depends on secretion of digestive juices and on forcing substances through tubular organs by rhythmic changes in their diameters. The internal economy depends on the action of _____ _____ and _____.

6-18

6-19
← To p. 36

---

(1) striated
    muscles
(2) glands
(3) smooth
    muscles
(4) glands

6-23

Salivation and sweating are actions of (1) _____. Constriction of the pupil, vomiting, blushing, and blanching are actions of (2) _____ _____. Both types of response are (3) _____ by appropriate stimuli.

6-24
← To p. 36

---

(1) striated
(2) reflex

6-28

The principle of the simple reflex applies to responses by _____ _____ and _____ as well as some reflexes involved in posture, locomotion, and protective skeletal responses.

6-29
← To p. 36

We commonly lack "self-knowledge" in the sense that we cannot describe much of our past behavior. Many early childhood experiences cannot be recalled possibly because appropriate verbal behavior was not _____ (TT) at the time.

48-1

---

reinforced

48-5

A very young child cries in response to a painful stimulus. Although this may be in part unlearned, a parent _____ this behavior if he provides needed attention.

48-6

---

reinforced

48-10

When the verbal community reinforces first crying, next whining, and finally talking, behavior is being shaped through _____ _____ to a final form acceptable to the community.

48-11

---

cannot
(will not)

48-15

A driver carefully watching the road will later be unable to describe much of the roadside scenery. Watching the road is * * * looking at the scenery.

48-16

---

reinforced
(conditioned)

48-20

If talking about severely punishing situations generates strong aversive stimuli, we may be automatically _____ for talking about other things, as an example of avoidance behavior.

48-21

---

repressed

48-25

Self-knowledge is sometimes lacking because it is displaced by incompatible behavior which avoids the aversive stimuli generated by talking about punished responses. This kind of absence of self-knowledge has been called _____.

48-26

---

emitted

48-30

Inadequate self-knowledge may result because we have not been _____ to notice some aspect of our behavior.

48-31

when (if, after) 7-4	Reinforcement and behavior occur in the temporal order: (1) _____, (2) _____. 7-5
deprived of food (hungry) 7-9	If an animal's response is not followed by reinforcement, similar responses will occur _____ frequently in the future. 7-10
natural (non-deliberate) 7-14	Food is not reinforcing unless the animal has first been * * * food for some time. 7-15
einforce 7-19	In laboratory research, various devices are used to reinforce responses. Heat can be used to _____ the responses of a cold animal. 7-20
response (behavior) 7-24	The response of pressing a bar must be emitted at least once in order to be _____. 7-25
less frequent (become extinguished) 7-29	*No* eliciting stimuli are observed for bar pressing, flicking leaves in the park, etc. Therefore, responses of this type * * * classified as reflex behavior. 7-30

$S^D s$
(stimuli)

48-4

Discrimination results from a three-term contingency. Even though our behavior always generates potential stimuli, these are $S^D s$ only if a response has been _____ in their presence.

48-5

---

(1) is not
(2) is

48-9

When the *verbal community* (parents and others) considers a child too old to whine, whining is no longer _____, although saying, "my stomach hurts" in a normal voice may be.

48-10

---

reinforced

48-14

If we have never learned to notice an aspect of our own behavior, it * * * be described by us.

48-15

---

(1) conditioned
(reinforced,
shaped)
(2) incompatible

48-19

If self-observation produces aversive stimuli, behavior incompatible with noticing one's own behavior is automatically _____.

48-20

---

(1) aversive
(negative)
(2) reinforcing
(positive)

48-24

When a person cannot recall some previously punished behavior, we say he has _____ it.

48-25

---

(1) aversive
(negative,
punishing)
(2) repressed

48-29

Repressed behavior will not undergo extinction if the behavior is seldom _____ and therefore does not go unreinforced.

48-30

> Performing animals are sometimes trained with "rewards." The behavior of a hungry animal can be "rewarded" with _____.
>
> 7-1

---

1) behavior
2) reinforcement

7-5

> Food given to a hungry animal does not reinforce a particular response unless it is given almost immediately _____ the response.
>
> 7-6

---

less
(in-)

7-10

> To make sure an animal will perform, the trainer provides _____ for the response frequently.
>
> 7-11

---

deprived of
(without,
hungry for)

7-15

> Reinforcing a response produces an increase in the _____ that the response will occur again.
>
> 7-16

---

reinforce

7-20

> An electrically operated food magazine which presents food can be used to reinforce a(n) _____ of an organism deprived of food.
>
> 7-21

---

reinforced

7-25

> Since no eliciting stimuli are observed for such responses as flicking leaves or bar pressing, we *cannot* say that these responses are _____ by stimuli, as are the responses in reflexes.
>
> 7-26

(1) controlling (2) controlled 47-3	In putting candy out of sight to keep from eating it, the (1) _____ to be controlled is eating candy, and the (2) _____ which controls is putting candy out of sight. 47-4 ← To p. 303
(1) reinforces (2) aversive (negative) 47-8	In self-control, the (1) _____ response is reinforced by the (2) _____ of conditioned aversive stimuli associated with the controlled response. (TTs) 47-9 ← To p. 303
ositive (and) egative einforcing (and) versive] 47-13	A delicious but indigestible food generates not only reinforcing stimuli but aversive stimuli which can result in the _____ of a controlling response. 47-14 ← To p. 303
(1) voluntary (2) involuntary 47-18	The weight-reducing pill which is simply a piece of candy to be taken before a meal controls ingestive behavior slightly by decreasing _____. 47-19 ← To p. 303
(1) anxiety (2) aversive 47-23	When a man sets a clock radio to awaken him, he is arranging for a(n) _____ (TT) to occur at a specified time to control his behavior. 47-24 ← To p. 303
1) (controll-)ing 2) reinforced 47-28	A self-controlling response avoiding previously shamed behavior reduces the _____ _____ _____ generated by that behavior. 47-29 ← To p. 303
(1) does (can) (2) do not (need not) 47-33	**End of Set**

food 7-1	A technical term for "reward" is reinforcement. To "reward" an organism with food is to _____ it with food. 7-2
after 7-6	Unlike a stimulus in a reflex, a reinforcing stimulus * * * act to elicit the response it reinforces. 7-7
reinforcement(s) 7-11	A hungry pigeon in the park flicks dead leaves about with quick movements of its beak. This behavior is _____ whenever it uncovers bits of food. 7-12
probability (likelihood, chances) 7-16	We do not observe "probability" directly. We say that a response has become more probable if it is observed to occur more _____ under controlled conditions. 7-17
response 7-21	If the cold (or food-deprived) organism turns on an electrically operated heat lamp (or food magazine), the response of turning on will be _____. 7-22
elicited 7-26	Responses such as bar pressing, flicking leaves, etc., are said to be *emitted* rather than *elicited* since there * * * (are or are no?) observed eliciting stimuli. 7-27

(1) decrease (reduce, lower) (2) probability 47-2	In analyzing cases in which one response controls another, we distinguish between the controlling response and the controlled response. Putting candy out of sight is the (1) _____ response; eating candy is the (2) _____ response. 47-3
einforcing (and) versive positive (and) egative] ITHER ORDER) 47-7	Candy in the mouth (1) _____ the behavior of reaching for candy and putting it in the mouth. This behavior has (2) _____ consequences associated with gaining weight. 47-8
controll-)ed 47-12	A delicious food may later cause severe indigestion. "Nature" has arranged both _____ and _____ consequences of eating such a food. 47-13
(1) operant (2) respondent (reflex) 47-17	The layman calls weeping "involuntary" and putting onion juice near one's eyes "voluntary." In these terms, the actress's technique shows (1) "_____" control over (2) "_____" behavior. 47-18
) (controll-)ing) (controll-)ed 47-22	An overly anxious man may "take to drink." In technical terms, he uses the drug, alcohol, to reduce the emotional state of (1) _____, which is frequently one effect of conditioned (2) _____ stimuli. 47-23
conditioned 47-27	Behavior which "avoids sin" is (1) controll- _____ behavior which is (2) _____ by the reduction of conditioned aversive stimuli. 47-28
reinforces 47-32	A man (1) * * * resist temptation by engaging in controlling behavior which is itself reinforced by external events. We * * * interpret this as the exercising of an inner power called "will." 47-33

reinforce 7-2	*Technically* speaking, a thirsty organism can be _____ with water. 7-3
does not (will not) 7-7	A reinforcement does not elicit a response; it simply makes it more _____ that an animal will respond in the same way again. 7-8
reinforced 7-12	A pigeon is occasionally reinforced for flicking leaves about because of the common natural arrangement of leaves over _____. 7-13
frequently (often) 7-17	When a response has been reinforced, it will be emitted _____ frequently in the future. 7-18
reinforced 7-22	The response of turning on the electrically operated heat lamp or food magazine will be emitted more _____ in the future if the organism is cold or hungry. 7-23
are no 7-27	If pressing the bar does not operate the food magazine, the response * * * reinforced. 7-28
/	

) control) conditions (variables, contingencies) 47-1	A mother may put candy out of sight to _____ the probability that her child will ask for it. She may do the same thing to reduce the (2) _____ that *she* will eat candy. 47-2
controls (prevents, avoids) 47-6	Self-control is often involved when the response to be controlled has both _____ and _____ consequences. 47-7
reinforcement 47-11	The controll-_____ response usually has both positive and negative consequences. 47-12
(1) operant (2) reflex (respondent) 47-16	When the actress puts onion juice near her eyes, a(n) (1) _____ controls a(n) (2) _____. 47-17
emotional 47-21	A man who is bothered by his own aggressive behavior toward others may take a "tranquilizer." Taking the drug is the (1) controll-_____ response; aggressive behavior is the (2) controll-_____ behavior. 47-22
paired 47-26	In shaming a man for unethical or immoral behavior, aversive stimuli are paired with the stimuli generated by that behavior and hence are _____ as aversive stimuli. 47-27
reinforcement (conditioning) 47-31	In ethical training, we are taught that certain behavior is "wrong." This behavior later generates conditioned aversive stimuli whose reduction _____ a variety of responses called "resisting temptation." 47-32

reinforced (NOT: rewarded) 7-3	The trainer reinforces the animal by giving it food _____ it has performed correctly. 7-4 To p. 41
probable (likely) 7-8	Food is probably not reinforcing if the animal is not * * *. 7-9 To p. 41
food (seed, insects, reinforcers) 7-13	The reinforcement used by animal trainers is deliberately arranged, while the arrangement of leaves and food in the park is * * *. 7-14 To p. 41
more 7-18	To get an animal to emit a response more frequently, we _____ the response. 7-19 To p. 41
frequently (often) 7-23	In a typical apparatus, the depression of a horizontal bar automatically operates a food magazine. The apparatus selects "bar pressing" as the _____ to be reinforced. 7-24 To p. 41
is not (will not be) 7-28	Reinforcement makes responses more frequent while failure to receive reinforcement makes responses * * *. 7-29 To p. 41

▷

A man may (1) _____ the behavior of another man by arranging relevant conditions. Also, he may control his own behavior by arranging the same kinds of (2) _____ .

47-1

---

1) controls
   (weakens,
   avoids)
2) removing
   (taking away,
   avoiding)   47-5

In exerting self-control by putting candy away to avoid eating it, one response _____ another response.

47-6

---

1) reinforces
   (conditions)
2) (controll-)ing

47-10

The response to be controlled is often strong because it has received powerful _____ .

47-11

---

1) (controll-)ing
2) elicits

47-15

Putting a handkerchief containing onion juice near one's eyes is (1) _____ behavior; weeping tears is (2) _____ behavior.

47-16

---

1) (controll-)ing
2) decrease
   (decline,
   disappear)
47-20

In "counting to ten" before acting in anger, we make use of the fact that a(n) _____ state often rapidly grows weak.

47-21

---

reinforcement

47-25

In shaming a man for unrestrained, unethical, or immoral behavior, stimuli generated by the behavior are being _____ with the aversive stimuli of shaming so that they will later generate anxiety or "feelings of guilt."

47-26

---

1) (controll-)ing
2) (controll-)ed

47-30

In so-called self-control, the controlling response is established through _____ , just like any other response.

47-31

Set 8

The Standard Experimental Situation

Estimated time: 14 minutes

See exhibit on preceding page
Turn to next page and begin

---

(1) operant
(2) responses

8-4

When the first peck on the key is _____ (TT) by food, the probability of another peck on the key is increased.

8-5

---

(1) stimulus
(2) response

8-9

It might be said that "the pigeon has acquired the habit of pecking the key," but the only thing observed is an increased _____ of responding after reinforcement.

8-10

---

not

8-14

If a pigeon has not been in the box for a long time, its rate of responding upon returning to the box will be lower than previously in the box. This *forgetting* is due to the passage of _____ during which the response is not emitted.

8-15

---

operates upon
(acts upon,
changes,
affects,
influences) 8-19

In the experiment described on the exhibit, the pecking response slightly moves the key. This is an instance of the fact that an operant * * * the environment.

8-20

---

reinforced

8-24

A psychologist fed her infant son when he emitted a faint "cooing" sound. The rate of "cooing" when hungry was expected to (and did) _____ as a result of this reinforcement.

8-25

---

(1) operant
(2) reinforced
    (acceptable:
    conditioned)
    8-29

When you are thirsty and near a drinking fountain, it is (1) _____ that you will walk to the fountain because such behavior has been (2) _____ in the past, under a similar condition of deprivation.

8-30

← To p. 298

(1) response (2) stimulus 46-3	The usual effects of reflexes explain the evolution of such mechanisms. The reflex of vomiting * * * survival value because organisms which possess it remove dangerous materials from their stomachs. 46-4 ← To p. 298
survival 46-8	Dust in the eyes elicits lachrymal secretion. Tears further the survival of the organism by washing out dust. Any organism not possessing this ____ would probably suffer damage to its vision. 46-9 ← To p. 298
operant 46-13	The sneezing little boy who "only does it to annoy" exhibits (1) ____ behavior rather than (2) ____ behavior. 46-14 ← To p. 298
(1) reflex (respondent) (2) operant 46-18	When we keep from coughing by sucking a soothing or narcotic cough drop or sipping a little water, we control a reflex by removing or minimizing its ____. 46-19 ← To p. 298
stimulus 46-23	Vomiting in response to a feather in the throat is a(n) (1) ____; the behavior of tickling the throat with a feather is a(n) (2) ____. 46-24 ← To p. 298
(1) involuntary (2) voluntary 46-28	The term voluntary is a misleading description of operant behavior because operants * * * controlled through relevant variables as completely as respondents. 46-29 ← To p. 298

When a pigeon is first placed in the experimental space, there is a low _____ that a peck on the key will soon be emitted.

8-1

---

reinforced

8-5

When pecking the key is followed immediately with food, the _____ of the response is *observed* to increase.

8-6

---

rate
(frequency)

8-10

When a peck is followed by food, the event is described by saying, "The peck was followed by (1) reinforce-_____." The food is called a(n) (2) _____. (TT)

8-11

---

time

8-15

Forgetting and extinction are technical terms for different processes. The response is *emitted* without reinforcement only in the process called (1) _____. The response is *not emitted* in the process called (2) _____.

8-16

---

operates upon
(acts upon,
changes,
affects)

8-20

There are two classes of behavior, *operant* and *respondent*. (1) _____ behavior is influenced by the consequences of previous, similar responses whereas in (2) _____ behavior, a stimulus precedes the response.

8-21

---

increase
(rise)

8-25

The mother who feeds her baby when he "coos" increases the rate of "cooing." When the rate of "cooing" has increased because of the reinforcement, the operant has become _____. (TT)

8-26

---

(1) probable
    (likely)
(2) reinforced
    (acceptable:
    conditioned)

8-30

If a water fountain consistently fails to operate, you cease to go to it when thirsty. Because of the lack of (1) _____ (TT), the operant has been (2) _____. (TT)

8-31

reduces (eliminates) 46-2	When a man pulls his hand away from a hot stove, the (1) _____ terminates the (2) _____ which elicited it. <div align="right">46-3</div>
sneezing (coughing) 46-7	In struggling against an inadequate supply of air, "gasping for air" is respondent behavior which supplements defective respiration and increases the chances of _____ of organisms possessing this reflex. <div align="right">46-8</div>
operant 46-12	In general, "operant reinforcement" of glandular responses has no direct effect. *Vocal* "crying for attention," however, is clearly a(n)_____. <div align="right">46-13</div>
(1) avoid (2) operant 46-17	To keep from "flinching" when firing a pistol, we can oppose the (1) _____ response of flinching with an incompatible strong (2) _____ response of holding the hand and arm steady. <div align="right">46-18</div>
is not (cannot be) 46-22	By tickling his throat with a feather or drinking an irritating solution of mustard and water, a man can regurgitate poisonous food. The operant behavior of tickling or drinking controls a respondent by producing the _____ for it. <div align="right">46-23</div>
control 46-27	Reflex behavior is commonly called *involuntary*; operant behavior is called *voluntary*. Thus, vomiting is said to be (1) _____, while emptying one's plate into a garbage disposer is called (2) _____. <div align="right">46-28</div>

probability	To say that there is, at first, a low probability of pecking the key, means that the pigeon will emit pecks at a low _____ or _____ . (GIVE BOTH)
8-1	8-2

rate (frequency) (NOT: probability)	After the pigeon pecks the key and receives food, it begins to peck steadily. Presenting food is said to have _____ pecking, which has now become con- ditioned.
8-6	8-7

(1) (reinforce-) ment (2) reinforcer (reinforcing stimulus)	When food no longer follows pecking, the (1) _____ of emitting the response is observed to decline gradually. This process is called (2) _____ .
8-11	8-12

(1) extinction (2) forgetting	Pecking the key is an example of behavior which operates upon the environment. Thus it is a(n) _____ .
8-16	8-17

(1) Operant (2) respondent (reflex)	The diameters of visceral organs are changed by (1) _____ muscles. Parts of the skeletal frame are moved by (2) _____ muscles.
8-21	8-22

conditioned	The mother can reinforce an infant's vocal behavior only after at least one vocalization has been _____ .
8-26	8-27

1) reinforcement 2) extinguished	**End of Set**
8-31	

stimulus 46-1	Heavy exercise overheats the body and produces sweating. The cooling effect of the evaporation of sweat from the skin _____ the stimulating condition which elicited the response of sweating. 46-2
survival value 46-6	Roughly speaking, the purpose of the reflex called _____ is to remove irritants from the *upper* respiratory passages. 46-7
is 46-11	If shedding tears increased in frequency when followed by displayed affection, we would call crying a conditioned _____ response. It is doubtful, however, that the case is ever that simple 46-12
(1) respondent (reflex) (2) operant 46-16	The yawning reflex often offends one's companions. We stifle a yawn by holding our jaw rigid in order to (1) _____ aversive social consequences. Holding the jaw rigid is a(n) (2) _____. 46-17
(1) terminated (eliminated, escaped) (2) avoids (prevents) 46-21	A man is told that food he has just eaten is dangerously spoiled; he does not regurgitate the food in a manner which resembles throwing food away. Vomiting * * * directly controlled by avoidance contingencies. 46-22
(1) avoids (2) reduces (terminates, escapes) 46-26	The operant "holding the breath" under water exerts control over reflex breathing. But the operant is itself under the _____ of avoidance contingencies. 46-27

rate (or) frequency (GIVE BOTH) 8-2	REFER TO THE FOOTNOTE ON THE EXHIBIT. A given peck on the key is a(n) (1) _____. The general behavior of "pecking a key" is a(n) (2) _____. 8-3
reinforced 8-7	In operant behavior, the temporal order of the response and the reinforcing stimulus is first the (1) _____ (TT) and then the (2) _____ _____. (TT) 8-8
(1) rate (frequency) (2) extinction 8-12	When the rate of pecking has returned to its initial low level as a result of withholding food, the operant is said to have been _____. 8-13
operant 8-17	Operant behavior has direct effects on the environment. One consequence which results in an increase in the subsequent rate of the operant response is called a(n) _____. (TT) 8-18
(1) smooth (2) striated (striped, skeletal) 8-22	Action upon the environment usually results from movement of the skeletal frame. Operants are usually contractions of _____ muscles. 8-23
emitted (made) 8-27	The psychologist fed the baby when he emitted "coos," but *not* when he cried. We should expect that crying when hungry would be (1) _____ because of the withholding of (2) _____. 8-28

A reflex response may change the stimulus which elicits it. When coughing dislodges a bit of food in the throat, the response eliminates its own ____.

46-1

---

survival

46-5

The *purpose* of sneezing is the effect which gives the reflex ____ ____.

46-6

---

did not

46-10

The temporal relation between a child's weeping and a resulting display of parental affection * * * like the principal contingency in operant conditioning.

46-11

---

respondent (reflex)

46-15

When a movie script calls for violent coughing, the director may ask a mediocre actor to inhale irritating fumes. He gets "realism" by demanding (1) ____ behavior rather than (2) ____ behavior.

46-16

---

response

46-20

A man is told that food he is starting to eat may be dangerously spoiled; he immediately throws it away. A conditioned aversive stimulus is thus (1) ____. This operant response (2) ____ actual poisoning.

46-21

---

(1) operant
(2) respondent (reflex)

46-25

In holding one's breath under water, the operant which opposes reflex breathing (1) ____ the irritation of inhaled water and (2) ____ conditioned aversive stimuli established by previous inhalation of water.

46-26

---

(1) operant
(2) respondent (reflex response)

46-30

Breathing rapidly to hyperventilate before swimming under water is "voluntary" or (1) ____ breathing; the swimmer surfaces before "involuntary" or (2) ____ breathing becomes too powerful to be suppressed by an operant.

46-31

(1) response (2) operant 8-3	The experiment described on the exhibit is concerned with (1) _____ (TT) behavior. The apparatus reinforces specific (2) _____ (TT) when they are emitted. 8-4 ← To p. 47
) response) reinforcing stimulus (reinforcer, reinforcement) 8-8	A stimulus elicits a response in *respondent* (reflex) behavior. In respondent behavior, the temporal order is first the (1) _____, then the (2) _____. 8-9 ← To p. 47
extinguished 8-13	A response is said to be extinguished when its rate has returned to its initial low level because responses have been emitted but _____ followed by reinforcement. 8-14 ← To p. 47
reinforcement 8-18	The word *operant* is a noun or an adjective indicating something which is operative or has an influence. Operant behavior * * * the environment. 8-10 ← To p. 47
striated (striped, skeletal) 8-23	*After* a hungry infant begins crying, he is fed; soon he cries regularly when hungry. Feeding is said to have _____ crying which has now become conditioned. 8-24 ← To p. 47
extinguished (decreased) reinforcement (food) 8-28	Vocalizations are classed as (1) _____ behavior when they act upon the environment (social, in this case). In that case, their frequency depends on whether or not they are (2) _____. 8-29 ← To p. 47

has (is of) 46-4	When overheating causes the small blood vessels in the skin to enlarge and suffuse the skin with blood ("flushing"), heat is more rapidly lost. The reflex has ____ value in lowering dangerous body temperatures. 46-5
reflex 46-9	When a child's tears lead to a display of parental affection, the reflex response is followed by a consequence which probably * * * figure in its evolutionary development. 46-10
(1) operant (2) respondent (reflex) 46-14	When an actor imitates "gasping for air" in a scene in a disabled submarine, he engages in operant behavior, the topography of which closely approximates ____ behavior. 46-15
stimulus 46-19	When we choke back a sob, we control a reflex with an incompatible response. The operant "choking back" suppresses a reflex ____. 46-20
(1) respondent (reflex) (2) operant 46-24	In holding one's breath under water, (1) ____ behavior is controlling (2) ____ behavior. 46-25
are 46-29	Taking snuff to induce a sneeze might be called the "voluntary" control of "involuntary" behavior. The whole act represents a chain, the first member of which is a(n) (1) ____ response which produces a stimulus for a(n) (2) ____. 46-30

Set 9

Positive and Negative Reinforcement

Estimated time: 14 minutes   **Turn to next page and begin** ▶

---

negative

9-4

Turning off a television commercial is reinforced by the *termination* of a(n) (1) _____ reinforcer; turning on a very funny program is reinforced by the *presentation* of a(n) (2) _____ reinforcer.

9-5

---

(1) positive
    reinforcer
(2) negative
    reinforcer

9-9

A man turns his face away from an ugly sight. Turning away is reinforced by the _____ of the ugly sight (a negative reinforcer).

9-10

---

reinforced
(acceptable:
conditioned)

9-14

"What does he see in her?" might mean "How does she _____ his courting behavior?" (TT)

9-15

) not reinforcing
   (extinguishing)
) incompatible

9-19

A school teacher is likely, when possible, to dismiss a class when her students are rowdy because she has been _____ by elimination of the stimuli arising from a rowdy class.

9-20

) decreases
) extinguished
   (not reinforced)

9-24

Absenteeism increases if employees are not sufficiently _____ with wages and suitable working conditions. (TT)

9-25

---

reinforcer
(reinforcing
stimulus)

9-29

End of Set

reinforced (conditioned) 45-3	As described in (A) and (B), it appears that the dog threw itself against the door primarily because of Mrs. Frazier's subsequent action in * * *. 45-4 ← To p. 293
intermittent 45-8	If Mrs. Frazier acts in (B) to stop the dog's whining and banging *while* it is happening, her own behavior is an example of _____ behavior. 45-9 ← To p. 293
continuous 45-13	In (E), another new contingency has developed which can influence Mrs. Frazier's behavior. Spending so much time opening the door * * * an aversive condition for Mrs. Frazier. 45-14 ← To p. 293
rates (frequencies) 45-18	Mrs. Frazier controlled the dog's behavior in a satisfactory way principally through positive re-inforcement. She * * * resort to aversive control or punishment. 45-19 ← To p. 293
positive (and) negative (EITHER ORDER) 45-23	Removing the card while the dog was watching would _____ (TT) whatever the dog was doing. 45-24 ← To p. 293
avoidance 45-28	The result as described in (H) was to prevent further damage to the door by eliminating certain behavior with an (1) S____. Only when the (2) S____ was present did Mrs. Frazier need to open the door at the first whine. 45-29 ← To p. 293

A hungry pigeon pecks a key and is immediately given food. The (1) _____ of the pecking response will increase since presenting food (2) * * * a reinforcement.

9-1

---

(1) negative
(2) positive

9-5

A stimulus is called a negative reinforcer if its _____-tion reinforces behavior.

9-6

---

termination
(end, removal)

9-10

A food-deprived child will probably ask for food if the response "asking for food" has been (1) _____ in the past. This is an example of (2) _____ reinforcement.

9-11

---

reinforce

9-15

The man who brings candy to his wife to end an argument may find later that his wife argues _____ (more or less?) frequently. An appeaser has worked as a reinforcer.

9-16

---

reinforced
(negatively
reinforced)

9-20

The teacher who dismisses a class when it is rowdy probably causes the frequency of rowdy behavior to (1) _____, since dismissal from class is probably a(n) (2) _____ for rowdy children.

9-21

---

reinforced

9-25

In looking for lost car keys, one may search the same littered table top several times before this behavior is _____ through consistent failure to find them.

9-26

---

increased 45-2	The dog may have mechanically opened some other door by throwing its forelegs against the door. If so, the response was _____ previously by a natural contingency. 45-3
(1) in(-side) (2) out(-side) 45-7	In (B), "occasionally" means that Mrs. Frazier provided _____ reinforcement. 45-8
(1) escape (2) avoidance 45-12	When, in (D), Mrs. Frazier starts opening the door after the dog's *first* faint whine, the dog's whining is on the schedule called _____ reinforcement. 45-13
was not (is not) 45-17	The dog's "asking to be let in" soon occurred with two very different _____ depending on whether the card was or was not in place. 45-18
(1) $(S)^\Delta$ (2) $(S)^D$ 45-22	*Removing* an S^Δ or *presenting* an S^D are two ways of describing the same change of stimulus. It is reinforcement although the distinction between _____ and _____ reinforcement cannot be made. 45-23
$(S)^\Delta$ 45-27	In "turning back" in (J), the dog avoids an S^Δ which would have occurred if it had gone out on that occasion. We may interpret this "turning back" as _____ behavior. 45-28
negative 45-32	**End of Set**

(1) rate
    (frequency)
(2) is
    (constitutes,
    acts as)   **9-1**
	If, instead of presenting food after the pigeon pecks the key, a loud noise is turned *on*, the rate of pecking will *not* increase. Presenting a loud noise * * * a reinforcement.
	
	9-2

mina(-tion) imina(-tion)] **9-6**	Elimination of a television commercial may be a negative reinforcement. If so, the television commercial is a(n) _____ reinforce-_____. **9-7**
reinforced (conditioned) positive **9-11**	Both positive and negative reinforcement _____ the rate of response. **9-12**
more **9-16**	The man who brings his wife candy when she is especially agreeable may find that she argues * * *. He has reinforced responses which are incompatible with arguing. **9-17**
increase reinforcement **9-21**	A teacher who dismisses a class when it is quiet (1) _____ the probability of rowdy behavior. She is reinforcing responses which are (2) _____ with rowdiness. **9-22**
extinguished **9-26**	If people continue to buy books, music, and works of art, we conclude that these objects _____ the behavior of purchasing them. **9-27**

respondents (reflex responses) 45-1	We can say that whining is an operant if we can show that its frequency_____ as the result of Mrs. Frazier's opening the door in (B). 45-2
reinforced (conditioned) 45-6	(B) describes reinforcement only if being outside is reinforcing when the dog is (1) _____-side, and being inside when the dog is (2) _____-side. 45-7
slowly 45-11	(D) suggests that Mrs. Frazier's own behavior is no longer (1) _____ behavior (which *terminates* whining and scratching) but (2)_____ behavior (which *prevents* door scratching). 45-12
discrimination 45-16	The word "NO" on the card * * * more effective than, say, an equally conspicuous geometrical pattern. 45-17
S^D 45-21	Removing the card is a case of removing an (1) S_____ and presenting an (2) S_____. 45-22
accidental 45-26	(I) may be interpreted as the avoidance of a long S_____ period which by that time often occurred when the dog was outside. 45-27
reinforcing 45-31	In general, the dog reinforced Mrs. Frazier's own behavior by using_____reinforcement since the dog stopped whining and scratching. 45-32

is not 9-2	When pecking a key *turns off* a very loud noise for a few moments, frequency of pecking in the presence of the noise may be observed to *increase*. In that case ending the loud noise * * * a reinforcement. 9-3
negative (reinforce-)r 9-7	If a funny program is a positive reinforcer, presenting the program is a(n) _____ _____. 9-8
increase 9-12	When an infant emits the sounds "da-da," his father fondles him. We classify fondling as a reinforcer when we note that the infant (1) _____ this response more (2) _____. 9-13
less frequently (less often, less) 9-17	Two responses are incompatible when they cannot be emitted at the same time. A wife who reinforces her husband when he is agreeable may find the rate of arguments decreasing because arguments are _____ with being agreeable. 9-18
decreases incompatible 9-22	If we consistently get no answer when we dial a number, we stop dialing. This process is called (1) _____, and is due to lack of (2) _____. 9-23
reinforce (acceptable: condition) 9-27	To stop a dog from begging for food, one should _____ the operant by never again feeding it when it begs. 9-28

We cannot be sure that whining is an operant. It may be one of the many ____ which occur in an emotional state generated when a strong response cannot be executed.

45-1

---

would not

45-5

The expression "asking to be let out" suggests that the dog's behavior is similar to a human verbal response such as "open the door." Both responses are ____ by the action of a second organism.

45-6

---

variable (-)ratio

45-10

The schedule suggested in (B) should make the dog's behavior extinguish very ____ if reinforcement were discontinued.

45-11

---

(1) s^Δ
(2) s^D

45-15

When, in (F), Mrs. Frazier opened the door if the card wasn't in place but not if it was in place, she was establishing a(n) ____.

45-16

---

s^Δ

45-20

In (F), the door *without* the card became a(n) ____ for asking to be let in.

45-21

---

reinforce

45-25

The "silently" in (G) is important because it was advisable to remove the card without stimulating the dog in order to prevent ____ contingencies of reinforcement which might establish undesired superstitious behavior.

45-26

) extinction
) control
   (discrimination)

45-30

Occasionally letting the dog in when the card was in place would spoil the result by ____ the response in the presence of s^Δ, thus breaking down the discrimination.

45-31

is 9-3	Reinforcement which consists of *presenting* stimuli (e.g., food) is called *positive* reinforcement. In contrast, reinforcement which consists of *terminating* stimuli (e.g., painful stimuli) is called _____ reinforcement. 9-4 ← To p. 52
positive reinforcement 9-8	The rate of an operant can be increased by presenting a(n) (1) _____ _____ or by ending a(n) (2) _____ _____. 9-9 ← To p. 52
(1) emits (2) frequently (often) 9-13	When the father fondles the infant after it has said "da-da," the infant may smile, repeat "da-da," etc. If he continues to fondle the infant frequently, we assume that the smile, etc., have _____ the father's behavior. 9-14 ← To p. 52
incompatible 9-18	An undesired response can be eliminated by (1) * * * the response, or by reinforcing other responses which are (2) * * * with it. 9-19 ← To p. 52
extinction reinforcement 9-23	If an airplane spotter never sees the kind of plane he is to spot, his frequency of scanning the sky (1) _____. In other words, his "looking" behavior is (2) * * *. (TT) 9-24 ← To p. 52
extinguish 9-28	A stimulus which follows a response is called a(n) _____ if the rate at which similar responses are emitted is observed to increase. 9-29 ← To p. 52

Set 45

A Problem in Behavioral Engineering

Estimated time: 13 minutes

See exhibit on preceding page
Turn to next page and begin ▶

---

opening
the door
(reinforcing it)

45-4

If the dog pushed the door open and slipped through without help, we * * * say that the dog was "asking to be let out."

45-5

---

escape

45-9

If Mrs. Frazier acts in (B) only when there has been so much whining and banging that she "can't stand it any more," the dog is probably being reinforced on a(n) ____ - ____ schedule.

45-10

---

is (may be, was)

45-14

The card on the door became a(n) (1) ____ for the response of asking to be let in, and the door without a card became a(n) (2) ____ for the response.

45-15

---

did not

45-19

Because whining was never reinforced when the card was on the door, the card became a(n) ____ for the response of asking to be let in.

45-20

---

reinforce

45-24

It was important *not* to remove the card when the dog was whining or jumping against the door because that would ____ this behavior.

45-25

---

(1) $(S)^\Delta$
(2) $(S)^D$

45-29

A similar result could be achieved by completely extinguishing responses to the door, but the dog's "asking to be let in" was sometimes useful to Mrs. Frazier. Hence, (1) ____ was less suitable than establishing stimulus (2) ____.

45-30

increases 10-4	The receipt of candy as a result of "throwing a tantrum" is an example of _____ reinforcement. 10-5
incompatible with 10-9	Two ways of effectively preventing unwanted conditioned behavior are: to (1) _____ it by withholding reinforcement and to condition some (2) _____ behavior. 10-10
rate (frequency) (acceptable: probability) 10-14	Other things being equal, an operant which has been observed to occur at a high rate in the past has a high _____ of occurring at some future time. 10-15
(1) less (2) extinction 10-19	Reaching for a glass of water and saying "Water, please" are (1) _____; any specific instance of such behavior, however, is called a(n) (2) _____. 10-20
Operant 10-24	_____ usually control the internal economy of the organism. 10-25
emitted 10-29	In forgetting, a response decreases in probability with the passage of time during which it * * * emitted. 10-30

(A) Mrs. Frazier owned a dog which "asked to be let out or in" by whining softly and then standing on its hind legs and throwing its forepaws noisily against the door.

(B) Mrs. Frazier occasionally opened the door when the dog "asked to be let in or out."

(C) After the house was repainted and the door beautifully refinished, it became important for Mrs. Frazier to keep the dog from scratching the door.

(D) So Mrs. Frazier started responding to the dog's *first* faint whine, not waiting for the jump against the door.

(E) It was so easy to get in and out that the frequency of the behavior increased, and Mrs. Frazier began to spend a good share of the day letting the dog in and out.

(F) Mrs. Frazier solved the problem by hanging a card bearing the letters NO outside the door. The door was never opened when the card was in place; but when the card was *not* in place, the door was opened as soon as the dog whined.

(G) The card could be silently removed from the door through the mail slot.

(H) The dog quickly stopped "asking to be let in" when the card was in place. During this period, damage to the door was repaired. Henceforth, when it was convenient to let the dog in, Mrs. Frazier would remove the card. At other times the dog stayed outside without whining or throwing itself against the door.

(I) Because it was no longer easy to get back in, the dog now "asked to be let out" only infrequently.

(J) Sometimes, after asking to be let out, the dog would see Mrs. Frazier pick up the card to put on the door and would turn back and stay in the house.

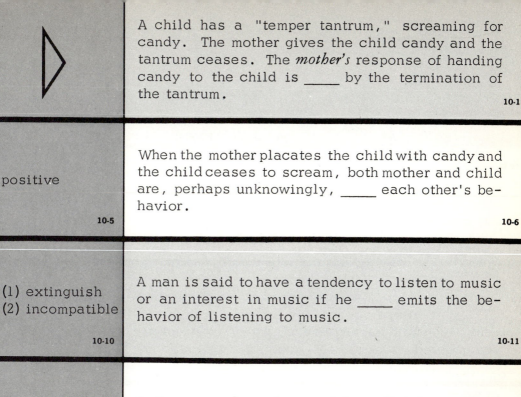

▷	A child has a "temper tantrum," screaming for candy. The mother gives the child candy and the tantrum ceases. The *mother's* response of handing candy to the child is _____ by the termination of the tantrum.
	10-1

positive	When the mother placates the child with candy and the child ceases to scream, both mother and child are, perhaps unknowingly, _____ each other's behavior.
10-5	10-6

(1) extinguish (2) incompatible	A man is said to have a tendency to listen to music or an interest in music if he _____ emits the behavior of listening to music.
10-10	10-11

probability (likelihood)	A pigeon pecks a key and immediately receives food. After this, it is more _____ that the pigeon will again emit the response.
10-15	10-16

(1) operants (2) response	After a response has been reinforced, the _____ is high that it will be repeated.
10-20	10-21

Respondents (Reflexes, smooth muscles, and glands)	The pairing of two stimuli is necessary to condition (1) _____ behavior; reinforcement is necessary for conditioning (2) _____ behavior.
10-25	10-26

is not	When, because a response is no longer followed by reinforcement, the response is emitted at a lowered rate, we say that _____ has taken place.
10-30	10-31

effect (result) **44-3**	A man paid for tearing down walls is insulted by his employer. In working, he swings his sledge hammer with great vigor. The money he is paid affects this behavior as a(n) (1) _____, the insult as a(n) (2) _____ stimulus. **44-4** ← To p. 287
many (multiple, more than one) **44-8**	As we write a paragraph, we create an elaborate chain of verbal stimuli which alter the probabilities of other words to follow. Sustained verbal behavior almost always involves _____ causes. **44-9** ← To p. 287
(1) multiple (several, different) (2) multiple (several, different) **44-13**	Two responses which cannot be emitted simultaneously are _____ responses. **44-14** ← To p. 287
algebraic summation **44-18**	A dog approaches a strange object. If the object is a positive reinforcer, (1) _____ the object is reinforced; if it is a negative reinforcer, withdrawing from the object is (2) _____. **44-19** ← To p. 287
approach **44-23**	An organism may oscillate between approach and withdrawal. When a dog first approaches, then withdraws, and then approaches again, it is _____ between two responses. **44-24** ← To p. 287
oscillation **44-28**	Many highly reinforced responses are also punished. A second response which terminates the conditioned aversive stimuli generated by a punished response may also be strong. These two responses are _____. **44-29** ← To p. 287
) incompatible (conflicting)) always (continuously, constantly) **44-33**	**End of Set**

reinforced 10-1	If termination of a temper tantrum reinforces a mother's response of giving candy to her child, the cessation of noise is an example of _____ reinforcement. 10-2
conditioning (acceptable: reinforcing) 10-6	To avoid conditioning temper tantrums, the mother should not _____ such behavior when it is emitted. 10-7
frequently (often) 10-11	We do not observe a "tendency" to listen to music or a "trait" such as a love for music. What we actually observe is that a man frequently _____ the behavior of listening to music. 10-12
probable (likely) 10-16	A pigeon pecks a key and immediately receives food. Technically speaking, the response is followed by _____. 10-17
probability 10-21	There *is* an eliciting stimulus for _____ behavior. 10-22
(1) respondent (reflex) (2) operant 10-26	The magnitude of the response is related to the intensity of the preceding stimulus in _____ behavior. 10-27
extinction 10-31	When, as a result of the *passage of time* with no opportunity to emit the response, a response is emitted at a lowered rate, we say that _____ has taken place. 10-32

can 44-2	A restaurant hires a pretty waitress and serves good food. Two different reinforcers, good food and a view of a pretty waitress, have a common _____ in increasing patronage. 44-3
s^Ds (stimuli) 44-7	A word which "expresses multiple meanings" is controlled by * * * stimuli. 44-8
s^D (stimulus, variable) 44-12	A single event may have (1) _____ effects on behavior and (2) _____ events may have a common effect. 44-13
withdrawing 44-17	The separate probabilities of two conflicting responses may combine in *algebraic summation*. A timid man standing at the edge of a dance floor may show _____ _____ of the conflicting responses of approach and withdrawal. 44-18
withdraw (turn back) 44-22	After the dog turns away from a strange object, the variables controlling approach may increase and the variables controlling withdrawal may decrease. The dog may again _____ this object. 44-23
(1) algebraic summation (2) oscillation 44-27	In trying to decide about a purchase, we show _____ when we tentatively decide to buy, then not to buy, and then to buy, etc. 44-28
anxiety (emotion) 44-32	We might infer that an "anxiety neurosis" results when two (1) _____ responses are strong. Conditioned aversive stimuli are more or less continuously generated; hence the organism is nearly (2) _____ in a state of anxiety. 44-33

negative 10-2	With reference to the influence of the temper tantrum on the mother's behavior, the tantrum is a negative (1) reinforc-____; its cessation is a negative (2) reinforc-____. 10-3
reinforce 10-7	If temper tantrums have been previously conditioned, the mother can (1) ____ the response by consistently not (2) ____ it. 10-8
emits 10-12	We call a man a golf "enthusiast" if he frequently ____ the operant behavior of playing golf. 10-13
reinforcement 10-17	When a pigeon is reinforced for pecking a key, the (1) ____ at which the response is (2) ____ increases. 10-18
respondent (reflex) 10-22	There *is no* eliciting stimulus for ____ behavior. 10-23
respondent (reflex) 10-27	Most (1) ____ behavior involves the activity of smooth muscles and glands. Most (2) ____ behavior involves the activity of striated muscles. 10-28

two (both) 44-1	Two reinforcers * * * (can or cannot?) have a common effect in increasing the probability of a given operant. 44-2
the same (one, a single, a given) 44-6	The verbal response "house" may be under the control of an actual house, a printed word, a spoken word, or words which frequently precede the word, as in completing "the White. . ." Many _____ exert control over the same response. 44-7
prompt 44-11	In puns, verbal slips, etc., the "multiple meaning" of a word is important. By "multiple meaning" we imply that more than one _____ (TT) is contributing to the probability of the response. 44-12
probability 44-16	If uncomplicated by other variables, a dog's history of negative reinforcement for withdrawing from strange objects determines its probability of _____ from another strange object. 44-17
algebraic summation 44-21	As a dog approaches a strange object, the variables controlling withdrawal may increase. When in algebraic summation, the tendency to withdraw exceeds the tendency to approach, the dog will _____. 44-22
increases 44-26	When a dog stands "not too close and not too far" from a strange object, its behavior shows (1) _____ _____. When it approaches, jumps back, approaches, etc., it shows (2) _____. 44-27
anxiety (emotion) 44-31	When one or more of the variables controlling a response is aversive, prolonged conflict may result in a sustained state of _____. 44-32

) (reinforc-)er
) (reinforc-)ement

10-3

When a temper tantrum results in the receipt of candy, the probability that the child will have a tantrum in the future _____.

10-4

← To p. 57

---

(1) extinguish
(2) reinforcing

10-8

In addition to extinguishing temper tantrums, the mother may frequently reinforce "playing quietly." This would help to eliminate tantrums by conditioning behavior which is * * * them.

10-9

← To p. 57

---

emits

10-13

Many so-called traits (aggressiveness, persistence, friendliness, etc.) are simply ways of indicating an individual's _____ of emitting certain types of behavior.

10-14

← To p. 57

---

(1) rate
    (frequency)
(2) emitted

10-18

If a previously reinforced response is no longer reinforced, it soon occurs (1) _____ frequently. This is called (2) _____.

10-19

← To p. 57

---

operant

10-23

_____ (Operant or Respondent?) behavior usually acts upon the external environment.

10-24

← To p. 57

---

(1) respondent
(2) operant

10-28

In operant conditioning, a response can be reinforced only after it has been _____.

10-29

← To p. 57

Two "causes" may have a common effect. An operant reinforced with two reinforcers appropriate to two different deprivations will vary with _____ deprivations.

44-1

---

two
(multiple)

44-5

We may light a cigarette (a) on smelling cigarettes, (b) after seeing a friend light one, or (c) when watching a television advertisement for cigarettes. Three S^Ds can exert control over * * * response.

44-6

S^Ds (stimuli)

44-10

An actor may be unable to complete the recitation of a soliloquy until prompted. The soliloquy is a chain of verbal responses. The _____ (i.e., the added S^D) given to the actor is an additional source of stimulus control.

44-11

---

incompatible
(conflicting)

44-15

If uncomplicated by other variables, a dog's history of positive reinforcement for approaching strange objects determines its _____ of approaching another strange object.

44-16

---

approach (and)
withdrawal
(EITHER ORDER)

44-20

When incompatible responses are *diametrically opposed*, there may be a(n) _____ _____ of their independent probabilities, as when a soldier moves slowly into combat.

44-21

---

oscillation

44-25

There is oscillation in behavior when the act of beginning to execute a response _____ the strength of variables controlling a response diametrically opposed to it.

44-26

---

oscillate

44-30

When behavior which is both reinforced and punished shows oscillation, conditioned aversive stimuli are repeatedly generated. These stimuli may in turn generate a state of _____.

44-31

Read exhibit now and refer to it as needed during the first half of this lesson.

(A) A pigeon is deprived of food for some time.

(B) The pigeon is placed in a standard experimental space where a feeding mechanism filled with grain is presented occasionally for a few seconds.

(C) The feeding mechanism or "food magazine" makes a characteristic noise, and the food is illuminated while available.

(D) Noise and light from the magazine initially have no power to reinforce behavior.

(E) On the other hand, food does reinforce any behavior it may follow. (Food is an *unconditioned* or *primary reinforcer*.)

(F) When the magazine has been operated many times, the pigeon immediately responds to the noise and light by approaching and eating.

(G) All food is removed from the feeding mechanism.

(H) The empty magazine now operates only when a key is pecked.

(I) Although the magazine is empty, the rate of pecking the key increases. The sound and light of the magazine have evidently become *conditioned reinforcers* (sometimes called *secondary reinforcers*).

(J) The sound and light became *conditioned reinforcers* when they were repeatedly paired with food.

(K) When pecking the key continues to operate the empty magazine, the rate declines.

(L) The sound and light of the magazine are no longer paired with food and, through extinction, lose the power to reinforce.

Set 44

Multiple Causes and Conflicting Responses

Estimated time: 12 minutes

Turn to next page and begin ▶

---

(1) reinforcer
(2) aversive
    (emotional)

44-4

A man paid for tearing down walls is insulted by his employer. His great vigor in swinging his sledge hammer may reflect the combined effect of _____ variables.

44-5

---

multiple
(many,
several)

44-9

A quizmaster may give hints or prompts to a contestant. He is providing additional _____ to make the answer more probable.

44-10

---

incompatible

44-14

In the condition we call "conflict," the variables active at the moment strengthen two or more _____ responses.

44-15

---

(1) approaching
(2) reinforced

44-19

A dog approaches a strange object slowly. (Strange objects in the past have provided both reinforcing and aversive stimuli.) The slow approach represents algebraic summation of the probabilities of _____ and _____.

44-20

---

oscillating

44-24

Frequently "changing one's mind" about a purchase is an example of _____ between two responses.

44-25

---

incompatible
(conflicting)

44-29

When behavior is both strongly reinforced and severely punished, the organism may _____ between early phases of the two incompatible responses.

44-30

Set 11

Conditioned Reinforcers

See exhibit on preceding page

Estimated time: 26 minutes

Turn to next page and begin ▶

---

paired with
(followed by)

11-8

After (G), operation of the food magazine will pro-duce sound and light, but approaching the maga-zine will no longer be _____ by food.

11-9

---

paired

11-17

In the usual experiment, a peck operates a noisy magazine containing food. The peck is reinforced by both _____ and _____ reinforcement. (TTs)

11-18

---

conditioned
reinforcer

11-26

The exhibit experiment demonstrates that an op-erant can be conditioned *without* using a(n) _____ reinforcer.

11-27

---

e paired with
re followed by,
ightly precede)

11-35

When the chimpanzee drops tokens into the peanut vending machine, the tokens become (1) _____ re-inforcers because they slightly precede the food, a(n) (2) * * *.

11-36

---

two (both)

11-44

If tokens have been paired with unconditioned re-inforcers appropriate to many states of deprivation, there are _____ conditions of deprivation under which tokens reinforce behavior.

11-45

---

generalized
reinforcers

11-53

A parent's *attention* can _____ (TT) the behavior of a child.

11-54

S^Ds (stimuli) 43-3	In (C), the taste of candy probably _____ (TT) the behavior of putting candy in the mouth. 43-4 ← To p. 282
(1) (B) (2) (C) (3) multiple (several, three)　43-8	In the laboratory, it (1) * * * possible to isolate simple functional relations; but in interpreting most events outside of the laboratory, we must be alert to the possibility of (2) _____ effects in complex situations. 43-9 ← To p. 282
(1) satiating (2) emotional 43-13	The event of presenting a single bit of candy had _____ effects on the child's behavior. 43-14 ← To p. 282
isolate (analyze, study) 43-18	An experimenter often holds all independent variables constant except the one he is investigating. In this way, he is * * * the effect this variable has upon the dependent variable. 43-19 ← To p. 282
reinforced (conditioned) 43-23	By reinforcing some specific behavior with small amounts of attention for a few moments, we can (1) _____ the behavior without producing satiation. In this way, we can (2) _____ the two effects of attention.　43-24 ← To p. 282
decrease 43-28	Oscillation, or alternation, of emotional effects in extinction after continuous reinforcement produces a record showing a(n) _____ in response rate as well. 43-29 ← To p. 282

(A) is necessary if _____ is to be used as a reinforcer.

11-1

---

reinforced

11-9

After (G), the sound of the food magazine is no longer paired with the _____ reinforcer. (TT)

11-10

---

onditioned (and)
nconditioned
:ITHER ORDER)

11-18

When the magazine operates after a peck, the pigeon approaches it and eats. Since approaching the magazine takes time, there is a short delay between the response and the _____ reinforcement. (TT)

11-19

---

unconditioned

11-27

When you are reinforced for services by a check, the check is analogous to the * * * in the present experiment.

11-28

---

1) conditioned
2) unconditioned
   reinforcer

11-36

We can demonstrate that a token has become a conditioned reinforcer by delivering a token immediately _____ some new response has been emitted.

11-37

---

many

11-45

A reinforcer which is not dependent on any one specific deprivation is called a generalized reinforcer. A conditioned reinforcer becomes a generalized reinforcer when paired with * * * unconditioned reinforcers.

11-46

---

reinforce
(hence:
condition)

11-54

Feigning illness and being conspicuous (exhibitionism) often get attention. In other words, the attention of others _____ (TT) feigning illness and acting conspicuously.

11-55

elicits 43-2	In (C), visual stimuli from the candy are the _____ for eating the candy. 43-3
(1) decrease 　　(lower) (2) S^Ds 43-7	The single piece of candy which elicited a reflex response in (1) _____ (USE LETTER) was an S^D for ingestive behavior in (2) _____ (USE LETTER) and an S^D for verbal behavior in (E). Thus, this single event had (3) _____ effects. 43-8
reinforcer 43-12	The child may eat less in (H) partly because of the (1) _____ effect of eating the candy, (C), and partly because of the (2) _____ effect described in (G). 43-13
isolated (analyzed, separated, distinguished) 43-17	By using simple organisms with controlled histories in simple environments, we hold many variables constant in order to _____ one effective variable at a time. 43-18
satiation 43-22	If a child who has stopped misbehaving after receiving much attention is *more* likely to misbehave on future occasions, then "attention" _____ (TT) misbehaving. 43-23
increase 43-27	As an emotional effect wears off, the organism returns to a higher rate of responding even though extinction is still proceeding. This means that more responses are now going unreinforced. The emotional effect may therefore return. There is another _____ in rate. 43-28

food 11-1	In (B), approaching the food magazine is _____ by food, provided the pigeon reaches the magazine in time to eat. 11-2
unconditioned (acceptable: primary) 11-10	In (H), the key is connected with the magazine for the first time. Thus the response to be conditioned can not have had a previous history of _____. 11-11
unconditioned 11-19	When a peck on the key operates a full magazine, a little time elapses between the response and the unconditioned reinforcement because of the time needed for the pigeon to * * *. 11-20
noise and/or light (conditioned reinforcer) 11-28	You will not continue to work for checks which "bounce" because the (1) _____ reinforcing power disappears in (2) _____. (TT) 11-29
after 11-37	Tokens are shown to be reinforcers if they _____ the subsequent rate of response similar to a response they have followed. 11-38
several (many) 11-46	If a chimpanzee exchanges tokens for food, water, a mate, and escape from pain, a token becomes a(n) _____ _____. 11-47
reinforces (hence: conditions) 11-55	"Paying attention" or "looking interested" when someone talks will usually increase the (1) _____ at which he talks since "attention" is a(n) (2) _____ _____ for most persons. 11-56

effects (results, consequences) 43-1	(B) describes the effect of candy as a stimulus which _____ a reflex response. 43-2
(1) decreases (lowers) (2) increase (raise) 43-6	Even though (C) should slightly (1) _____ the deprivation level, the child now asks for candy at (E) although he did not at (A). This is due to the fact that the sight and taste of candy are (2) _____ for asking for more. 43-7
withholds (doesn't give, removes) 43-11	(G) describes an emotional effect produced by the withholding of a(n) _____, where reinforcement has previously been continuous. 43-12
decrease 43-16	We deliberately arrange experimental conditions to analyze (or isolate) the effects of a single variable. By changing the conditions specified in (D), the effect of stimulus control can be _____ from the effect of deprivation. 43-17
multiple (several) 43-21	A child who misbehaves to get attention will stop when suddenly given almost constant attention. Here the most obvious effect of giving attention is an example of _____ rather than reinforcement. 43-22
decline (decrease) 43-26	The emotional effect of failure to receive reinforcement may wear off and the rate will _____ somewhat. 43-27

reinforced [conditioned (by being reinforced)] 11-2	In (C), the noise and light of the magazine are being paired with _____. 11-3
...ditioning ...nforcement) 11-11	In (I), when a first peck to the new key is emitted, it is followed by the sound of the magazine. Since the magazine is empty, its presentation * * * followed by an unconditioned reinforcer. 11-12
approach the magazine (go to food) 11-20	When a peck operates the magazine, the noise of the magazine operation occurs immediately. The (1) _____ reinforcement is immediate, whereas the (2) _____ reinforcement is slightly delayed. 11-21
(1) conditioned (secondary) (2) extinction 11-29	A stimulus which acquires the property of a reinforcer is called a(n) _____ reinforcer. 11-30
increase 11-38	When a chimpanzee who has exchanged tokens for peanuts presses a telegraph key, a token is delivered. If the token is a conditioned reinforcer, the _____ of the response, pressing the key, will be observed to increase. 11-39
generalized reinforcer (conditioned generalized reinforcer) 11-47	After the chimpanzee has exchanged tokens for food, water, a mate, etc., the tokens * * * effective if the chimpanzee is well-fed but deprived of water. 11-48
rate (frequency) (conditioned) generalized reinforcer 11-56	People frequently show *approval* just before they provide many different types of reinforcers. Smiles, the word "good," and other "signs of approval" become conditioned _____ _____. 11-57

The single event described in (A) has several different _____.

43-1

---

are (were)

43-5

Ingestion of food produces satiation, an operation which (1) _____ the probability of "asking for food." At the same time, the discriminative stimuli generated by eating (2) _____ the probability of that response.

43-6

---

multiple effects (several, many, three effects)

43-10

Although the verbal response "asking for more," (E), has been maintained by nearly continuous reinforcement, in (F), the parent _____ the positive reinforcer, candy.

43-11

---

would not

43-15

When stimuli from candy no longer serve as S^Ds, we should observe a decrease in the probability of asking for candy after eating a little candy. The decrease would be due to a(n) _____ in deprivation.

43-16

---

(1) is not
(2) is

43-20

A single aversive stimulus used in punishment elicits respondents, conditions other stimuli to elicit these respondents, and makes possible the conditioning of avoidance behavior. The single aversive stimulus has _____ effects.

43-21

---

decrease (lower, reduce)

43-25

The single operation of withholding positive reinforcement has two effects; both effects are a(n) _____ in rate.

43-26

food (reinforcement) 11-3	In (D), before being paired with food, the noise of the magazine * * * reinforce a response which it follows. 11-4
is not 11-12	In (I), because the rate of key pecking increases when followed by the sound of the empty food magazine, we conclude that this sound is a(n) _____ _____ 11-13
) conditioned) unconditioned 11-21	The conditioned reinforcer (noise of the magazine) occurs (1) _____ after a response to the key, but the unconditioned reinforcer is (2) _____ until the pigeon reaches the magazine. 11-22
conditioned (secondary) 11-30	A stimulus which has the property of a reinforcer without prior conditioning is called a(n) * * *. 11-31
rate (frequency) 11-39	The chimpanzee is being "paid" with tokens for pressing the key. Technically, we say its responses of pressing the key are _____. 11-40
are (will be, remain) 11-48	The effectiveness of a generalized reinforcer is relatively independent of the organism's condition of _____ at any given moment. 11-49
generalized reinforcers 11-57	You may show affection or approval to _____ (TT) a response you want another person to emit more frequently. 11-58

Set 43

Multiple Effects

See exhibit on preceding page

Estimated time: 15 minutes

Turn to next page and begin ▶

---

reinforces
(conditions)

43-4

Because of (D), the sight and taste of one piece of candy * * * S^Ds for asking for more candy.

43-5

---

(1) is
(2) multiple
(many,
various)

43-9

Events in everyday situations are often complex in that a single event may have multiple effects. In the episode described in the exhibit, the piece of candy had _____ _____.

43-10

---

multiple
(several)

43-14

If, once each day, we gave a single piece of candy (never followed by additional candy), the stimuli from the candy * * * serve as an S^D for asking for more.

43-15

---

analyzing
(isolating)

43-19

The relation between (A) and (E) is often called "whetting the appetite." It (1) * * * an example of a change in deprivation; it (2) * * * an illustration of the role of the candy in providing an S^D for further behavior.

43-20

---

(1) reinforce
(condition)
(2) isolate
(analyze,
separate)
43-24

When reinforcement is withheld after continuous reinforcement, response rate declines in extinction. Emotional behavior also occurs, and if this is incompatible with the response, it will _____ the rate further.

43-25

cannot (will not, would fail to) 11-4	In (E), food is termed an unconditioned reinforcer (or primary reinforcer) because its reinforcing power * * * depend on previous conditioning. 11-5
conditioned reinforcer (acceptable: secondary reinforcer) 11-13	Because the sound of the magazine *acquired* its power to reinforce, it is called a(n) ____ ____ . 11-14
(1) immediately (quickly) (2) delayed 11-22	In (I), the noise of the magazine will reinforce a response only if the pigeon is deprived of food. Both ____ and ____ reinforcers depend on food deprivation. 11-23
unconditioned reinforcer 11-31	If a conditioned reinforcer is not occasionally paired with an unconditioned reinforcer, its effectiveness as a reinforcer is ____ . 11-32
reinforced (acceptable: conditioned) 11-40	If the chimpanzee can no longer use tokens in the vending machine, tokens will (1) ____ their power to reinforce through the process called (2) ____ . 11-41
deprivation (acceptable: satiation, hunger) 11-49	A conditioned reinforcer can become a(n) * * * by being paired with *several* unconditioned reinforcers appropriate to various kinds of deprivation. 11-50
reinforce (condition) 11-58	You may withhold affection or approval to ____ (TT) behavior you don't want another person to emit. 11-59

(A) A parent gives a child a small piece of candy, although the child has not recently asked for candy.

(B) The child salivates and

(C) eats the candy.

(D) In the child's history, getting and eating one piece of candy has usually been followed by getting another piece.

(E) The child asks for more candy; but

(F) although the parent usually gives more candy when asked, this time no more candy is given.

(G) The child cries, his face grows red, and finally he has a temper tantrum.

(H) Dinner is served a few minutes later, and the child eats less than usual.

does not	A synonym for "unconditioned reinforcer" is "_____ reinforcer."
11-5	11-6

conditioned reinforcer (secondary reinforcer)	A synonym for "conditioned reinforcer" is "_____ reinforcer."
11-14	11-15

conditioned (and) unconditioned (EITHER ORDER)	A conditioned reinforcer which has acquired its capacity to reinforce by being paired with food is effective only when the animal is * * *.
11-23	11-24

extinguished (decreased)	A chimpanzee drops tokens into a vending machine which delivers peanuts. The peanuts are _____-ed reinforcers which increase the frequency of depositing tokens into the machine.
11-32	11-33

(1) lose (2) extinction	Food will reinforce a response only if the chimpanzee is deprived of food. Similarly, if the tokens have been paired only with food, they will be effective as reinforcers only if the chimpanzee is * * *.
11-41	11-42

generalized reinforcer (conditioned generalized reinforcer)	A generalized reinforcer is nearly _____ of the specific state of deprivation of the organism.
11-50	11-51

extinguish	Mr. X succeeds in coercing people into reinforcing him in many *different* ways. Signs of submissiveness in others then become _____ _____ which increase the frequency of new forms of coercion, independent of the particular deprivation.
11-59	11-60

behavior

42-3

A meteorologist who attempts to bring about rain by "seeding" clouds with dry ice is attempting to _____ the weather.

42-4
← To p. 276

---

(1) predicting
(2) controlling
(3) interpreting

42-8

A phenomenon is explained scientifically when we can state how it can be _____, _____, or _____.

42-9
← To p. 276

---

dependent

42-13

A scientist manipulates (1) _____ variables to determine whether they affect the (2) _____ variable in which he is interested.

42-14
← To p. 276

---

(1) independent
variable
(2) dependent
variable
(EITHER ORDER)

42-18

In a reflex, response magnitude is a(n) _____ of stimulus intensity.

42-19
← To p. 276

---

(1) independent
(2) dependent
(3) functional
relation
(4) law

42-23

When a functional relation is known, we may be able to manipulate the (1) * * * to control the (2) * * *.

42-24
← To p. 276

---

interpretation

42-28

By saying that nature is lawful, we mean that there are _____ relations between variables.

42-29
← To p. 276

---

is

42-33

End of Set

primary 11-6	In (F), approaching the magazine when it operates has been _____ because it has been consistently followed by an unconditioned reinforcer (food). 11-7
secondary 11-15	In (L), when the sound of the magazine is never followed by food, its capacity to reinforce is _____. (TT) 11-16
deprived of food (hungry) 11-24	Establishing a conditioned reinforcer is similar to respondent conditioning in that both require that two stimuli be _____. 11-25
ncondition(-ed) 11-33	When the chimpanzee drops tokens into a vending machine, the visual and tactual stimuli provided by the token occur, in time, slightly _____ the food. 11-34
deprived of food (hungry) 11-42	The chimpanzee has "bought" only peanuts with tokens. If he has just eaten his fill of peanuts, the tokens * * * be capable of reinforcing. 11-43
independent 11-51	Money buys many things. Money is a(n) * * *. It must have acquired this property by being frequently paired with many *different* reinforcers in the behavior we call "buying." 11-52

goals (aims, purposes, functions) 42-2	A science of behavior has as its goal the prediction, control, and interpretation of the ____ of living organisms. 42-3
interpret 42-7	The astronomer who gives the date of the next eclipse of the moon is (1) ____ an event; when he puts a satellite in orbit he is (2) ____ an event; when he explains the craters on the moon he is (3) ____ a thing or event. 42-8
(1) dependent (2) independent 42-12	A variable which a science attempts to explain is called a(n) ____ variable. 42-13
a function of 42-17	In a functional relation, there is an observed systematic relation between a(n) (1) * * * and a(n) (2) * * *. 42-18
law 42-22	We sometimes speak of cause-and-effect relations. A "cause" is a(n) (1) ____ variable, and an "effect" is a(n) (2) ____ variable. The relation is a(n) (3) ____ ____ and, when well established, it is formulated as a(n) (4) ____. 42-23
(1) predictions (2) control 42-27	When we show that an established relation between behavior and a given set of conditions may be exemplified in a given case, we engage in ____. 42-28
were not (was in-) 42-32	As a science succeeds in discovering functional relations, the assumption of lawfulness * * * confirmed. 42-33

conditioned (acceptable: reinforced)	In (F), the sound of the magazine is repeatedly being * * * food in the mouth.
11-7	11-8 ← To p. 63

extinguished	In the usual experiment, the magazine always contains grain. The conditioned reinforcer (noise) is not extinguished because the conditioned and unconditioned reinforcers continue to be ____.
11-16	11-17 ← To p. 63

paired	Pavlov's dog salivated when a tone (conditioned stimulus) sounded. An operant could probably have been conditioned by letting the response produce the tone because the tone would be a(n) ____ ____ as well.
11-25	11-26 ← To p. 63

before (prior to)	When the chimpanzee regularly "buys" food with tokens, the tokens become conditioned reinforcers since the tokens repeatedly * * * food.
11-34	11-35 ← To p. 63

will not (should not)	If the chimpanzee has exchanged tokens for food when food-deprived and for water when water-deprived, then tokens will be able to reinforce behavior under ____ (HOW MANY?) kinds of deprivation(s).
11-43	11-44 ← To p. 63

generalized reinforcer (conditioned generalized reinforcer)	A parent "pays attention" when he approaches a child, looks at him, touches him, etc. These activities generate stimuli affecting the child. The parent also provides food, water, loving care, etc. The stimuli arising from parental "attention" become (conditioned) ____ ____ for the child.
11-52	11-53 ← To p. 63

prediction 42-1	Prediction, control, and interpretation are the _____ of science. 42-2
predict 42-6	Pavlov became interested in conditioning when he noticed spontaneous secretion of saliva when no food was in the mouth. As a result of his experiments, he could _____ these spontaneous secretions as possibly resulting from conditioned stimuli. 42-7
dependent 42-11	In operant behavior, probability of response is the major (1) _____ variable; a condition of deprivation is one of the (2) _____ variables. 42-12
(1) dependent (2) independent 42-16	When a functional relation exists between a dependent and an independent variable, the dependent variable is said to be a function of the independent variable. Rate of emission of an operant is * * * the level of deprivation. 42-17
law 42-21	An established functional relation is a scientific _____. 42-22

(1) predict
    (determine,
    deduce)
(2) dependent
    variable 42-26
	When we state the probability of occurrence of a given response under a given set of conditions, we engage in (1) _____. When we arrange a set of conditions under which behavior has an assigned probability, we engage in (2) _____.
	
	42-27

(1) lawful (2) assuming 42-31	A science would not be successful in discovering functional relations if the assumption of lawfulness * * * valid. 42-32

Do not study exhibit in advance; use exhibit as needed in answering items.

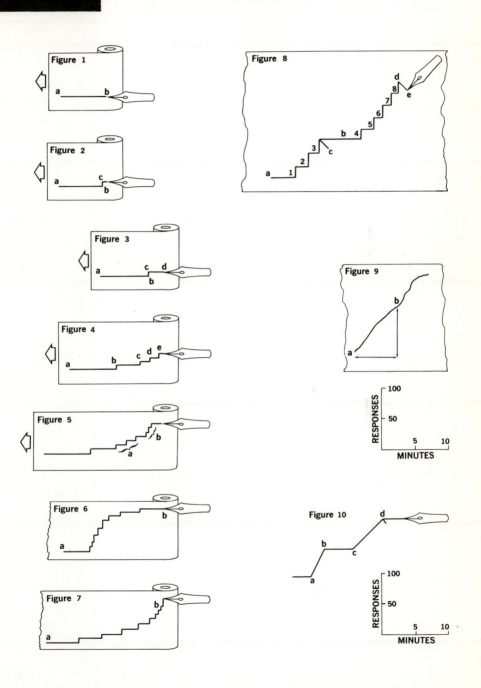

Figure 1

Figure 2

Figure 3

Figure 4

Figure 5

Figure 6

Figure 7

Figure 8

Figure 9

Figure 10

Science has as its goal the prediction, control, and interpretation of natural events. A meteorologist makes a(n) _____ when he forecasts tomorrow's weather.

42-1

---

control

42-5

In a reflex, if we know the intensity of a stimulus, we can _____ the magnitude and latency of the response.

42-6

---

(1) stimulus
(2) dependent

42-10

In operant behavior, the frequency of a response is _____ upon reinforcement history, states of deprivation, and stimulus conditions.

42-11

---

functional
relation

42-15

When an independent variable is shown to affect a dependent variable, the (1) _____ variable is said to be a function of the (2) _____ variable.

42-16

---

independent

42-20

The statement of the functional relation between velocity of a freely falling body and time of fall is called "the _____ of gravity."

42-21

---

(1) predict
(2) control
(3) interpret

42-25

If we know the values assumed by an independent variable; we can (1) _____ the values of the (2) * * *.

42-26

---

(1) functional
     relations
(2) lawful
     (determined,
     ordered)
42-30

In the beginning, a science merely assumes that its subject matter is (1) _____. Behavioral science begins by (2) _____ that behavior is lawful.

42-31

Set 12

The Cumulative Recorder

See exhibit on preceding page

Estimated time: 11 minutes   **Turn to next page and begin** ▷

---

(1) **a**
(2) **d**

12-4

In Figure 3, the time which elapsed between **a** and **b** is _____ than the time which elapsed between **c** and **d**.

12-5

---

(1) shorter
(2) shorter

12-9

In Figure 5, the higher the rate of responding, the (1) _____ the slope of the steplike line. We can determine the rate of responding from the (2) _____ of the steplike line.

12-10

7

12-14

Negative acceleration refers to a(n) (1) _____ in rate. Negative acceleration is shown in either Figure 6 or Figure 7. (WHICH?) Figure (2) _____.

12-15

---

3 (and) 8

12-19

In Figure 10, a response was reinforced at _____.

12-20

---

proximately) 5

12-24

In Figure 10, the animal emitted about _____ responses between **a** and **b**.

12-25

---

(1) vertical
(2) horizontal

12-29

In a cumulative curve, the *slope* is a record of the animal's * * *.

12-30

Set 42

Goals and Techniques of Science

Estimated time: 12 minutes   **Turn to next page and begin** ▶

---

control

42-4

A respondent is always under the _____ of a stimulus.

42-5

---

predicted,
controlled, (or)
interpreted

42-9

In a reflex, response magnitude is *dependent* upon the intensity of the (1) _____. The stimulus intensity is called the independent variable, and the response magnitude the (2) _____ variable.

42-10

---

(1) independent
(2) dependent

42-14

When changes in an independent variable provide systematic changes in a dependent variable, there is a functional relation between them. In reflexes, there is a(n) _____ _____ between stimulus intensity and response magnitude.

42-15

---

function

42-19

A law of behavior is a statement of an established functional relation between responding and one or more of the _____ variables which control it.

42-20

---

(1) independent
variable
(2) dependent
variable

42-24

Knowing a set of conditions, we can (1) _____ behavior; manipulating a set of conditions, we can (2) _____ behavior; knowing an effect, we might be able to (3) _____ it in relation to its causes.

42-25

---

functional

42-29

A science is only possible if there are (1) _____ _____ between variables, i.e., a science is possible only if its subject matter is (2) _____ as opposed to unlawful or capricious.

42-30

In Figure 1, a broad strip of paper is unwinding from a roll. The end of the paper is moving slowly toward the left. A pen held against the paper in a fixed position has drawn a line beginning at (1) _____ and ending at (2) _____.

12-1

---

longer
(greater,
more)

12-5

In recording the behavior of an organism, the pen moves upward and draws one short vertical line each time a response is made. In Figure 4, an experiment began when the pen was at **a**. The first response was made at _____.

12-6

---

(1) steeper
   (higher,
   greater)
(2) slope

12-10

In Figure 6, responding begins at a relatively high rate at **a**. The time between successive responses grows progressively _____.

12-11

---

(1) decrease
(2) 6

12-15

An increase in rate is called (1) _____ _____, and a decrease in rate is called (2) _____ _____.

12-16

---

d

12-20

If the paper moves slowly and if each vertical step is small, we cannot see the steplike record of a single response. The _____ of the curve at any point is still a valid indicator of rate of responding.

12-21

(about) 50

12-25

In Figure 10, the animal paused about (1) _____ minutes between positions (2) _____ and _____.

12-26

do not (cannot) Set 31 **41-2**	When the hold-up victim turns over his wallet, he (1) _____ a threat and (2) _____ physical injury. **41-3** ← To p. 272
activation syndrome Set 30 **41-6**	Punishment is effective in preventing a response when behavior which (1) _____ the punished behavior is established. But when this behavior has been extinguished, the (2) _____ response will again be emitted. **41-7** ← To p. 272
lower Set 40 **41-10**	In avoidance behavior, the longer the response postpones the aversive stimulus, the _____ the rate. **41-11** ← To p. 272
(1) A (2) B (3) C (4) y (5) z **41-14** Set 35	Reinforcement consists of (1) _____ a positive reinforcer or (2) _____ a negative reinforcer. Punishment consists of (3) _____ a positive reinforcer or (4) _____ a negative reinforcer. **41-15** ← To p. 272
(1) aversive (2) reinforcing Set 36 **41-18**	It is poor technique to shape skillful behavior with (1) _____ reinforcers because the aversive stimuli, which must be presented in order to be terminated, elicit many respondents which (2) * * * the behavior to be shaped. **41-19** ← To p. 272
decrease (reduce) Set 33 **41-22**	A person "can't remember" a very aversive childhood experience. This is called (1) _____. It can be interpreted as a case of engaging in other responses which (2) * * * thinking about the aversive experience. **41-23** ← To p. 272

(1) **a**
(2) **b**

12-1

In Figure 2, the slow movement of the paper under the fixed pen has drawn the horizontal line (1) _____ - _____. At the end of **a - b**, the pen suddenly moved a short vertical distance to (2) _____.

12-2

---

b

12-6

In Figure 4, three responses were made fairly quickly (closely together) at _____, _____, and _____.

12-7

---

longer
(greater)

12-11

In Figure 6, the slope of the curve drawn by the pen near **a** indicates a(n) _____ initial rate of responding.

12-12

) positive
   acceleration
) negative
   acceleration

12-16

To record other events, the pen moves quickly "to the southeast" and back again. In Figure 8, the pen is shown in the process of drawing a line from (1) _____ to _____. The point of the pen will immediately return to (2) _____.

12-17

---

slope

12-21

In Figure 10, the rate was highest between (1) _____ and _____, zero between (2) _____ and _____, and intermediate between (3) _____ and _____.

12-22

---

(1) (about) 5
(2) **b** (and) **c**

12-26

In the cumulative curves shown in the figures, time is shown by the (1) _____ distance traversed by the pen, and the number of responses by the (2) _____ distance.

12-27

Set 34 41-1

is

The reflex activities comprising the activation syndrome occur together in emotions. We * * * define any one specific emotion (anger or fear) by listing the reflexes involved.

41-2

---

(1) not be
(2) is (will be)

Set 40 41-5

Organisms in situations we call "emotional" frequently show the ____ ____.

41-6

---

extinction (or)
adaptation
(EITHER ORDER)

Set 36 41-9

With continuous punishment of a response maintained by positive reinforcement, the greater the severity of the punishment (after some minimum intensity is surpassed), the ____ the response rate.

41-10

---

(1) quickens
(2) dilate
(3) begins
(increases)

Set 30 41-13

(1) ____ Control session
(2) ____ Stimulant injected
(3) ____ Tranquilizer injected
(4) ____ Buzzer onset
(5) ____ Shock

41-14

) useful
(advantageous)
) useless
(harmful, disadvantageous)

Set 30 41-17

The exhilarating emotional reaction from riding a roller coaster or being in a speeding car is a reaction to stimuli which are often (1) ____ but in this instance are (2) ____ (TT).

41-18

---

is

Set 31 41-21

The teacher who uses strong aversive control to get students to study may ____ the probability that they will study after graduation.

41-22

---

(1) **a** (–) **b** (2) **c** 12-2	In Figure 3, the paper has moved on from the position shown in Figure 2. The fixed pen has drawn a second horizontal line _____ – _____. 12-3
c, **d**, (and) **e** 12-7	In Figure 5, the three responses recorded at **a** were emitted _____ rapidly than the three at **b**. 12-8
high (rapid) 12-12	In Figure 7, the rate increases fairly steadily from a low value near (1) _____ to a high value near (2) _____ . 12-13
(1) **d** (to) **e** (2) **d** 12-17	In Figure 8, the short mark ("hatch" or "pip") at _____ was made by a movement of the pen like the one shown at **e**. 12-18
(1) **a** (and) **b** (2) **b** (and) **c** (3) **c** (and) **d** 12-22	When the steps are small, we cannot count responses. But in Figure 9, the scale *at the right* tells us that approximately _____ responses were made between **a** and **b**. 12-23
(1) horizontal (2) vertical 12-27	The rate of responding is indicated by the _____ of the cumulative record. 12-28

In the experiment demonstrating shock avoidance, the low initial rate suggests that anxiety * * * necessary for adequate avoidance.

41-1

extinction

Set 38   41-4

The rate of a response maintained by positive re-inforcement may (1) * * * decreased by a *mild* con-tinuous punishment, but it (2) * * * decreased by a strong continuous punishment while punishment remains in effect.

41-5

s△

Set 33   41-8

If a timid person forces himself to attend many group meetings, his timidity may undergo the process of _____ or _____.

41-9

(1) eliminate
(2) decreases
(3) anxiety

Set 38   41-12

In the activation syndrome, inhalation (1) _____, bronchioles (2) _____, and adrenalin secretion (3) _____.

41-13

(1) avoidance
(2) escape

Set 32   41-16

The activation syndrome would usually be biolog-ically (1) _____ to a cave man, and it would usually be biologically (2) _____ to a public speaker.

41-17

1) slowly
   (seldom)
2) rapidly
   (frequently)
3) anxiety

Set 35   41-20

A given emotion * * * defined by the events which serve as reinforcers or by the increased probability of a group of responses.

41-21

c (–) d	In Figure 3, the pen has been in the four lettered positions **a**, **b**, **c**, and **d**. It occupied position (1) _____ first, and (2) _____ last.
12-3	12-4 ← To p. 73
less	The more rapid the responding, the (1) _____ the pauses between two responses and the (2) _____ the horizontal lines drawn by the pen.
12-8	12-9 ← To p. 73
(1) a (2) b	An increase in rate is called *positive acceleration*. Positive acceleration is shown in either Figure 6 or Figure 7. (WHICH?) Figure _____ .
12-13	12-14 ← To p. 73
c	The "southeast" mark or hatch is most often used to indicate that a response has been reinforced. In Figure 8, the responses numbered _____ and _____ were reinforced.
12-18	12-19 ← To p. 73
approximately) .00	If paper speed is very slow, we may not be able to accurately measure the time between any two responses; but in Figure 9, the scale tells us that responses at **a** and **b** were approximately _____ minutes apart.
12-23	12-24 ← To p. 73
slope	*Rate of responding* means responses/time (responses ÷ time). The slope of a cumulative record is (1) _____ distance/(2) _____ distance.
12-28	12-29 ← To p. 73

(1) escapes
(2) avoids

Set 33   **41-3**

In the experiment showing the ineffectiveness of punishment in removing a response from the repertoire, punishment was in effect for the first 10 minutes of _____ of a food-reinforced response.

41-4

---

1) avoids (is incompatible with)
2) punished

Set 39   **41-7**

A pigeon reinforced with food for pecking a key during an S^D but not during an S^Δ will peck a second key which delays the appearance of _____.

41-8

---

lower

Set 34   **41-11**

Punishment does not (1) _____ a response. Rate of responding temporarily (2) _____, in part, because punishment and the resulting conditioned aversive stimuli generate (3)_____.

41-12

---

1) presenting
2) terminating (removing)
3) terminating (removing)
4) presenting   **41-15**
Set 37

Operant behavior which postpones an *un*conditioned aversive stimulus is called (1) _____ behavior. Behavior which terminates an *un*-conditioned aversive stimulus is called (2) _____ behavior.

41-16

---

1) negative
2) are incompatible with (interfere with)
Set 32   **41-19**

In the presence of a conditioned aversive stimulus, a food-reinforced response is emitted more (1) _____, and a response with an avoidance history more (2) _____. These and similar changes define (3) _____.

41-20

---

1) repression
2) avoid (are incompatible with)
Set 39   **41-23**

End of Set

EXPERIMENT 1.

Preliminary treatment. A food-deprived pigeon is placed for the first time in a standard experimental box, and the feeding mechanism is operated *by the experimenter* from time to time. When the mechanism operates, there is a loud click. When first placed in the box, and for the first several clicks of the mechanism, the pigeon may jump, flap its wings, and rush about. After a while, this "emotional" behavior ceases. We say that *adaptation* has taken place. The pigeon eventually learns to turn toward and approach the feeding mechanism, or food magazine, whenever it hears the click.

Conditioned key pecking. A plastic disk is now attached behind a circular opening in the wall of the box above the feeding mechanism. The disk acts as an electric key. When the pigeon pecks the key, a circuit is closed causing the feeding mechanism to operate. (The experimenter no longer operates the mechanism.) Cumulative records of all responses to the key are made. Two examples are shown in Figures 1A and 1B. All responses were reinforced, but the usual sideward movements of the pen to indicate reinforcement are omitted.

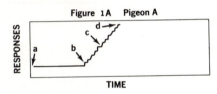

Figure 1A   Pigeon A

Figure 1B   Pigeon B

EXPERIMENT 2.

An inexperienced pigeon is placed in the box. No preliminary magazine training is given, that is, no attempt is made to adapt the pigeon to the box and the click, or to establish the click as a conditioned reinforcer. The key is connected to the feeding mechanism from the start. The cumulative record is shown in Figure 2.

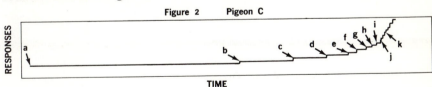

Figure 2   Pigeon C

"THE LEARNING CURVE"

Early investigators observed organisms in puzzle boxes, mazes, and similar situations. They measured successive delays in responding and plotted these in a "learning curve," believing that they were plotting the course of a basic learning process. Experiment 2 (Pigeon C) is comparable.

Plotted on the right are the delays between successive reinforced responses on the key.

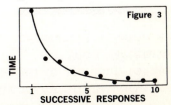

Figure 3

Page 78

← To p. 265

is not
(is no longer)

40-5

In Figure 1, the record for the control or "no punishment" procedure has many slight variations in
slopes which indicate some moment-to-moment
variation in (1) _____ of _____. Such variations (2)
* * * common in variable-interval reinforcement.

40-6
← To p. 265

---

punished

40-12

Figure 1. Except for the first 4 minutes, the slope
of the record for the tenth 1-hour session of continuous (1) _____ is about (2) * * * the slope for
the last of the "no punishment" sessions.

40-13
← To p. 265

---

higher

40-19

Experiment 2. On the first day of the stronger
punishment, the rate of responding is nearly _____.

40-20
← To p. 265

---

lower

40-26

When even more intense shocks were used, more
time was required to stabilize the rate. The more
intense the punishment the _____ the rise in rate to
a stable level.

40-27
← To p. 265

---

increased

40-33

Figure 3. Every response was again punished
beginning at the (1) _____ arrow. The response
rate immediately (2) _____.

40-34
← To p. 265

---

(1) increases
    (rises)
(2) higher

40-40

End of Set

Set 13

Factors Affecting Speed of Conditioning

See exhibit on preceding page

Estimated time: 24 minutes

Turn to next page and begin ▶

---

(1) adaptation
(2) conditioned
   reinforcer

13-8

After preliminary treatment, a key is connected to the feeding mechanism (magazine). For the first time in the history of the pigeon, a peck on the key will * * *.

13-9

---

shorter (less)

13-17

The rate of responding in Figure 1A (Pigeon A) between **b** and **c** is roughly the same as between _____ and _____ .

13-18

A

13-26

Experiment 2. Since the preliminary treatment was omitted for Pigeon C, there * * * opportunity for adaptation of unconditioned responses to the unfamiliar experimental box.

13-27

---

shorter

13-35

As the pigeon adapts to the click, the time elapsing between the click of the mechanism and contact with food decreases. This hastens the process of _____ the click as a reinforcer.

13-36

---

learning
curve

13-44

When the times between successive responses in Experiment 2 are plotted in a "learning curve" such as Figure 3, the falling curve means that these times are growing progressively _____ .

13-45

---

respondent
(reflex)

13-53

(1) _____ behavior maintains the internal economy of the organism. (2) _____ behavior affects the environment.

13-54

will not (cannot) 40-4	The variable-interval schedule, in (A), furnishes a base line on which the effects of added punishment can be observed. The experimenter maintains this base line long enough before introducing shock to be certain that the rate * * * changing. 40-5
(1) punished (2) the same as (equal to) 40-11	Experiment 1. The tenth session of punishment was preceded by nine 1-hour sessions during which each response was _____. 40-12
(1) variable-interval (2) stable (uniform, constant) 40-18	In Experiment 2, the same procedure was followed as in Experiment 1 except that the shock intensity was _____ in Experiment 2. 40-19
decrease 40-25	Experiment 2. When a sufficiently intense shock follows every response, rate of responding remains _____ than in the absence of a punishing contingency. 40-26
(1) discontinued (2) arrow 40-32	Figure 3. Within a very few seconds after punishment was discontinued, the rate of responding _____ drastically. 40-33
lower 40-39	Immediately after continuous punishment is discontinued, response rate (1) _____ and is, for a while, (2) _____ than that normally generated by the reinforcement schedule. 40-40

Experiment 1. During the preliminary treatment, "emotional" behavior is elicited by the strange box, the click of the magazine, etc. This "emotional" behavior * * * compatible with pecking the key or eating.

13-1

---

reinforced
operate feeding
mechanism,
sult in food)

13-9

The wiring of the apparatus is such that the click of the food mechanism as a(n) _____ _____ follows *immediately* upon the pigeon's response to the key.

13-10

---

c (and) d

13-18

Figure 1A shows that the reinforcement of the response at **b** produced an immediate, substantial increase in rate. This is shown by the change in the _____ of the curve at **b**.

13-19

---

was no

13-27

In Experiment 2, the first response produced a click of the magazine. Unconditioned emotional responses to the click have not undergone _____.

13-28

---

conditioning

13-36

One might say that Pigeon C learns much more slowly than A and B. The apparent slow learning of C is due to the time needed for (1) _____ of unconditioned responses and for establishing a(n) (2) _____ reinforcer.

13-37

---

shorter

13-45

Experiment 2 (Figure 2). Pigeon C's record does not reveal the speed of acquiring a key-pecking response because other processes are also involved. The pigeon must first _____ to the box and the click.

13-46

---

(1) Respondent
    (Reflex)
(2) Operant

13-54

(1) _____ behavior usually consists of the activity of striated muscle. (2) _____ behavior usually consists of the activity of smooth muscle and gland.

13-55

(1) activation
syndrome
(2) lowers

40-3

By inserting the electrodes beneath the skin, in (C), a shock of constant intensity can be delivered because variations in skin resistance * * * influence the voltage reaching the pain receptors.

40-4

---

increases
(rises,
becomes
steeper)

40-10

Figure 1. Although every response is (1) _____ during the punishment procedure, by the end of the first day the rate of responding is nearly (2) * * * the rate during the "no punishment" procedure.

40-11

---

(1) higher
(2) higher

40-17

In (H), responses continued to be reinforced on a(n) (1) * * * schedule without punishment until the experimenter was certain that the rate was (2) _____ at the value which prevailed before the introduction of shock.

40-18

---

lower

40-24

Experiment 2 indicates that if punishment is sufficiently intense it will _____ the rate of a response maintained on a variable-interval schedule of reinforcement.

40-25

---

uniform
(constant,
steady)

40-31

Experiment 3. As described in (K), punishment was (1) _____ at the point marked by the first (2) _____ in Figure 3.

40-32

---

(1) not be
(2) is (will be)

40-38

With continuous punishment of a response maintained by positive reinforcement, the greater the severity of the punishment (after some minimum intensity is surpassed), the _____ the response rate.

40-39

---

is not (is in-) 13-1	Experiment 1. We cannot relate the first reactions to the click and the box to any known history of conditioning. In that sense, this "emotional" behavior is _____ . 13-2
conditioned reinforcer 13-10	Experiment 1. Every peck on the key is *instantly* reinforced by the (1) _____ , but there is a short delay before reinforcement with (2) _____ because the bird must first bend down to the feeding mechanism. 13-1
slope 13-19	Pigeon A (Figure 1A) reached its maximal rate of responding after only _____ reinforcement(s). Conditioning was immediate. 13-20
adaptation 13-28	In Experiment 2, the click occurs at the very instant the response is emitted, but it is not yet a(n) _____ _____ , and little or no reinforcement occurs. 13-29
(1) adaptation (2) conditioned (secondary) 13-37	Pigeon A demonstrates that conditioning can occur very _____ when adaptation is already complete and when each response is immediately reinforced. 13-38
adapt 13-46	The click must also become a(n) _____ _____ before the key-pecking response can be conditioned effectively. 13-47
(1) Operant (2) Respondent (Reflex) 13-55	To condition an operant, a reinforcing stimulus is arranged to follow the _____ . 13-56

all 40-2	Aversive stimuli elicit the many respondents of the (1) ____ ____. One of these, sweating, (2) ____ the electrical resistance of the skin. 40-3
(1) lower (2) were not 40-9	Figure 1. During the first day of punishment, the slope of the record gradually * * * as the session progresses. 40-10
increased (rose) 40-16	In (G), the increased response rate was (1) ____ than while punishment was in effect and also (2) ____ than it had been in the session preceding the introduction of punishment. 40-17
were not 40-23	Figure 2. When every response is punished by a moderate intensity of shock, the rate of responding after daily 1-hour sessions is substantially ____ than it was without punishment. 40-24
positive acceleration 40-30	Figure 3. During the second 15 minutes of the session, rate of responding has become relatively ____. 40-31
higher 40-37	The rate of a response maintained by positive re-inforcement may (1) * * * decreased by a *mild* con-tinuous punishment, but it (2) * * * decreased by a strong continuous punishment while punishment remains in effect. 40-38

unconditioned (unlearned) 13-2	Experiment 1. As adaptation proceeds, the "emotional" behavior ceases. The elimination of this behavior is similar to the _____ of conditioned behavior. 13-3
) click (conditioned reinforcer)) food (unconditioned reinforcer) 13-11	The click is effective as a reinforcer for pecking the key because it follows the response (1) _____, whereas there is a short (2) _____ before the appearance of the unconditioned reinforcer. 13-12
one 13-20	Experiment 1. In everyday terminology, we would say that Pigeon A shows a(n) _____ speed of learning to peck the key. 13-21
conditioned reinforcer 13-29	In Figure 2, the pause **a – b** is (1) _____ than in Figure 1A mainly because unconditioned behavior to the experimental box had to undergo (2) _____. 13-30
fast (quickly, rapidly) 13-38	Pigeon C's record does not show a difference in speed of conditioning so much as (a) the lack of (1) _____ to the box and click, and (b) the lack of a conditioned reinforcer (2) _____ following early responses. 13-39
conditioned reinforcer (secondary reinforcer) 13-47	Does the "learning curve" of the early investigators actually reveal the learning process for the key-pecking response as an isolated bit of behavior? 13-48
response (behavior, operant) 13-56	To condition a respondent, a neutral stimulus is paired with the _____ _____ repeatedly. 13-57

stable (uniform, constant) 40-1	As indicated in (B), the 1-minute variable-interval schedule was in effect at * * * times during Experiments 1, 2, and 3. 40-2
reinforced 40-8	Figure 1. During the first half-hour of the first day of punishment, response rate is considerably (1) _____ than it was on the previous day when responses (2) * * * being punished. 40-9
was not (is not) 40-15	NOW READ EXPERIMENT 2. In (G), when punishment was discontinued, the response rate _____ for a while. 40-16
thirty-second 40-22	Figure 2. For Days 22, 27, and 32 there were many irregularities in response rates but the over-all rates * * * very different. 40-23
(1) reinforced (2) punished 40-29	Figure 3. During the first 15 minutes of the session, the response rate showed a gradual change found in most of the sessions with this combination of variable-interval food reinforcement and continuous punishment (e.g., Figures 1 and 2). Specifically the rate showed a(n) _____ _____. 40-30
punished 40-36	Figure 3. The response rate between the arrows is much higher than this schedule normally generates. When continuous punishment is discontinued, the response rate is, for a while, _____ than it would have been had there been no punishment. 40-37

extinction 13-3	Adaptation differs from extinction, however, in that no previous ____ of the behavior has taken place, so far as we know. 13-4
immediately delay (interval) 13-12	In Figure 1A at **a**, the key was connected and the recorder started. Pigeon A emitted the first peck at point ____ . 13-13
high (rapid, great) 13-21	In Figure 1B (Pigeon B), the first response occurred at ____ . 13-22
(1) longer (2) adaptation 13-30	The relatively long pauses between **b** and **c** and between **c** and **d** in Figure 2 are partly explained by the need for ____ to both the box and the click. 13-31
adaptation quickly (closely, immediately) 13-39	After looking at Pigeon C's record, we may suspect that Pigeon B also may not have undergone complete (1) ____ to the click as a novel stimulus, or that the click was not fully established as a(n) (2) * * *. 13-40
No 13-48	A "learning curve" for Pigeon A in Experiment 1 would drop to a low constant level after only ____ response(s). 13-49
unconditioned stimulus 13-57	A conditioned reinforcer acquires its power by being ____ with an unconditioned reinforcer. 13-58

(A) describes the schedule used throughout all three experiments. When uncomplicated by other variables, this schedule generates a(n) _____ and moderate rate of responding.

40-1

---

every (each)

40-7

Experiment 1. While punishment is in effect, every response is followed by shock. Responses are also still _____ on a variable-interval schedule.

40-8

---

acceleration

40-14

Experiment 1. By the tenth day of punishment, after many thousands of responses have been mildly punished, the over-all rate of responding * * * appreciably lowered.

40-15

---

higher

40-21

Experiment 2. The highest over-all rate during punishment shown in Figure 2 occurred on the _____ day of punishment.

40-22

---

stronger
(more intense)

40-28

NOW READ EXPERIMENT 3. Pecking the key was (1) _____ on a variable-interval schedule. Except for the 10-minute period described in (K), every response was (2) _____.

40-29

---

no

40-35

Figure 3. The rate of responding during the 10 minutes without punishment was substantially higher than during the parts of this session in which responses were _____.

40-36

nditioning
arning)
cceptable:
inforcement)

13-4

Experiment 1. The preliminary procedure is important because it provides an opportunity for *un*conditioned emotional behavior to undergo _____.

13-5

---

b

13-13

Throughout Experiment 1, the click of the magazine, a conditioned reinforcer, is followed by _____, an unconditioned reinforcer.

13-14

---

b

13-22

The record for Pigeon B differs from that for Pigeon A mainly in the fact that a(n) _____ time elapsed between the first, second, and third responses.

13-23

---

adaptation

13-31

Figure 2 shows a fairly smooth _____ acceleration. (positive or negative?)

13-32

---

(1) adaptation
(2) (conditioned) reinforcer

13-40

On the day following the experiment in Figure 2, Pigeon C was again placed in the box. It responded immediately. All emotional responses to the box which might be incompatible with the behavior had evidently undergone full _____.

13-41

---

one

13-49

The "learning curve" for Pigeon C could be interpreted as showing the gradual strengthening of a key-pecking "habit." But Experiment 1 shows that the acquisition of key pecking does not always occur _____-ly.

13-50

---

paired

13-58

A stimulus paired with food acquires the power to _____ an operant response.

13-59

Oct 40   Effects of Continuous Punishment
See exhibit on preceding pages
Estimated time: 21 minutes
Turn to next page and begin ▶

(1) rate (of) responding (2) are 40-6	Experiment 1. In (E), a brief, mild shock follows _____ response. 40-7
(1) punishment (2) the same as 40-13	Figure 1. During the first 4 minutes of the tenth day, the response rate shows positive _____. 40-14
zero 40-20	Experiment 2. By the fifth day of the stronger punishment, the over-all response rate is _____ than on the first day. 40-21
slower 40-27	When a shock stronger than that in Experiment 2 was used, the stable rate eventually reached was lower than that of the thirty-second day in Experiment 2. The _____ the punishment, the lower the stable rate of responding. 40-28
(1) second (2) decreased (dropped, declined) 40-34	Figure 3. As described in (K), between the points marked by the arrows _____ response was punished. 40-35

adaptation 13-5	Experiment 1. During the preliminary treatment, the pigeon is eventually conditioned to approach the feeding mechanism just after hearing the click. Two stimuli, _____ and food, therefore tend to occur close together. 13-6
food 13-14	Since food follows the click throughout the experiment, the reinforcing property of the click does not undergo _____ . (TT) 13-15
longer (greater) 13-23	Figure 1B. Pigeon B reaches a constant rate of responding after _____ responses have been reinforced. 13-24
positive 13-32	The positive acceleration in Figure 2 simply means that, in general, the intervals between successive responses become progressively _____ . 13-33
adaptation 13-41	The pigeon is also likely to respond immediately on the second day because it has been _____ many times for pecking the key. 13-42
gradual(-ly) [slow(-ly)] 13-50	In Experiment 1, it is important to establish the click as a reinforcer, *not* because a conditioned reinforcer is more effective than an unconditioned reinforcer, but because the click follows the response more _____ . 13-51
reinforce 13-59	A stimulus paired with food acquires the power to _____ a respondent. 13-60

Do not read Experiment 3 until instructed
to do so.

EXPERIMENT 3.

(J) A pigeon was reinforced with food on a 1-minute variable-interval schedule. A moderately intense shock followed each response, as in Experiment 2.

(K) Halfway through a session, punishment was abruptly discontinued for 10 minutes and then reinstated. The cumulative record is shown in Figure 3.

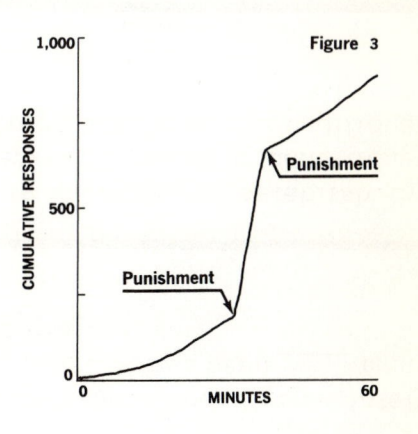

Figure 3

click 13-6	Experiment 1. In the preliminary procedure, the click becomes a conditioned reinforcer because the click and food are being _____ . 13-7
extinction 13-15	In Figure 1A, the time elapsing before the pigeon made the first response can be determined by the length of the part of the curve between _____ and _____ . 13-16
three 13-24	Figure 1B. Some evidence that the reinforcement of the response at **b** was effective is obtained from a comparison of distance **a** – **b** with distance _____ – _____ . 13-25
shorter 13-33	In Experiment 2, the "startle reflex" elicited by the click of the feeding mechanism takes a few seconds to subside. There is, therefore, a slight _____ before the occurrence of the unconditioned reinforcer. 13-34
reinforced 13-42	The early procedure for obtaining learning curves, exemplified by Figure 3 in the exhibit, is most like that for the pigeon labeled _____ . 13-43
quickly (rapidly, closely) 13-51	A "learning curve" * * * (does or does not?) describe the acquisition of an isolated response because it reflects, in part, a change in a conditioned reinforcer which only eventually provides immediate reinforcement. 13-52
elicit 13-60	A rat in an experimental apparatus is presented with food by a feeding mechanism which makes a noise. The noise acquires the power to (1) _____ salivation and to (2) _____ pressing a lever. 13-61

Do not read Experiment 2 until instructed
to do so.

EXPERIMENT 2.

(G) At the end of Experiment 1 punishment was discontinued. For the first few sessions, the rate of responding was actually *higher* than before punishment was introduced.

(H) After several sessions without punishment, the rate of responding dropped to the original level and again became stable. The cumulative record from the last day of this period without punishment is shown in Figure 2 labeled "No Punishment."

(I) Each response was then followed by a shock as in Experiment 1, but a moderately strong shock was used, 50 volts instead of the milder 30 volts. Cumulative records from many days under this procedure are shown in Figure 2 (Days: one through thirty-two).

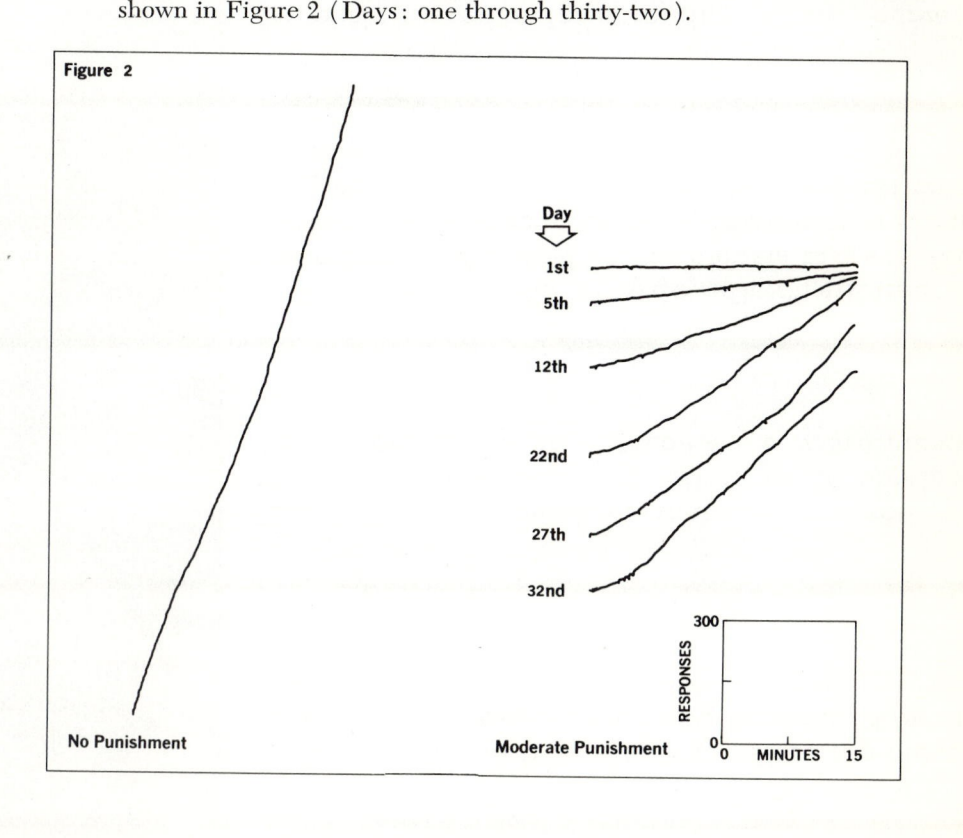

Figure 2

No Punishment

Day

1st
5th
12th
22nd
27th
32nd

Moderate Punishment

RESPONSES

300

0

0   MINUTES   15

paired 13-7	Experiment 1. The preliminary treatment has two effects important for later conditioning of key pecking. It allows time for (1) _____ of the "un-conditioned" behavior, and it establishes the click as a(n) (2) _____ _____. 13-8 ← To p. 79
a (and) **b** 13-16	The time elapsing between the first and second responses in the record for Pigeon A, Figure 1A, is very much _____ than the time elapsing before the first response. 13-17 ← To p. 79
b (–) **c** 13-25	Speed of conditioning is sometimes thought to indicate "intelligence." The pigeon is surely less intelligent than a man, yet a man cannot acquire a comparable response more rapidly than the pigeon labeled _____ on the exhibit. 13-26 ← To p. 79
delay (interval of time) 13-34	As "startle" responses to the click disappear, the times between the peck and the unconditioned re-inforcer grow _____. 13-35 ← To p. 79
C 13-43	In the procedures of earlier investigators, the basic learning process was thought to be shown graphically in a(n) _____ _____. 13-44 ← To p. 79
does not 13-52	Pecking a key is an example of operant behavior, and, as such, is to be distinguished from _____ behavior. 13-53 ← To p. 79

EXPERIMENT 1.

(A) A food-deprived pigeon was placed in a standard experimental chamber each day for a 1-hour session. Key pecking was reinforced with food on a variable-interval schedule (average interval of 1 minute) until rate of responding was stable from one day to the next.

(B) This schedule of food reinforcement remained in effect throughout all the experiments which follow.

(C) Small electrodes were inserted beneath the pigeon's skin. Through these electrodes a brief shock (lasting 100 milliseconds) could be delivered.

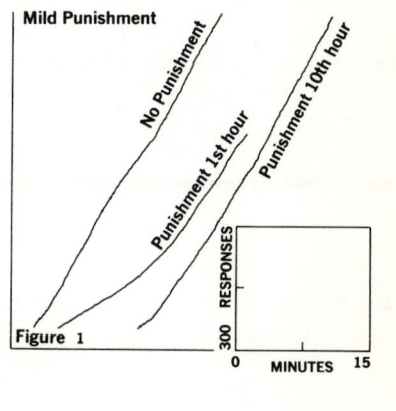

Figure 1

(D) The last day of the variable-interval schedule uncomplicated by punishment can be seen in Figure 1 where it is labeled "No Punishment."

(E) On the next day, *every* response was followed by a brief mild shock (30 volts). The cumulative record from this session is labeled "Punishment (1st hour)" in Figure 1.

(F) Every response continued to be punished through many daily sessions, and the variable-interval schedule of food reinforcement remained in effect. The cumulative record from the tenth session of continuous punishment is shown in Figure 1.

The experimenter places several pigeons in separate experimental boxes. A food magazine delivers a small amount of food to each pigeon every 15 seconds regardless of what the pigeon is doing. When the experimenter returns later, he finds one bird sitting very still, another hopping from one foot to the other, another bowing, another turning around and around, another raising and lowering its head, etc. Each bird continues to repeat its own "ritual" between deliveries of food.

← To p. 257

) decreases
) incompatible
   with
 	
          39-3
	Whether a shock is delivered following a response or independently of any response, it is effective in temporarily (1) ____ the rate of food-reinforced behavior. In either case, shock produces a(n) (2) ____ state.
	                                             39-4
	← To p. 257

(1) reinforced
(2) probability
 	
        39-8
	A pinched child may not giggle for a while. Even though the pinch had not followed his giggle closely, the effect would have been * * *.
	
	                           39-9
	← To p. 257

) conditioned
   aversive
) termination
  (reduction,
  elimination)
        39-13
	Situations in which responses have been punished generate conditioned aversive stimuli. Behavior which terminates these stimuli is ____.
	
	                         39-14
	← To p. 257

avoid
 	
        39-18
	Punishment eventually leads to the reinforcement of "doing something else." Because "doing something else" prevents the occurrence of unconditioned aversive stimuli, it is an example of ____ behavior.
	                         39-19
	← To p. 257

) extinction
:) occur
  (be emitted,
  appear)
        39-23
	When incompatible behavior is extinguished, the punished response emerges in full strength. The punished response has not been emitted while in competition with the incompatible behavior, and hence extinction of this behavior * * * occurred.
	                         39-24
	← To p. 257

) avoid
:) repression
 	
        39-28
	A person described as "awkward," "timorous," or "inhibited" is often actively "not behaving," thereby avoiding the execution of behavior which has been ____ in the past.
	                         39-29
	← To p. 257

Set 14

PART III Operant Conditioning: Precise Contingencies

Accidental Contingencies and
Superstitious Behavior   See exhibit on preceding page
Estimated time: 17 minutes   **Turn to next page and begin** ▶

ccident(-ally)
unintention(-ally)]

14-7

In the "accidental contingency experiment," the feeding mechanism operates every 15 seconds *regardless* of what the pigeon is doing. This differs from the usual experiment because _____ is not contingent upon any specific response.

14-8

---

reinforcement

14-15

A response reinforced often enough to be emitted at a high rate continues to be reinforced even though there is no deliberate connection between the _____ and the operation of the food magazine.

14-16

---

superstitions

14-23

A student may scratch his head while trying to solve a problem. If he finds a solution at that moment, the response of scratching his head will be _____ .

14-24

---

reinforced

14-31

The accidental nature of the reinforcing contingency explains the variety of _____ conditioned in experiments on "accidental contingencies."

14-32

---

reinforcement

14-39

You may rub a rabbit's foot because you have been told it will bring good luck. Being told it will bring good luck makes it more likely that you will _____ (TT) the response for the first time.

14-40

---

often
(frequently)

14-47

We have already seen that, under ideal conditions, a pigeon may reach a high stable rate after only _____ reinforcement of a very simple response.

14-48

1) unconditioned aversive stimulus 2) activation syndrome 39-2	A shock is delivered to a rat which has received food for lever pressing. Even if the shock is not contingent on the response, the rate immediately (1) _____ because the resulting emotional condition is (2) * * * lever pressing. 39-3
aversive stimulus 39-7	The parent who pinches the child for giggling is (1) _____ by the termination of the giggling. The (2) _____ is increased that the parent will use punishment in similar situations in the future. 39-8
reinforced 39-12	As the early components of a frequently punished chain of responses are emitted, they generate (1) _____ _____ stimuli. Any behavior of "doing something else instead" will be reinforced by the (2) _____ of these stimuli. 39-13
avoidance (incompatible) 39-17	By actively holding still, you may _____ making a movement which resembles one which has been punished. 39-18
reinforcement (conditioning) 39-22	When punishment is discontinued, the avoidance behavior resulting from earlier punishment undergoes (1) _____. The previously punished behavior may then (2) * * *. 39-23
1) repression 2) incompatible with 39-27	A person may "talk about other things" (or just not talk) and thereby (1) _____ talking about aversive situations. We need not refer to this as a process of (2) _____ which forces response out of "consciousness." 39-28

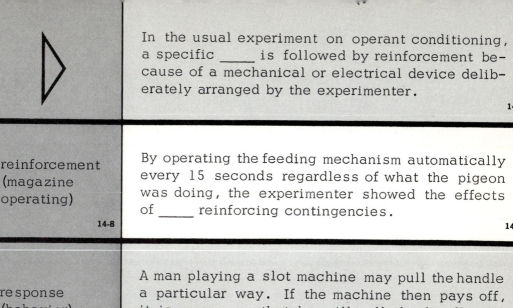

In the usual experiment on operant conditioning, a specific _____ is followed by reinforcement because of a mechanical or electrical device deliberately arranged by the experimenter.

14-1

---

reinforcement
(magazine
operating)

14-8

By operating the feeding mechanism automatically every 15 seconds regardless of what the pigeon was doing, the experimenter showed the effects of _____ reinforcing contingencies.

14-9

---

response
(behavior)

14-16

A man playing a slot machine may pull the handle a particular way. If the machine then pays off, it is more _____ that he will pull the handle the same way on the next play.

14-17

---

reinforced
(hence:
conditioned)

14-24

If a student solves a problem while scratching his head, he is (1) _____ likely to scratch when he has another problem, and the behavior has a good chance of being (2) _____ again by the solving of the new problem.

14-25

---

responses
(rituals,
superstitions)

14-32

A man who has occasionally thrown a seven while calling "Come, seven!" may call the same words for some time during a losing streak, but if he never again gets a seven, the response will eventually be _____.

14-33

---

emit

14-40

If you receive good news shortly after rubbing a rabbit's foot, the superstitious behavior is accidentally _____.

14-41

---

one

14-48

A response accidentally reinforced is unlikely to be accidentally reinforced again if the first reinforcement resulted in a(n) _____ rate of responding.

14-49

(1) eliminate 　　(get rid of 　　weaken) (2) decreases 　　(declines) (3) anxiety　　**39-1**	A shock delivered to the feet of a rat is a(n) (1) ___ ___ ___ which will elicit the respondents characteristic of the (2) ___ ___. **39-2**
is not **39-6**	The child who is pinched for giggling during a ceremony stops giggling immediately. Pinching is a(n) ___ ___; the responses to it are incompatible with giggling. **39-7**
(1) punished (2) conditioned 　　aversive 　　stimuli 　　**39-11**	A response which terminates an aversive stimulus is ___. **39-12**
incompatible **39-16**	Any behavior which "displaces" a frequently punished response prevents the appearance of the unconditioned aversive stimulus. The response which replaces the usually punished response is an example of ___ behavior.　　**39-17**
punished **39-21**	Punishment *in*directly lowers the rate of the punished response by providing conditions for the ___ of incompatible avoidance behavior. **39-22**
incompatible with (displacing) 　　**39-26**	A person "can't remember" a very aversive childhood experience. The clinician calls this (1) ___. It is probably, in part, the effect of other responses which are (2) * * * "thinking about" the aversive experience.　　**39-27**
(1) reinforced (2) may not be 　　(is not) 　　**39-31**	**End of Set**

response 14-1	When the experimenter deliberately arranges reinforcing contingencies, it * * * accidental that reinforcement follows a particular response. 14-2
accidental 14-9	When the magazine operates independently of the pigeon's behavior, it is only by accident that any particular _____ is reinforced. 14-10
probable (likely) 14-17	A bowler may snap his fingers just as the ball hits the pins. Although this behavior has no effect on the ball, a "strike" will _____ snapping the fingers. 14-18
(1) more (2) reinforced 14-25	Head scratching, pencil chewing, table tapping, etc., do not actually solve problems; thus, they are generally (1) _____ forms of behavior resulting from (2) _____ contingencies of reinforcement. 14-26
extinguished 14-33	When *termination* of a stimulus increases the rate of a contingent response, it is a case of _____ reinforcement. 14-34
reinforced 14-41	If rubbing the rabbit's foot had not been emitted, it could not have been reinforced. Once the verbally suggested superstitious behavior has been (1) _____, it is possible for (2) _____ reinforcement to follow. 14-42
low 14-49	A particularly slow learner may require many reinforcements before developing a high rate of responding. He is _____ likely to develop superstitious behavior than a faster learner. 14-50

Mild unsustained punishment does not permanently (1) _____ an operant. Rate of responding temporarily (2) _____ because punishment, and the resulting conditioned aversive stimuli, generate (3) _____.

39-1

---

(1) contingent
  (dependent)
(2) aversive
  stimulus
  (negative
  reinforcer)₃₉₋₅

For an aversive stimulus to lower the rate of a positively reinforced response, it * * * necessary for the stimulus to be response-contingent.

39-6

---

is not

39-10

When a response is followed immediately by an aversive stimulus, the response is said to have been (1) _____. Stimuli which accompany punishment become (2) _____ _____ _____.

39-11

---

conditioned
aversive

39-15

By getting out of a situation in which punishment is common, a man can prevent the occurrence of the punished behavior and the resulting aversive stimuli. This is a case of avoidance. The behavior is _____ with the punished behavior.

39-16

---

extinction

39-20

While displaced by an avoidance response, a punished response is not extinguished. When incompatible behavior is extinguished, the _____ response will be emitted again.

39-21

---

incompatible
(avoidance)

39-25

When a response prevents the occurrence of punished behavior, the clinician may say that the punished behavior is "repressed." Repression may be interpreted as avoidance behavior which is * * * the punished behavior.

39-26

---

(1) reinforced
(2) decrease
  (decline)

39-30

Since the behavior of punishing others is (1) _____ by its quick effects, it is frequently repeated even though the effect (2) * * * permanent.

39-31

Page 258

is not 14-2	The environment provides many natural contingencies of reinforcement. An animal stalks its prey silently because a silent response is often reinforced. This * * * an example of a natural contingency. 14-3
response (behavior, operant) 14-10	Whether accidentally or deliberately arranged, the operation of the food magazine _____ (TT) whatever a bird happens to be doing. Therefore, the rate of emitting this response increases. 14-11
reinforce 14-18	A bowler may make movements as though he controlled the ball after it has left his hand. These movements are frequently reinforced by a(n) _____ (accidental or natural?) reinforcement even though they do not actually affect the ball. 14-19
superstitious accidental 14-26	A desperate man playing roulette may shout his number as the wheel turns. If he then wins, he will * * * shout the next time he plays. 14-27
negative 14-34	A man has a cold. A friend recommends a "cure" which is in fact worthless. The man tries it and feels fine the next day. This *termination* of the "miseries of a cold" is an example of _____ reinforcement. 14-35
(1) emitted (2) accidental 14-42	Accidental *respondent* conditioning is also possible. In a city under bombardment, the odor of a bomb shelter may be _____ with unconditioned stimuli for the pattern of respondents in "fear." 14-43
ess 14-50	An "intelligent" person may be defined as one who learns quickly even under less than ideal conditions. Thus, he is especially prone to developing _____. 14-51

Set 39

---

(1) decreasing
(reducing,
lowering)
(2) emotional

39-4

The rate of positively reinforced behavior is low-ered by an aversive stimulus whether response-contingent or not. In punishment, an aversive stimulus is (1) ____ upon a response, but the emo-tional effect is the same as with a non-contingent (2) ____ ____ .

39-5

---

the same
(decreased
giggling)

39-9

To lower the rate of giggling temporarily, it * * * necessary for a pinch to follow a giggle closely (to be response-contingent).

39-10

---

reinforced

39-14

A situation in which some response has been pun-ished frequently or severely provides ____ ____ stimuli.

39-15

---

avoidance

39-19

If punishment is repeatedly avoided by executing incompatible behavior, the conditioned negative reinforcer undergoes ____ and the incompatible behavior is no longer reinforced.

39-20

---

has not
(did not,
would not have)

39-24

A person may be unable to talk about a very aver-sive experience. The experience is sometimes said to be "forced into the unconscious" in a process called "repression." We may interpret repression as the displacement of punished behavior by ____ behavior.

39-25

---

punished

39-29

When we ridicule a man for doing something we find undesirable, our behavior is (1) ____ by an immediate (2) ____ in the frequency of the un-desirable behavior.

39-30

is	Under both natural and arranged contingencies, reinforcement occurs just _____ a given response.
14-3	14-4

reinforces	If a bird happens to raise its head just before the magazine operates, then * * * is reinforced.
14-11	14-12

accidental	A poker player leaves the table briefly. Upon his return he gets a very good hand. A good hand is shown to be a(n) (1) _____ if his frequency of leaving the table (2) _____.
14-19	14-20

probably	Since in the experiment the relation between receipt of food and ritualistic behavior is accidental, we say the behavior is _____.
14-27	14-28

negative	A man tries a cold "cure" which has *no* medicinal value; if he then feels better, relief from the "miseries of a cold" is an example of a(n) _____ (accidental or natural?) contingency involving a negative reinforcement.
14-35	14-36

paired	When the odors, colors, etc., of a particular bomb shelter are paired with unconditioned stimuli resulting from an air raid, it is an example of a(n) _____ pairing.
14-43	14-44

superstitions	**End of Set**
14-51	

punished 38-3	Experiment 1. A second group described in (E) (1) * * * punished. Their extinction curve provides a control in determining the effects of (2) _____. 38-4 ← To p. 252
higher (steeper) 38-8	Experiment 1. Punishment results in a(n) (1) _____ rate while the punishing contingency is in effect, and the rate continues to be (2) _____ for a while after punishment ceases. 38-9 ← To p. 252
is not (cannot be) 38-13	Experiment 1. Slapping the forepaws is an aversive stimulus which elicits many respondents of the (1) _____ _____. If these respondents (2) * * * compatible with lever pressing, the lowered rate during punishment is, in part at least, explained. 38-14 ← To p. 252
punished 38-18	Experiment 2. During (H), various stimuli in the experimental situation were (1) _____ with an aversive stimulus, a slap on the forepaws. The stimuli became (2) _____ _____ stimuli as in Experiment 1. 38-19 ← To p. 252
disappeared (been extinguished, decreased) 38-23	Experiment 2. During the 2 hours described in (I), lever pressing could not be extinguished because the lever was * * *. 38-24 ← To p. 252
(1) decreases (2) increases (3) anxiety 38-28	If the experimental box had had a door, a punished rat would have been reinforced for leaving through the door since this response would have _____ the conditioned aversive stimuli generated by the box. 38-29 ← To p. 252

after	Giving food to a food-deprived organism is always temporally related to *some* behavior (perhaps just the behavior of standing still) and must, therefore, function to _____ that behavior.
14-4	14-5

head raising (that, that behavior)	In the "accidental contingency experiment," if head raising has been accidentally reinforced once, it is much more (1) * * * that the pigeon will be raising its head just before the next (2) _____, 15 seconds later.
14-12	14-13

(1) reinforcer (2) increases	A player throwing dice when a great deal of money is at stake exclaims "Come on, baby!" and wins. The verbal behavior has no effect on the (1) _____, but the outcome of the throw may have an effect on the player's (2) _____.
14-20	14-21

superstitious	If a previously reinforced response is never again reinforced, it is eventually _____.
14-28	14-29

accidental	A loud disturbing noise from an electrical appliance ended just as a man barely touched a dial. If touching the dial actually had no effect, this was an example of a(n) (1) _____ contingency involving a(n) (2) _____ reinforcement.
14-36	14-37

accidental	If the odor of a bomb shelter later elicits the respondent pattern of "fear," it is an example of a(n) (1) _____ reflex which is superstitious because the stimulus pairing was (2) _____-al.
14-44	14-45

extinction 38-2	Experiment 1. During the first 10 minutes of ex-tinction as described in (C), one group of four rats was _____ (TT) for each lever-pressing response. 38-3
punished (slapped) 38-7	Experiment 1. During the second hour, the record for the punished group showed a somewhat _____ slope than the record for the unpunished group. 38-8
(1) lower (2) number 38-12	Other things being equal, behavior * * * perma-nently eliminated by punishment if the punishment is discontinued in the immediate future. 38-13
(1) punished (2) extinction 38-17	For the first 10 minutes of extinction in Experiment 2 (described in H), the procedure was the same as for the _____ group in Experiment 1. 38-18
aversive 38-22	Experiment 2. During the 2 hours described in (I), the state of anxiety should have _____. 38-23
(1) extinction (2) punishment 38-27	In anxiety, behavior reinforced with food (1) _____ and avoidance behavior (2) _____. Thus, the tem-porary decreases in Experiments 1 and 2 seem to be examples of the type of change which we call (3) _____. 38-28

reinforces (hence: conditions) 14-6	In the experiment on accidental reinforcing contingencies described in the exhibit, the feeding mechanism operated every 15 seconds regardless of what the pigeon was doing. A response was only _____ -ally reinforced. <div align="right">14-7 ← To p. 89</div>
extinguished 14-14	Since substantial conditioning is produced by a single reinforcement, it is highly probable that a response accidentally reinforced will occur again and receive additional _____. <div align="right">14-15 ← To p. 89</div>
superstitious 14-22	Pulling a slot-machine handle in a fancy way, talking to dice, etc., are examples of _____ because they depend on accidental reinforcement. <div align="right">14-23 ← To p. 89</div>
extinction 14-30	If the experiment on accidental contingencies is repeated with many different pigeons, each pigeon develops its own "ritual." Each pigeon does whatever it was accidentally _____ for doing. <div align="right">14-31 ← To p. 89</div>
reinforcement [(reinforcing) contingency] 14-38	A response which is never emitted cannot be followed by _____ and, hence, cannot be conditioned. <div align="right">14-39 ← To p. 89</div>
is (will be, may be) 14-46	If a single reinforcement has only a small effect, it is unlikely that a response followed by one accidental reinforcement will occur sufficiently _____ to be accidentally reinforced again. <div align="right">14-47 ← To p. 89</div>

Experiment 1. In (A), lever pressing was maintained on a fixed-interval schedule of (1) _____. *Presentation* of food following a response is defined as (2) _____ reinforcement.

38-1

---

(1) reinforced
(2) punished

38-5

Experiment 1. While responses were being punished, the response rate was _____ for the punished rats than for the unpunished rats.

38-6

---

higher

38-10

Experiment 1. By the end of the second extinction day, the two groups had made approximately * * * total number of responses.

38-11

---

(1) conditioned
(2) anxiety
    (emotion)

38-15

Experiment 1. When punishment is discontinued, we expect the rate to remain low until the stimuli provided by the situation cease to be conditioned aversive stimuli through _____.

38-16

---

could not
(would not)

38-20

Experiment 2. During 2 hours, in the absence of the lever, the forepaws were not slapped. This means that the conditioned aversive stimuli in the box were not being paired with the _____ _____ stimulus, the slap.

38-21

---

(1) had
(2) had no
    (did not
    have an)

38-25

Experiment 2. Conditioned aversive stimuli from the lever (and from the behavior of pressing it), which could not be (1) _____ under condition (I), probably caused the slight (2) _____ in rate described in (K).

38-26

Example: How to train a dog to touch a doorknob with its nose.

You will need a reinforcer which can be presented very quickly when the behavior is emitted. A *conditioned* reinforcer is most convenient, for example, an *auditory* stimulus such as the sound of a dime-store noisemaker or "cricket." Condition the dog by sounding the cricket just before tossing a small piece of food into a dish. Repeat until the dog goes to the dish as soon as the cricket sounds.

You could condition the desired response by waiting until the dog's nose touched the knob and then reinforcing, but you might have to wait a long time. To avoid this, *shape* (or *differentiate*) the behavior. At first, reinforce any response remotely related to the final form. For example, the dog may be sitting still, and it will never touch the knob doing that. Therefore, reinforce *any slight movement* by sounding the toy cricket as soon as the dog moves, tossing a small scrap of food into the dish. (The advantage of an *auditory* conditioned reinforcer is that it reaches the dog instantly no matter where the dog is looking.) When the dog is moving about, reinforce movements in the general direction of the door and withhold reinforcements for movements in any other direction (*differential reinforcement*). Gradually shape the behavior of moving closer to the door and then closer to the knob. Then reinforce bringing the head closer to the knob. Finally deliver a reinforcement only when the dog is touching the knob with its nose. This gradual shifting of the criterion of differential reinforcement is known as *successive approximation*. The entire process should take only a few minutes.

Although the goal is to get the dog's nose to touch the doorknob, a large pattern of behavior is strengthened by reinforcement. The dog must approach the door, assume a particular posture, and so on. The various *elements* of the total response must all be conditioned in the shaping process.

If we now want to condition a different response, a first response may be a help or a hindrance, depending on whether the two responses share *common elements*.

---

(1) was not
(2) punishment

38-4

Experiment 1. While the data shown in the figure were being collected, responses were not (1) _____. For the first 10 minutes each response by one group was (2) _____. (TT)

38-5

---

(1) lower
    (decreased)
(2) lower (low)

38-9

Experiment 1. During the second day of extinction, the group which had been punished showed a slightly _____ over-all rate as indicated by the slopes.

38-10

---

(1) activation
    syndrome
(2) are not
    (are in-)

38-14

Experiment 1. During punishment, the stimuli provided by the experimental box, the rat's behavior, the lever, etc., are paired with an aversive stimulus. Thus, they become (1) _____ aversive stimuli and produce a state of (2) _____.

38-15

---

(1) paired
(2) conditioned
    aversive

38-19

Experiment 2. When the lever was removed at (I), further responses could not be emitted, and therefore extinction * * * be completed.

38-20

---

absent
(not present,
removed)

38-24

Experiment 2. Only the lever was absent during the 2-hour period. The conditioned aversive stimuli from other parts of the box (1) * * * an opportunity to be extinguished while those from the lever (2) * * * opportunity to be extinguished.

38-25

---

terminated
(removed,
escaped from)

38-29

Leaving the box would have lowered the rate of lever pressing because it would have been incompatible with lever pressing. Merely turning away from the bar is also reinforced as avoidance behavior and is also * * * lever pressing.

38-30

Set 15

PART IV Shaping

Principles of Shaping New Behavior

See exhibit on preceding page

Estimated time: 20 minutes

Turn to next page and begin ▶

does not
(will not)

15-7

In training a high jumper, the coach reinforces *successive approximations* to good form by _____ the crossbar a little, after a few successful jumps.

15-8

---

differential

15-15

There are two aspects in shaping skillful behavior: (a) reinforcing only certain responses, which is called (1) _____ _____; and (b) gradually raising the requirement for reinforcement, which is called (2) _____ _____.

15-16

---

successive
approximation

15-23

A brief technical way of saying, "We reinforce movements toward the door and do not reinforce movements away from the door" is: "We _____ _____ movements toward the door."

15-24

---

temporal

15-31

Touching the knob of a door is similar to touching some other part—say, the hinge; the two behaviors have common _____. (TT)

15-32

---

time
(delay,
interval,
wait)

15-39

Bowling and many similar skills are shaped rather slowly because of the lack of an effective reinforcer which _____-ly follows the behavior.

15-40

---

shaping

15-47

On the rifle range, we begin at close range and move to longer and longer ranges as we become more skilled. Moving to longer ranges applies the principle of * * *.

15-48

Experiment 1.

(A) Eight rats were reinforced with food on a fixed-interval schedule for pressing a lever.

(B) After three daily sessions of 1 hour each, food reinforcement was discontinued. Responses made without reinforcement were recorded for two sessions of 2 hours each.

(C) For four rats, the apparatus was so arranged that each lever-pressing response during the first 10 minutes of extinction resulted in a slap on the forepaws by a return kick of the lever.

(D) After 10 minutes, the rats were no longer slapped.

(E) The other four rats were not slapped at all.

(F) The averaged cumulative records for the two groups of rats for the two extinction sessions are presented in Figure 1.

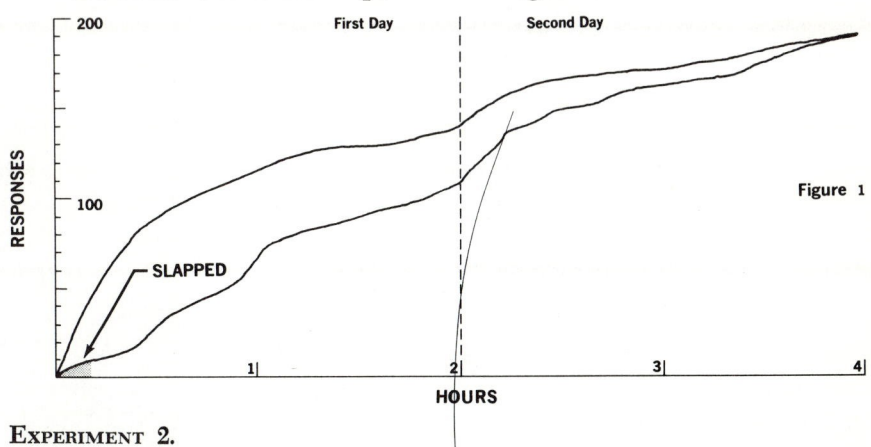

Experiment 2.

(Wait until instructed to read Experiment 2.)

(G) A group of new rats were treated like the punished group in Experiment 1 until the extinction session.

(H) For the first 10 minutes in extinction, every response was followed by a slap.

(I) After this short period of punishment, each rat was left in the box for 2 hours, but the lever was removed.

(J) Two hours later, the lever was replaced and extinction continued with *no* further slapping of the forepaws.

(K) Except for a very slight initial depression in rate,

(L) the extinction curve was like that for the unpunished rats in Experiment 1.

The high-jump star in a track meet is reinforced for clearing the crossbar. The height of the crossbar determines which form or energy of response will be successful and hence _____.

15-1

---

raising

15-8

Gradually shifting the criterion as to what form of response will be reinforced alters behavior through *successive approximation*. By requiring a slightly higher jump each time, behavior is gradually shaped through _____ _____.

15-9

▶ differential reinforcement
▶ successive approximation

15-16

In differential reinforcement, one form of behavior is (1) * * * and other, possibly rather similar, forms are (2) * * *.

15-17

---

differentially reinforce

15-24

It is more than simple conditioning when we differentially reinforce successive approximations to a final form of behavior. When we follow the procedure, we are said to be _____ behavior.

15-25

---

elements

15-32

Response differentiation * * * a synonym for shaping.

15-33

---

immediate(-ly)
[quick(-ly)]

15-40

Eventually the *stimuli* resulting from successful movements of the bowler's body (i.e., the "feel" of bowling) become conditioned as a (n) _____ through being paired with falling pins.

15-41

(1) presented (2) withdrawn	Reinforcement, whether it be presenting a positive reinforcer or removing a negative reinforcer, _____ the rate of a response it follows.
37-3	37-4 ← To p. 246
(1) B (2) positive	One procedure, which we call punishment, is to _____ a positive reinforcer immediately after a response.
37-8	37-9 ← To p. 246
(1) positive (2) negative	Removing an aversive stimulus is a(n) (1) _____ -ment. Presenting an aversive stimulus is a(n) (2) _____ -ment.
37-13	37-14 ← To p. 246
D A reinforcement	A response might be followed by a change from S^D to S^Δ. Terminating S^D might be classed as (1) _____ (USE LETTER) and presenting S^Δ might be classed as (2) _____. (USE LETTER) Both cases are (3) _____.
37-18	37-19 ← To p. 246
emotional	If an emotional state elicited by punishment is incompatible with the operant behavior punished, the frequency of the incompatible operant will _____ so long as the emotional state continues.
37-23	37-24 ← To p. 246
conditioned aversive stimuli (conditioned negative reinforcers) 37-28	When a buzzer sounds for 3-minute periods and is consistently followed by shock, behavior with an avoidance history (1) _____ and food reinforced behavior (2) _____ in frequency.
	37-29 ← To p. 246

reinforced 15-1	In practicing the high jump, a form of jump which clears the crossbar is reinforced while a slightly different form which does not clear the bar is * * *. 15-2
successive approximations 15-9	When the crossbar is relatively low, many different _____ of responses are reinforced. 15-10
reinforced (conditioned) not reinforced (extinguished) 15-17	READ THE EXHIBIT ON PAGE 97 NOW AND REFER TO IT AS NEEDED. In the experiment described in the exhibit, we differentially reinforce the dog for moving about by withholding (1) _____ until the dog (2) _____. 15-18
shaping (differentiating) 15-25	The very first step in the procedure described in the exhibit is to establish an auditory stimulus as a(n) (1) _____ reinforcer by repeatedly pairing it with a(n) (2) * * *. (TT) 15-26
is 15-33	The procedure with which we train the dog to touch the doorknob is called (1) _____-ing or response (2) _____. 15-34
reinforcer 15-41	When "feedback" from the bowler's body has become a conditioned reinforcer, it _____-ly reinforces bowling behavior. 15-42

D	Reinforcement may be either positive as when a positive reinforcer is (1) _____, or negative as when a negative reinforcer is (2) _____. (CAUTION, REFER TO EXHIBIT)
37-2	37-3

present	Making a child go without dinner for drawing on the wallpaper is an example of _____ (USE LETTER) since food is a(n) _____ reinforcer.
37-7	37-8

reinforcement (reinforcing)	Punishment is the withdrawal of a(n) (1) _____ reinforcer or the presentation of a(n) (2) _____ reinforcer following a response.
37-12	37-13

is not	A response may be followed by a change from S^Δ to S^D. Terminating S^Δ might be classed as (1) _____ (USE LETTER) and presentation of S^D might be classed as (2) _____. (USE LETTER) Both cases are (3) _____.
37-17	37-18

punishment (B)	An aversive stimulus such as shock elicits a(n) _____ state.
37-22	37-23

activation syndrome	Stimuli accompanying or just preceding a punished response become _____ _____ _____ by being paired with the punisher.
37-27	37-28

not reinforced (extinguished) 15-2	The term *differential* reinforcement indicates that only responses surpassing some specific criterion are reinforced. In high jumping, the height of the crossbar sets the criterion for the _____ reinforcement of jumps. 15-3
forms (types) 15-10	In raising the bar after a few successful jumps, the coach is raising the criterion for differential _____. 15-11
) reinforcement (food)) moves (responds) 15-18	The behavior of a dog in sitting and looking at a person who often feeds it is (probably unintentionally) _____ by the novice trainer. 15-19
) conditioned) unconditioned reinforcer 15-26	The auditory conditioned reinforcer is useful because (as explained in the exhibit) a reinforcement is most effective if it occurs * * * after a response. 15-27
) shap(-ing)) differentiation 15-34	Any operant response which occurs immediately (1) * * * reinforcement increases in (2) _____. 15-35
immediate(-ly) [quick(-ly)] 15-42	Learning to bowl is speeded up if an instructor immediately says "good" when the form is good, but not when it is not. In reinforcing only relatively good form, he is * * * (TT) good form. 15-43

A 37-1	A rat presses a lever and escapes shock. This is an example of ____ in the table. (USE LETTER) 37-2
(1) C (2) presentation (3) negative 37-6	One procedure, which we call punishment, is to ____ a negative reinforcer immediately after a purpose. 37-7
increases 37-11	In defining punishment as B and C in the table, we do not refer to any effect on behavior. Punishment refers to procedures which are the reverse of those which have proved to be ____. (TT) 37-12
opposite (reverse) 37-16	We discover the effects of punishment only by carrying out an experiment. Unlike reinforcement, punishment * * * defined in terms of any particular effect on behavior. 37-17
(1) $(S)^\Delta$ (2) $(S)^D$ (3) reinforced 37-21	A child is refused permission to go out because he has misbehaved. If "outside" is a positive reinforcer, this is an example of ____. 37-22
punished 37-26	Regardless of the effectiveness of punishment, an aversive stimulus used as a punisher will elicit the respondents (sweating, increased heart rate, etc.) comprising the ____ ____ which occurs in many emotional states. 37-27
punished 37-31	A passenger on the "Andrea Doria" pressed a light switch just as the ship collided with the "Stockholm." The response was (1)____. This was a(n) (2) ____-al contingency. 37-32

differential 15-3	Differential reinforcement is the reinforcement of one form or magnitude of a response when other rather similar forms or magnitudes * * * reinforced. 15-4
reinforcement 15-11	In gradually _____ his standards, the coach is differentially reinforcing successive approximations to the desired behavior. 15-12
reinforced (conditioned) 15-19	When reinforcement for sitting still is withheld, the dog soon _____ sitting still. 15-20
immediately (instantly, quickly) 15-27	Food tossed into a dish will not immediately stimulate the dog if it is not looking, but a(n) _____ stimulus, such as the sound of a "cricket," affects the dog immediately. 15-28
(1) before (prior to) (2) rate (frequency) 15-35	After the behavior of "touching the doorknob" has been shaped, we can quickly condition "touching the hinge." We profit from the previously reinforced elements which the two behaviors * * *. 15-36
differentially reinforcing 15-43	If the bowling instructor says "good" at the very instant the learner completes a movement, reinforcement is _____ and thus most effective. 15-44

A pigeon pecks a key and a food magazine operates. This is an example of _____ in the table. (USE LETTER)

37-1

---

increases

37-5

Spanking a child for drawing on the wallpaper is an example of (1) _____ (USE LETTER) because spanking constitutes the (2) _____ of a (3) _____ reinforcer.

37-6

---

(1) response
(2) withdrawal
(3) presentation

37-10

A reinforcement is defined as an event which _____ the rate of a response which it follows.

37-11

---

punishing
(punishment)
reinforcing
(reinforcement)

37-15

Punishment is defined as a procedure which is the _____ of reinforcement.

37-16

---

reinforcement
punishment

37-20

A child is not permitted to go outside to play until he cleans his room. "Inside" is an (1) S_____ for playing and "outside" an (2) S_____. Cleaning the room will, therefore, be (3) _____ by presentation of S^D and withdrawal of S^Δ.

37-21

---

reinforced

37-25

When pressing a lever turns *on* a shock, pressing the lever is being _____.

37-26

---

(1) decreases
(2) increases

37-30

A child reaches out and touches a flame. The child's behavior was _____ by a natural contingency.

37-31

are not

15-4

We speak of differential reinforcement when we want to indicate that some responses are (1) * * * (TT), and some rather similar responses are (2) * * *. (TT)

15-5

---

aising

15-12

In gradually shifting the criteria of differential reinforcement, the coach is shaping the desired behavior through successive _____.

15-13

---

stops (quits)

15-20

Moving and sitting still are incompatible. When we reinforce moving, the dog stops sitting still, not only because one response (sitting still) is extinguished but because a different response (moving) which is * * * sitting still is reinforced.

15-21

---

auditory

15-28

An auditory conditioned reinforcer (the "cricket") is especially convenient in shaping behavior because the sound reaches the dog- * * * delay.

15-29

---

have in common (share)

15-36

After shaping "touching the doorknob," we shall be handicapped in shaping "lying in the corner" since we shall first have to _____ the incompatible behavior of "touching the doorknob."

15-37

---

immediate

15-44

The instructor should not wait for perfect form before saying "good." He should use both the principles of differential reinforcement and successive approximation to _____ good form.

15-45

Set 37

PART XI Punishment

Basic Concepts

Estimated time: 13 minutes

See exhibit on preceding page
Turn to next page and begin ▷

---

increases

37-4

Reinforcement may be positive as in A or negative as in D. In either case it _____ the future rate of the response.

37-5

---

withdraw
(remove)

37-9

In punishment, a(n) (1) _____ is followed by (2) _____ of a positive reinforcer or (3) _____ of a negative reinforcer.

37-10

---

reinforce(-ment)
punish(-ment)

37-14

Removing a positive reinforcer after a response is (1) _____. Presenting a positive reinforcer after a response is (2) _____.

37-15

---

(1) B
(2) C
(3) punishment

37-19

When contingent upon a response, a change from S^{Δ} to S^D is (1) _____, and a change from S^D to S^{Δ} is (2) _____.

37-20

---

decrease
(decline, fall)

37-24

When pressing the lever turns *off* a shock, pressing the lever is _____ (TT) by termination of the shock.

37-25

---

(1) increases
(2) decreases

37-29

The conditioned aversive stimuli generated by regularly punished behavior will result in a state of anxiety in which positively reinforced behavior (1) _____ and avoidance behavior (2) _____ in frequency.

37-30

einforced
1ot reinforced
(extinguished)
HER ORDER)

15-5

We must speak loudly to be heard at a noisy party. At a noisy party, loud speech is _____ (TT) reinforced.

15-6

pproximations

15-13

Complex skills must be shaped very gradually. As the criterion for differential reinforcement is shifted, _____ _____ to the final behavior are made.

15-14

ncompatible
vith

15-21

When we reinforce movements toward the door *but not movements* in other directions, we are _____ _____ movements toward the door.

15-22

vithout (with
irtually no)

15-29

Using a "cricket" to reinforce the dog's responses is superior to merely tossing pieces of food into a dish because the temporal relation between _____ (TT) and _____ (TT) can be better controlled.

15-30

xtinguish

15-37

In learning to bowl, a specific pattern of movements must be shaped. The falling pins _____ the behavior.

15-38

hape
differentiate)

15-45

When the instructor slowly raises his standards for saying "good," he is making _____ _____ to the desired form.

15-46

Read exhibit now and refer to it as needed.

The table refers to different possible *contingencies* between a response and events which *immediately follow* a response. You may find it convenient to reproduce this table on scratch paper, using abbreviations, for reference in answering items.

	PRESENTATION	WITHDRAWAL
POSITIVE REINFORCER	A. Positive Reinforcement	B. Punishment
NEGATIVE REINFORCER	C. Punishment	D. Negative Reinforcement

differentially 15-6	In learning the high jump, you begin with the crossbar fairly low and gradually raise it. If a jump barely clears the bar when it is low, this same jump * * * clear it when it is higher. 15-7 ← To p. 98
successive approximations 15-14	The high jumper is reinforced if he clears the crossbar, but not if he does not. The height of the crossbar automatically selects the criterion for _____ reinforcement. 15-15 ← To p. 98
differentially reinforcing 15-22	In shaping any given behavior, we gradually change the criterion of what to reinforce. The desired behavior is approached by * * *. 15-23 ← To p. 98
response (and) reinforcement (EITHER ORDER) 15-30	For best results in shaping behavior, the conditioned reinforcer should be presented in a close _____ relation to the response. 15-31 ← To p. 98
reinforce (differentially reinforce) 15-38	In bowling, there is a relatively long _____ between the release of the ball and the fall of the pins. 15-39 ← To p. 98
successive approximations 15-46	When the bowling instructor differentially reinforces closer and closer approximation to good form, we call the process _____ behavior. 15-47 ← To p. 98

reinforcer 36-2	When we say that a man is "suffering from" anxiety, we imply that a(n) _____ state is aversive. 36-3 ← To p. 241
(1) extinction (2) adaptation 36-6	In recommending that a man should change his job to get relief from worrying about his work, we propose to change an emotional condition by removing the * * *. 36-7 ← To p. 241
reinforcing 36-10	By slowing down, the speeding driver * * * the conditioned aversive stimuli which his speeding has elicited. 36-11 ← To p. 241
negative 36-14	A man can sometimes get rid of the aversive effects of hating someone by getting away from him. The emotion is reduced or eliminated by removing its _____. 36-15 ← To p. 241
incompatible 36-18	An emotional reaction may quickly grow weaker as time passes. "Counting to ten" before acting in anger _____ the magnitude of the reaction by making it more remote from the inciting event. 36-19 ← To p. 241
increase 36-22	When an employee is severely criticized for an error made during a period of anxiety, the probability of errors may _____ as a result of the increase in anxiety. 36-23 ← To p. 241

---

differentially

16-4

When parents differentially reinforce a young child only for the sounds of their language, these sounds (1) * * * in frequency while "foreign" sounds (2) * * *.

16-5

---

(1) elements
(2) reinforced

16-9

When we push a heavy object, it moves only if our push exceeds a given force. The contingencies determining which force of pushing will be _____ _____ are determined by the physical properties of the situation.

16-10

---

(1) is
(2) is

16-14

If the shot-put coach never *reinforces* unless the world's record is broken, he (1) * * * using successive approximation; he (2) * * * have a criterion which, if reached, would direct him to provide differential reinforcement.

16-15

---

shaping
(response
differentiation)

16-19

Most of the elements of newly shaped behavior have already been followed by _____ in earlier approximations.

16-20

---

immediately
(quickly)

16-24

A baseball pitcher acquires skill slowly, in part, because there is some _____ between his throwing movements and the reinforcement of seeing the ball cross the plate, seeing the batter swing and miss, or hearing the umpire call "Strike!"

16-2

emotional 36-1	In saying that someone "enjoys a good cry," we imply that an emotional state or some stimulus accompanying it is a(n) _____. (TT) 36-2
(1) positive (2) negative (EITHER ORDER) 36-5	If a timid person forces himself to attend many group meetings, his timidity may undergo the process of (1) _____ (if the emotion was conditioned) or (2) _____ (if it was unconditioned). 36-6
onditioned versive stimuli aversive stimuli, egative einforcers) 36-9	Strong conditioned anxiety generated by speeding may make a driver drive slowly. The anxiety is aversive rather than _____. 36-10
reinforcing 36-13	When getting rid of a strong emotion is reinforcing, it is an example of _____ reinforcement. 36-14
incompatible 36-17	Doing good to someone who "despitefully uses" you is _____ with the emotional behavior usually strengthened by "despiteful use." 36-18
aversive (emotional) 36-21	The employee who makes an error because of anxiety may be criticized by his boss. This will probably _____ his anxiety. 36-22
intermittent 36-25	**End of Set**

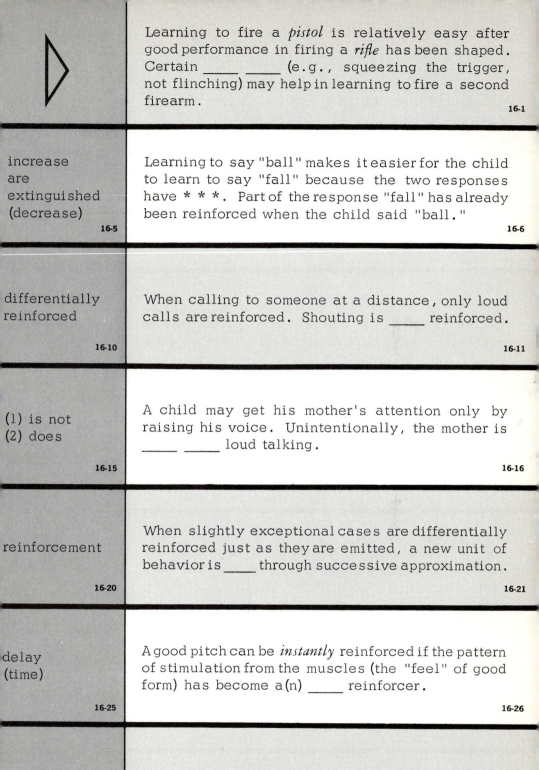

Learning to fire a *pistol* is relatively easy after good performance in firing a *rifle* has been shaped. Certain _____ _____ (e.g., squeezing the trigger, not flinching) may help in learning to fire a second firearm.

16-1

increase
are
extinguished
(decrease)

16-5

Learning to say "ball" makes it easier for the child to learn to say "fall" because the two responses have * * *. Part of the response "fall" has already been reinforced when the child said "ball."

16-6

differentially
reinforced

16-10

When calling to someone at a distance, only loud calls are reinforced. Shouting is _____ reinforced.

16-11

(1) is not
(2) does

16-15

A child may get his mother's attention only by raising his voice. Unintentionally, the mother is _____ _____ loud talking.

16-16

reinforcement

16-20

When slightly exceptional cases are differentially reinforced just as they are emitted, a new unit of behavior is _____ through successive approximation.

16-21

delay
(time)

16-25

A good pitch can be *instantly* reinforced if the pattern of stimulation from the muscles (the "feel" of good form) has become a(n) _____ reinforcer.

16-26

A "tear-jerker" is a book, play, or movie designed to reinforce the reader or viewer by generating mild _____ effects.

36-1

---

aversive

36-4

Some types or degrees of emotional states are (1) _____ reinforcers and others are (2) _____ reinforcers.

36-5

---

reinforcing

36-8

When we warn someone of the dangers of fast driving, show him pictures of crashes, corpses, etc., we pair stimuli generated by speeding with aversive stimuli. The stimuli from speeding become * * *.

36-9

---

increases
(conditions)

36-12

A reduction in strong states of "rage," "anger," etc., is _____ (TT) to most people.

36-13

---

extinction

36-16

A man's hatred may be reduced if he can engage in emotional behavior which is _____ with hatred.

36-17

---

incompatible
with

36-20

Skilled behavior learned while one is calm may be disrupted in anxiety. "Putting the pressure on" an opposing baseball pitcher is using a(n) _____ stimulus in an effort to disrupt behavior.

36-21

---

reinforced
(conditioned)
extinction

36-24

The parent who attempts to extinguish a child's display of bad temper must be sure to ignore it *consistently*, otherwise he will maintain the behavior on _____ reinforcement.

36-25

common elements 16-1	An infant's operant behavior is composed of un-differentiated wiggles, squirms, waving of arms and legs, etc. Out of this activity, skilled movements of the child are very gradually _____ through differential reinforcement. 16-2
common elements 16-6	In learning a second language, new vocal patterns will already have been shaped through _____ reinforcement when the first language was learned. 16-7
differentially 16-11	The soft-loud range of normal speech is _____ by the use of differential reinforcement by members of the verbal community. 16-12
differentially reinforcing 16-16	When the mother becomes accustomed to the child's moderately loud voice, she may answer only still louder calls. The intensity of the child's voice gradually _____ through unintentional differential reinforcement. 16-17
shaped (differentiated) 16-21	A person skilled in one sport will probably be quick to acquire skill in a new sport if the two require "similar" movements, timing, etc. By "similar," we mean that the required responses have * * *. 16-22
conditioned (secondary) 16-26	The pitching coach who knows good form speeds learning by supplying _____ (TEMPORAL ANSWER) differential reinforcement, as by saying "Good!" 16-27

Set 36

PART X   Emotion II

Emotions as Reinforcing
and Aversive Conditions

Estimated time: 9 minutes

Turn to next page and begin ▶

---

emotional
(anxiety)

36-3

In going to a psychiatrist to get relief from worry, a man is escaping from an emotional condition which has the properties of a(n) _____ stimulus.

36-4

---

stimulus
(aversive
stimulus,
cause)

36-7

The exhilaration of riding a roller coaster or being in a speeding car is an example of an emotional condition which is _____.

36-8

---

escapes
(decreases,
terminates)

36-11

Society usually condemns strong emotional reactions such as "jealousy," "fear," "anger," "rage," "hatred," etc. Society's condemnation _____ the aversive properties.

36-12

---

stimulus
(cause)

36-15

If a person loses a conditioned hatred for someone as the result of frequently being near him under conditions which do not arouse hatred, the emotional condition disappears through _____.

36-16

---

decreases
(lowers)

36-19

"Love thine enemies" directs one to engage in emotional behavior * * * hatred.

36-20

---

increase

36-23

We may advise a parent to ignore a child's display of bad temper if we believe that the behavior has been (1) _____ (TT) by the parent's reactions and can therefore be eliminated through (2) _____. (TT)

36-24

shaped (differentiated) 16-2	In the nursery, crude vocal responses are reinforced. As the child grows, listeners reinforce increasingly accurate vocalizations. Requiring better speech at age three than at age two illustrates ____ ____ in shaping. 16-3
differential 16-7	When an American learns Chinese, skill in drawing characters must be shaped; but when he learns French, the required writing skills (1) * * * been shaped. French and English writing have many (2) ____ ____. 16-8
shaped (differentiated) (acceptable: conditioned) 16-12	If in teaching the shot-put, a coach is satisfied with *every* throw, no matter how bad, he (1) * * * using successive approximation, and he (2) * * * using differential reinforcement. 16-13
increases 16-17	We generate "new" forms of behavior by differentially reinforcing forms which gradually approximate the final form. We call this procedure ____ the behavior. 16-18
common elements 16-22	When we acquire skill in driving one car, the skill "transfers" to driving other cars. This is to be expected because the behaviors of driving the two cars * * * really very different. 16-23
immediate 16-27	Annoyance at hearing loud speech and failure to hear faint whispers, set the upper and lower limits of the intensity of verbal responses which the listener will ____ ____. 16-28

conditioned
aversive
(aversive)

35-3

Experiment 1. In (F), part of a pattern of behavior characterizing (1)____ is described. This pattern is now produced by a (2) ____ ____ stimulus.

35-4
← To p. 236

---

(1) decrease
(2) increase

35-8

Experiment 1. A stimulant (amphetamine, pronounced am-fet'-a-meen) ____ the rate when the buzzer is *not* sounding.

35-9
← To p. 236

---

lowers
(decreases)

35-13

Experiment 1. Under the tranquilizer, the buzzer (a conditioned aversive stimulus) has * * * influence on the rate.

35-14
← To p. 236

---

after

35-18

Experiment 2. In earlier sessions, pressing the lever had (1) ____ a shock. Therefore, lever pressing in this experiment is (2) ____ behavior.

35-19
← To p. 236

---

(1) high
(2) low

35-23

Figure 2. While the buzzer is sounding, as between points 2 and 3, the rate of the food-reinforced response is (1) ____ while the rate of the response having an avoidance history is (2) ____ than before the buzzer onset.

35-24
← To p. 236

---

(1) high
(2) decreases

35-28

Figure 2. Just before the onset of the buzzer (e.g., point 2) the rate of both responses is nearly ____ for a short while. Note the repetition of all the complex details of the record as the cycle repeats.

35-29
← To p. 236

successive approximation 16-3	The babblings of a very young child presumably contain all the basic sounds of all languages. But the parents _____ (TT) reinforce only the sounds of their own language. 16-4 ← To p. 106

1) have
  (have already)
2) common
  elements
 	
16-8
	Reinforcing one operant may often increase the strength of another. Common (1)_____ are strengthened when either operant is (2) _____.
	
	16-9
	← To p. 106

(1) is not (2) is not 16-13	If a shot-put coach says "good" each time a man makes a throw better than his last, he (1) * * * using successive approximation, and he (2) * * * using differential reinforcement. 16-14 ← To p. 106
shaping 16-18	It is true that to be reinforced a response must first be emitted; nevertheless, by the procedure called _____, it is possible to create complicated units of behavior which would never otherwise appear. 16-19 ← To p. 106
are not 16-23	To be most effective, reinforcement must follow a response _____. (TEMPORAL ANSWER) 16-24 ← To p. 106
differentially reinforce 16-28	When we walk on the deck of a ship at sea, a slightly different form of walking ("sea-legs") is shaped by the special contingencies determining which forms of walk will be _____ _____ on a slowly tilting surface. 16-29 ← To p. 106

adaptation 35-2	Experiment 1. The contingency described in (E) establishes the buzzer as a(n) * * * stimulus which will produce anxiety. 35-3
1) decreases (drops) 2) zero 35-7	Experiment 1. When the buzzer has sounded for a short time, the rat behaves in the manner described in (F). Thus, while there is a(n) (1) _____ in rate of food-reinforced behavior, there is a(n) (2) _____ in crouching, etc. 35-8
greater 35-12	Experiment 1. While the buzzer is absent, the tranquilizer (reserpine) _____ the over-all rate, as compared with the control session. 35-13
) fixed-ratio) high) pauses (breaks) 35-17	Experiment 2. Reinforcements are not marked in Figure 2. However, since the schedule is a fixed ratio of 12, the steplike character of the record between points 1 and 2 suggests that the very short horizontal sections occur just _____ reinforcement. 35-18
) was absent (was not present, was off)) was present (was on) 35-22	Experiment 2, Figure 2. When the conditioned aversive stimulus is absent, the rate of the food-reinforced response is (1) _____, and the rate of the response with an avoidance history is rather (2) _____. 35-23
) decreases) increases 35-27	Figure 2. Some additional "fine grain" effects can be seen. During most of the buzzer interval, the rate of avoidance behavior is (1) _____, but just before the shocks at points 1 and 3, the slope of the avoidance record (2) _____. 35-28

(1) negative
(2) positive

Set 9   17-5

Name the response systems involved in the following: walking to the table, putting food in the mouth and chewing it, (1) * * * muscle; moistening food with saliva, (2) * * *; passing food into stomach, (3) * * *; and providing stomach with digestive juices, (4) * * *.   17-6

---

temporal

Set 3   17-11

After a chimpanzee has exchanged tokens for food, water, a mate, etc., the tokens * * * effective as reinforcers if the chimpanzee is well-fed but deprived of water.   17-12

---

shaping

Set 15   17-17

Persistent head scratching, pencil chewing, table tapping, etc., while studying are frequently conditioned (1) _____ operants resulting from (2) _____ contingencies of reinforcement.   17-18

) adapted
) quickly
   (immediately)

Set 13   17-23

In shaping any given behavior, we gradually change the criterion for reinforced responses. The desired behavior is approached by * * *.   17-24

---

(1) respondent
    (reflex)
(2) operant

Set 10   17-29

Reaching for a glass of water or saying "Water, please" are examples of (1) _____ behavior; any specific instance of such behavior, however, is called a(n) (2) _____.   17-30

---

(1) dimensions
(2) internal

Set 6   17-35

A conditioned reinforcer can become a(n) * * * by being paired with several unconditioned reinforcers appropriate to various deprivations.   17-36

(1) variable- interval (2) uniform (steady, constant, stable) 35-1	Experiment 1. (C) describes the emotional effect of an unfamiliar stimulus. In (D), exposure to the buzzer has been sufficient for complete _____. 35-2
is no 35-6	Experiment 1. In the non-drugged control session, *after* the first half minute or so of the buzzer, the rate (1) _____ nearly to (2) _____ and remains there until the period ends with a shock. 35-7
(1) increases (2) decreases 35-11	Experiment 1. The anxiety shown by the suppres- sion of the response rate during the conditioned aversive stimulus is _____ in the stimulant ses- sions than in the normal (control) sessions. 35-12
(1) decreases (2) increases 35-16	READ EXPERIMENT 2 NOW. Experiment 2. Chain pulling was on a(n) (1) * * * schedule of food re- inforcement. This schedule produces a(n) (2) _____ and steady rate of responding with (3) _____ after reinforcement. 35-17
) conditioned aversive) shock (unconditioned aversive stimulus) 35-21	Experiment 2, Figure 2. Between points 1 and 2 (and the other comparable portions of the session), the conditioned aversive stimulus (1) * * *, and between points 2 and 3 it (2) * * *. 35-22
anxiety 35-26	In anxiety, the rate of food-reinforced behavior (1) _____ and the rate of avoidance behavior (2) _____. 35-27

On a cumulative record, the slope of the line indicates (1) * * *, and the hatch marks or pips usually indicate (2) * * *.

17-1

) striated
   (striped)
:) glands
) smooth muscle
) glands
Set 6   17-6

Many so-called traits ascribed to individuals (aggressiveness, persistence, friendliness, etc.) are simply alternate ways of indicating an individual's _____ of emitting certain types of behavior.

17-7

---

are (remain,
will be)

Set 11   17-12

Conditioned operants are eliminated in two contrasting ways: the response is emitted without reinforcement in the process called (1) _____, but is not emitted in the process called (2) _____.

17-13

) superstitious
) accidental

Set 14   17-18

Two ways of effectively preventing unwanted conditioned behavior are: (a) to (1) _____ it by withholding reinforcement, or (b) to condition some (2) _____ behavior.

17-19

---

successive
approximation

Set 15   17-24

To condition a reflex, a neutral stimulus is (1) _____ with a(n) (2) _____ _____.

17-25

---

(1) operant
(2) response

Set 10   17-30

Lying generates stimuli which have acquired the power to elicit the conditioned responses which occur in _____.

17-31

---

generalized
reinforcer

Set 11   17-36

The reinforcers used by animal trainers are (1) _____ arranged, but a pigeon foraging for food among leaves in a park is working under (2) _____ contingencies.

17-37

Experiment 1. In (A), the base line against which anxiety is to be observed is provided by a(n) (1) * * * schedule of reinforcement by water. This schedule yields a fairly moderate and (2) _____ rate of responding.

35-1

---

(1) buzzer
(2) down(-ward)

35-5

During the "normal" or control (saline) session (comparing the no-buzzer period with the first half minute of each buzzer period) there * * * change in response rate when the buzzer begins.

35-6

---

decrease

35-10

Experiment 1. The stimulant (1) _____ the rate of bar pressing while the conditioned aversive stimulus is absent, and it (2) _____ the rate of bar pressing in the presence of the conditioned aversive stimulus.

35-11

---

(1) conditioned
    aversive
    stimulus
(2) decreases

35-15

Experiment 1. By definition, a drug which decreases anxiety is one which (1) _____ the effect of a conditioned aversive stimulus. A drug which increases anxiety (2) _____ the effect of a conditioned aversive stimulus.

35-16

---

(1) end
(2) were not

35-20

Figure 2. At point 2, the buzzer began sounding. The buzzer had become a(n) (1) _____ _____ stimulus because of many earlier pairings with (2) _____, as at point 3.

35-21

---

anxiety

35-25

Figure 2 illustrates two changes occurring simultaneously in a single organism. These changes characterize a state of _____.

35-26

---

(1) conditioned
    aversive
(2) anxiety
(3) decrease
(4) increase 35-30

End of Set

1) rate (of responding) 2) reinforcements Set 12 17-1	(1) _____ behavior is strongly influenced by the consequences of previous similar responses, whereas (2) _____ behavior depends upon a preceding stimulus. 17-2
rate (frequency, probability) Set 10 17-7	In differential reinforcement, one form or magnitude of behavior is (1) * * * and other, possibly rather similar forms or magnitudes, are (2) * * *. 17-8
(1) extinction (2) forgetting Set 10 17-13	In conditioning a reflex, as the number of pairings of the conditioned and unconditioned stimuli increases, the latency of the conditioned reflex (1) _____ and the magnitude of the conditioned response (2) _____, until both reach a limit. 17-14
(1) extinguish (2) incompatible Set 10 17-19	A stimulus which elicits a response without previous conditioning is called a(n) (1) _____ _____; a stimulus which elicits a response only after conditioning is called a(n) (2) _____ _____. 17-20
) paired) unconditioned stimulus Set 3 17-25	In the usual experiment, when a peck operates the food magazine the (1) _____ reinforcement is immediate, whereas the (2) _____ reinforcement is slightly delayed. 17-26
fear (anxiety) Set 5 17-31	A particularly slow learner may require many reinforcements before developing a high rate of responding. He is _____ likely to develop superstitious behavior than a faster learner. 17-32
) deliberately) natural (non-deliberate) Set 7 17-37	When behavior decreases in frequency and when, so far as we know, no previous conditioning of the behavior has taken place, we call the process not extinction but _____. 17-38

Set 35

PART X   Emotion II

Experiments on Anxiety

See exhibit on preceding page

Estimated time: 17 minutes

Turn to next page and begin ▶

---

(1) anxiety
(2) conditioned
aversive

35-4

Figure 1. The short segments between the straight and broken arrows were recorded while the (1) _____ was operating. These portions of the records were displaced (2) _____ -ward slightly to isolate them from the rest of the record.

35-5

---

increases

35-9

Experiment 1. When the buzzer *is* sounding, the stimulant produces a(n) _____ in rate compared with the rate during the buzzer in the normal (or saline-control session).

35-10

---

little (no)

35-14

Experiment 1. The buzzer, as a(n) (1) * * * produces a state of anxiety shown by the fact that it (2) _____ the rate of bar pressing maintained by positive reinforcement.

35-15

---

(1) delayed
(postponed,
avoided)
(2) avoidance

35-19

Experiment 2. During this session (and several previous sessions like it), the only shocks were those at the (1) _____ of the buzzer periods. These were unavoidable shocks in the sense that they (2) * * * contingent upon an absence of avoidance behavior.

35-20

---

(1) low
(almost zero)
(2) higher

35-24

A conditioned aversive stimulus changes the probability of many responses. We call the change produced by a conditioned aversive stimulus a state of _____ .

35-25

---

zero

35-29

Experiment 2.   Conclusion: Presenting a(n) (1) _____ _____ stimulus results in a state of (2) _____ , shown in part by a(n) (3) _____ in food-reinforced behavior and a(n) (4) _____ in behavior which has an avoidance history.

35-30

(1) Operant (2) respondent (reflex) Set 10 17-2	In a conditioned reflex, when a conditioned stimulus is repeatedly presented alone, the magnitude of the conditioned response (1) _____ and the latency of the conditioned reflex (2) _____, until (3) _____ is complete. 17-3
reinforced (conditioned) not reinforced (extinguished) Set 15 17-8	The experimenter deliberately arranges reinforcement for key pecking, but superstitious behavior is conditioned by _____ reinforcement. 17-9
(1) decreases (2) increases Set 4 17-14	A psychologist fed a baby when he emitted "coos," but *not* when he cried. We would expect that crying when hungry would be (1) _____ (TT) because of the withholding of (2) _____. (TT) 17-15
unconditioned stimulus conditioned stimulus Set 3 17-20	If an airplane spotter never sees the kind of plane he is to spot, his frequency of scanning the sky (1) _____. In other words, his "looking" behavior is (2) * * *. (TT) 17-21
conditioned (secondary) unconditioned (primary) Set 13 17-26	In a reflex, the more intense the stimulus, the greater the (1) _____ of the response and the shorter the (2) _____ of the reflex. 17-27
less Set 14 17-32	Operant behavior has direct consequences on the environment. A consequence which results in an increase in the subsequent rate of the operant response is called a(n) _____. (TT) 17-33
adaptation Set 13 17-38	Learning to say "ball" makes it easier for the child to learn to say "fall" because the two responses have * * *. 17-39

Read Experiment 1 now. Wait until instructed
to read Experiment 2.

EXPERIMENT 1.

(A) A water-deprived rat is reinforced with water on a variable-interval schedule
until responding stabilizes at a moderate rate — a base line on which anxiety
is to be observed.

(B) Every 10 minutes a buzzer sounds for 3 minutes.

(C) When the buzzer is first sounded, the rate of
lever pressing is decreased.

(D) Soon, the buzzer has no effect on rate.

(E) The rat is now shocked at the end of each 3-
minute buzzer period.

(F) Soon, when the buzzer sounds, the animal
begins to crouch and remains fairly immobile.
Erection of hair, defecation, etc., occur.

(G) Sample records taken at this stage are given
in Figure 1 marked "SALINE." The straight
arrow indicates the onset of the buzzer. The
broken arrow indicates the brief shock,
followed immediately by termination of the
buzzer.

(H) To isolate the performance in the presence of
the buzzer, the record is displaced downward
between the arrows.

(I) Saline solution injected into the rat has no
effect. The performance is typical of unin-
jected rats.

(J) Reserpine is a tranquilizer.

(K) Amphetamine is a stimulant.

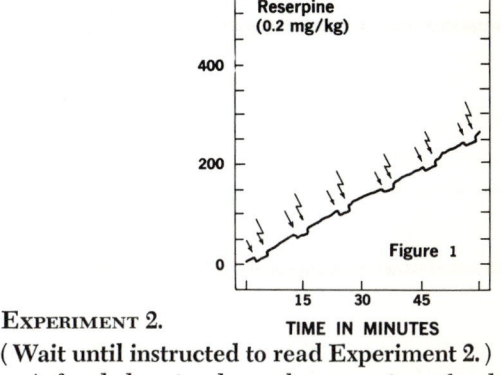

Figure 1

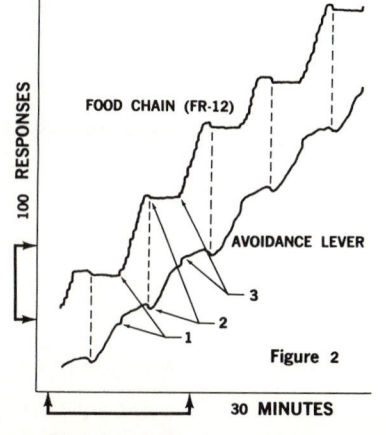

Figure 2

EXPERIMENT 2.

(Wait until instructed to read Experiment 2.)

A food-deprived monkey receives food
after every twelfth pull of a chain. At the
same time, a lever is present which in the
past has been used in an avoidance procedure
(a response to it delayed shock 20 seconds).
In the session represented by the record in
Figure 2, the avoidance contingency was *not*
in effect but extinction is not yet complete. Periods of quiet and buzzer-terminated-
by-shock were alternated every 6 minutes. Between points 1 and 2 on Figure 2
the buzzer and shock remained off; then at point 2, the buzzer was sounded, con-
tinuing to point 3; at 3, a brief shock was presented and the buzzer was terminated.

(1) decreases (declines) (2) increases (lengthens) (3) extinction	When a pigeon is reinforced for pecking a key, the reinforcing stimulus occurs (1) _____ a peck, and the (2) _____ at which this response is (3) _____ (TT) increases.
Set 4 17-3	17-4

(1) decreases (declines) (2) increases (lengthens) (3) extinction

Set 4   17-3

When a pigeon is reinforced for pecking a key, the reinforcing stimulus occurs (1) _____ a peck, and the (2) _____ at which this response is (3) _____ (TT) increases.

17-4

---

accidental

Set 14   17-9

In a reflex, the (1) _____ of a stimulus is the intensity which is barely sufficient to (2) _____ a(n) (3) _____.

17-10

---

extinguished reinforcement

Set 10   17-15

Certain groups of responses, such as those elicited by a sudden loud noise, are characteristic of a state of _____.

17-16

---

decreases extinguished (not reinforced)

Set 9   17-21

You will not continue to work if your pay checks "bounce" because the (1) _____ generalized reinforcing effect of such a check disappears in (2) _____.

17-22

---

(1) magnitude (2) latency

Set 1   17-27

When a response is elicited by a stimulus without previous conditioning, the sequence is called a(n) _____ _____.

17-28

---

reinforcer

Set 8   17-33

If in teaching the shot-put, a coach is "satisfied" with every throw, no matter how bad, he (1) * * * using successive approximation and he (2) * * * using differential reinforcement.

17-34

is not

34-3

Figure 1. The "hatch marks" or "pips" on the record indicate _____.

34-4
← To p. 230

---

lever pressing
(bar pressing)

34-8

Experiment 1. Pressing the lever does not generate the various conditioned aversive stimuli generated by other responses in the box. These other responses generate _____ which are paired with shock.

34-9
← To p. 230

4,000
(TO THE
NEAREST
THOUSAND)

34-13

Experiment 1. The animal must receive an occasional shock or the conditioned aversive stimuli generated by other behavior will lose their aversive properties through _____.

34-14
← To p. 230

---

2 minutes

34-18

Figure 2. Each point shows, for a particular session, the (1) _____ of responses on the key which (2) * * *.

34-19
← To p. 230

---

smaller
(lower)

34-23

Figure 2. During the early sessions, an S^Δ was presented whenever (1) * * * had elapsed after the last (2) _____.

34-24
← To p. 230

---

shorter
(lesser)

34-28

Experiment 2 demonstrates that a(n) (1) _____ may be an aversive stimulus capable of maintaining (2) _____ behavior.

34-29
← To p. 230

← To p. 111

(1) after
(2) rate
   (frequency)
(3) emitted

Set 8   17-4

Turning off a television commercial is reinforced by termination of a(n) (1) _____ reinforcer; turning on a very funny program is reinforced by the presentation of a(n) (2) _____ reinforcer.

17-5
← To p. 111

---

(1) threshold
(2) elicit
(3) response

Set 1   17-10

An important aspect of respondent conditioning is the _____ relation between presentations of the initially neutral stimulus and of the unconditioned stimulus.

17-11
← To p. 111

---

emotion
(fear,
anxiety)

Set 5   17-16

When we differentially reinforce successive approximations to a final form of behavior, we are _____ behavior.

17-17
← To p. 111

---

(1) conditioned
(2) extinction

Set 11   17-22

A simple operant can be conditioned very rapidly if the organism is (1) _____ to the situation and if a reinforcer follows the response (2) _____ .

17-23
← To p. 111

---

unconditioned
reflex

Set 3   17-28

The pairing of two stimuli is necessary for conditioning (1) _____ behavior; reinforcement is necessary for conditioning (2) _____ behavior.

17-29
← To p. 111

---

(1) is not
(2) is not

Set 16   17-34

Smooth muscles change the (1) _____ of various (2) _____ organs.

17-35
← To p. 111

(1) postpones 　　(delays, 　　avoids) (2) avoidance 34-2	Experiment 1. The rat has already responded under this procedure in many sessions. Thus, initial conditioning * * * shown in Figure 1. 34-3
conditioned aversive 34-7	Experiment 1. The only behavior in the box which is never accompanied by shock is * * *. 34-8
four 34-12	Experiment 1. Each full excursion of the pen across the paper represents about 1,000 responses. Once the animal begins responding, it presses the lever _____ times (TO THE NEAREST THOUSAND) before receiving another shock. 34-13
avoidance 34-17	Experiment 2. During Sessions 1-19 (excluding 2 and 12), if no response was made on the key which postponed S^Δ for as long as * * *, then a 1-minute S^Δ (or "time-out") occurred. 34-18
were not 34-22	Figure 2. The numbers of responses emitted during Sessions 2 and 12 were very much _____ than during the other sessions. 34-23
higher (greater) 34-27	Each response delayed the shock in Experiment 1 by only 8 seconds. The response rate was higher in Experiment 1 than in Experiment 2 partly because each response delayed the aversive stimulus for a(n) _____ period of time. 34-28

When every response is reinforced, we speak of *continuous reinforcement*. Often, however, an operant is reinforced only occasionally, that is, reinforcement is *intermittent*. In one type of intermittent reinforcement, a response is reinforced only after a certain number of responses have been emitted (*ratio reinforcement*). In another type, a response is reinforced only after a certain time has passed (*interval reinforcement*). A given schedule is programmed by apparatus composed of timers, counters, relays, etc.

Food-deprived pigeons were reinforced with food for pecking a key in a standard experimental box. Typical portions of actual cumulative records are given to show the rate, and changes in rate, at which each pigeon pecked the key under various schedules of reinforcement.

EXPERIMENT 1.

A **fixed-interval schedule.** The experimental equipment includes a timer which starts just after reinforcement. After 10 minutes has elapsed, the key and magazine are connected and the next response is reinforced. Responses during the 10-minute interval are not reinforced.

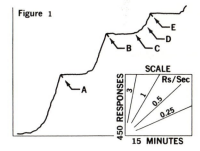

Figure 1

(1) 8 (2) response 34-1	Experiment 1. Pressing the lever (1) _____ shock for 8 seconds. Since the rat is not shocked if it presses the lever frequently enough, this is an example of (2) _____ behavior. 34-2

(1) aversive
    stimulus
    (negative
    reinforcer)
(2) anxiety
         34-6
	Experiment 1. Many responses emitted by the animal (except pressing the lever) have been followed by shock. Such behavior generates stimuli which are paired with shock and become _____ _____ stimuli.
	
	34-7

(1) is (2) deprivation 34-11	Experiment 1. After a few minutes, the rat begins to respond at a fairly high rate. No more shocks are received until the pen has traveled across the paper nearly _____ times. 34-12
(1) food (2) S^Δ 34-16	Experiment 2. Responses on one of the keys were effective only in avoiding S^Δ, therefore, responding on this key was an example of _____ behavior. 34-17
two 34-21	Experiment 2. During Sessions 2 and 12, S^Δs * * * presented. Responding on the key which previously postponed S^Δ had no effect. 34-22
increases 34-26	The shorter the period of postponement of an aversive stimulus, the _____ the response rate. 34-27
length of time (interval, period) 34-31	**End of Set**

Set 18

---

maintained

When reinforcement ceases altogether, the operant
* * *.

18-5   18-6

---

ratio
(variable-ratio)

A worker on "piecework" is paid $1 for every lot
of 20 articles he produces. When finishing a lot
is thus reinforced, the reinforcement is on a(n)
_____ schedule.

18-11   18-12

) 10 minutes
) reinforcement

Experiment 1. Another response is reinforced after
a fixed (1) _____ has elapsed since the last reinforcement. The schedule is called a(n) _____ - _____
schedule of reinforcement.

18-17   18-18

---

slopes

A rough estimate of the response rate represented
in a cumulative record can be obtained by comparing
the (1) _____ of the record with the slopes shown
in the (2) _____.

18-23   18-24

---

(1) reinforced
(2) after

Experiment 1. After B, the next reinforced response
is represented at (1) _____, and the indicated rate
just (2) _____ this point is about 2.5 responses per
second.

18-29   18-30

---

reinforced

Experiment 1. Responding "immediately after reinforcement" is extinguished through lack of _____
during this part of the interval. (Extinction under
one condition and not under another is called *discrimination* and is to be studied later.)

18-35   18-36

Experiment 1. The rat gets shocked only when more than (1) _____ seconds elapse after the last (2) _____ by the rat or the last shock.

34-1

---

(1) low
(2) shocks

34-5

Experiment 1. Shock is an unconditioned (1) _____ _____. A stimulus frequently preceding shock generates the emotional predisposition called (2) _____.

34-6

---

first (early)

34-10

Experiment 1. The low initial rate suggests that anxiety (1) * * * necessary for adequate avoidance behavior. This is similar to providing a condition of (2) _____ before using a positive reinforcer.

34-11

---

(1) avoidance
(2) avoids
    (postpones,
    delays)

34-15

READ EXPERIMENT 2 NOW AND REFER TO IT AS NEEDED. Experiment 2. There were two keys in this apparatus. Responses on one key were rein- forced with (1) _____ on a variable-interval schedule *except* when the (2) _____ (TT) was present.

34-16

---

(1) reinforced
(2) avoidance

34-20

Figure 2. During Sessions 1-19 (excluding 2 and 12) about _____ hundred responses per session were made on the S^Δ-avoidance key.

34-21

---

shortened
(decreased)

34-25

Figure 2. Decreasing the interval by which a re- sponse delays an S^Δ (from 2 minutes to 45 seconds) considerably _____ the number of responses per session.

34-26

---

rate
(frequency)

34-30

In avoidance behavior, one variable shown to be of considerable importance is the * * * during which the response postpones the aversive stimulus.

34-31

Page 231

The "acquisition," or conditioning, of behavior refers to an increase in frequency of occurrence of a response resulting from _____.

18-1

---

extinguished
decreases in
e, ceases)

18-6

When an operant is only occasionally followed by reinforcement, the schedule of reinforcement is said to be _____.

18-7

---

ratio
(fixed-ratio)

18-12

In a ratio schedule, the number of responses required per reinforcement may be constant (fixed-ratio schedule) or variable (variable-ratio schedule). Gambling is analogous to a(n) (1) * * * schedule and "piecework" to a(n) (2) * * * schedule.

18-13

---

(1) interval
    (period)
(2) fixed-
    interval

18-18

Experiment 1. The schedule is called a(n) (1) _____ - _____ schedule because only after 10 minutes have elapsed will another (2) _____ occur (and then, only if the organism (3) _____).

18-19

---

(1) slope
(2) scale

18-24

Experiment 1. Responses are reinforced at points B and E. The slope of the record from D to E is between the two slopes _____ and _____ shown on the scale.

18-25

---

(1) E
(2) before

18-30

Experiment 1. On a fixed-interval schedule of reinforcement, response rate is (1) _____-est just after reinforcement and (2) _____-est just before the next reinforcement.

18-31

---

reinforcement

18-36

Experiment 1. The pattern of responding, typical of the fixed-interval schedule, develops in part because of the _____ of responses occurring soon after reinforcement.

18-37

Set 34

PART IX   Avoidance and Escape Behavior

Avoidance Experiments

See exhibit on preceding page

Turn to next page and begin ▶

Estimated time: 17 minutes

shocks
(aversive
stimuli)

34-4

Experiment 1. In the first few minutes of the session, shown at **a** in Figure 1, the rate was (1) _____ and the animal received many (2) _____.

34-5

stimuli

34-9

Figure 1. In spite of a long history of avoiding shock, the rat receives many shocks during the _____ part of the session, as shown at **a**. These generate emotion.

34-10

extinction

34-14

Experiment 1 demonstrates (1) _____ behavior. This behavior (2) _____ the unconditioned aversive stimulus.

34-15

(1) number
(2) postponed S$^\Delta$
     (avoided S$^\Delta$)

34-19

Experiment 2. Responses in the presence of S$^\Delta$ were never (1) _____. Thus, postponing the loss of an opportunity to be reinforced on one key maintained (2) _____ behavior on the other key.

34-20

(1) 2 minutes
(2) response

34-24

Experiment 2. At the forty-fourth session, the interval between the last response and the presentation of an S$^\Delta$ was _____ to 45 seconds.

34-25

(1) S$^\Delta$
(2) avoidance

34-29

The length of time for which a response postpones an aversive stimulus is an important determinant of the _____ of an avoidance response.

34-30

reinforcement 18-1	A previously acquired operant which is consistently not reinforced will be _____. 18-2
intermittent 18-7	There are many different ways in which intermittent reinforcement may be scheduled. Under some schedules an operant may be extinguished; under others it will be _____ in strength. 18-8
(1) variable- ratio (2) fixed-ratio 18-13	When you telephone a friend at his home and there is no answer, time must elapse before he will have returned home to answer a second call. You are reinforced by getting an answer only if you call at the right _____. 18-14
fixed-interval reinforcement responds 18-19	On a cumulative recorder, the (1) _____ moves one small step with each response. Rate of responding is indicated by the (2) _____ of the line. 18-20
1 (and) 3 18-25	Experiment 1. The response rate represented by the record between D and E is approximately 2.5 _____ per _____. 18-26
(1) low(-est) (2) high(-est) 18-31	Experiment 1. After C there is a(n) (1) _____ in the slope, but between C and D the rate is still (2) _____ than between D and E. 18-32
-reinforcement tinction) 18-37	*Unlike* the "superstition" experiment, in a fixed-interval schedule of reinforcement a specific'response (e.g., pecking) must occur after the interval elapses. Reinforcement is contingent upon a(n) _____ in fixed-interval schedules. 18-38

Read Experiment 1 now and refer to it as needed.

EXPERIMENT 1.

A rat is placed in a standard experimental box, the floor of which is an electric grid through which the rat can be shocked. A brief shock occurs every 8 seconds unless the rat presses a lever; such a response postpones the shock for a full 8 seconds. The rat is shocked whenever it fails to emit a response within 8 seconds after the previous response or shock. The animal has been under the same contingencies for many sessions. (White space has been cut out of the record and the separate segments brought together to facilitate reproduction.) Occasional shocks are indicated by the short downward movements of the pen (not to be confused with the fragments of the reset lines).

Figure 1

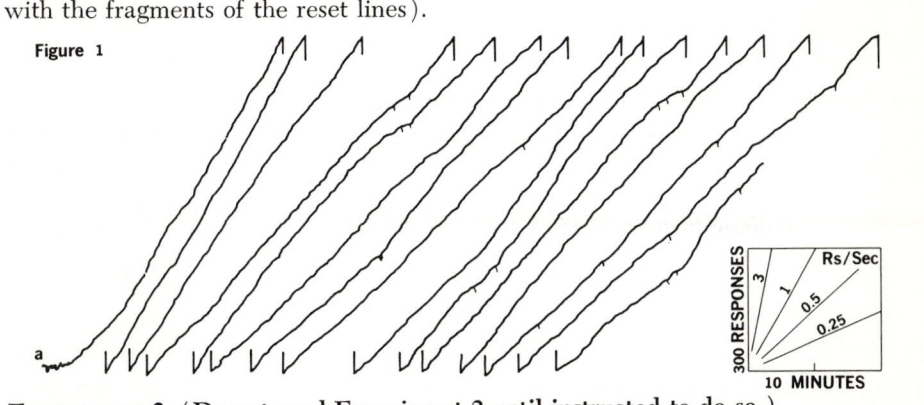

EXPERIMENT 2. (Do not read Experiment 2 until instructed to do so.)

In a standard apparatus a food-deprived pigeon pecked a key which delivered food on a variable-interval schedule when an S^D (lighted key) was present. In $S^\triangle$ responses produced no food. A second key was also present. Whenever the pigeon failed to respond on this key for a certain interval of time (2 minutes in first part of Figure 2 and 45 seconds in second part), $S^\triangle$ appeared for 1 minute on the food-reinforcement key. This procedure had been in effect for several days before data in Figure 2 were collected. In Figure 2 a point has been plotted for each session showing the total number of responses on the key which postponed $S^\triangle$. On days 2 and 12 (open circles) no $S^\triangle$s were presented whether or not the pigeon responded.

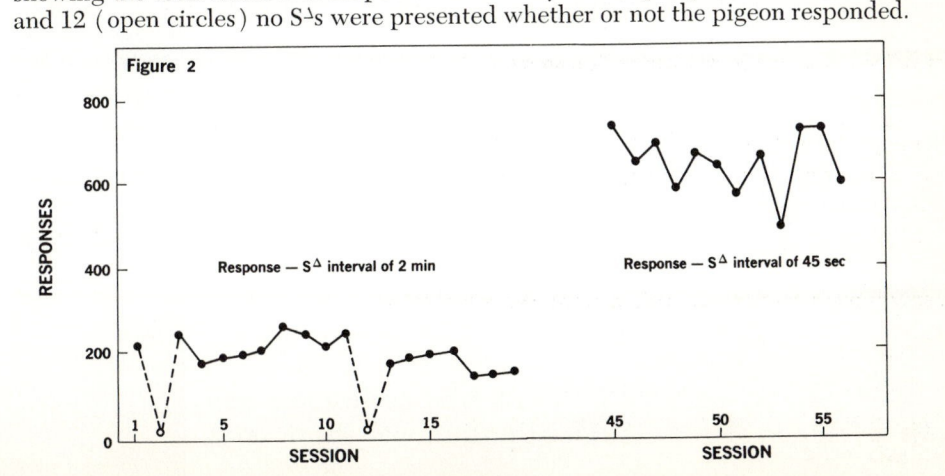

extinguished 18-2	Often, an operant is only occasionally reinforced, that is, reinforcement occurs ____ . 18-3
maintained 18-8	We do not always win at dice. Nor do we always get an answer when we telephone a friend. Reinforcement for these responses occurs ____ . 18-9
time (interval) 18-14	When reinforcement becomes available only after a lapse of time, it is said to be on an interval schedule. Using a telephone is often reinforced on a(n) ____ schedule. 18-15

(1) pen
  (needle,
  stylus, line)
(2) slope
  18-20
	Experiment 1. Reinforced responses occur at the points labeled * * *.
	
	18-21

responses (per) second 18-26	Experiment 1. Flat (horizontal) portions of the record indicate periods when ____ responses occurred. 18-27
(1) increase (2) lower 18-32	Experiment 1. A fixed-interval schedule of reinforcement results in (1) ____ responding just after reinforcement; the rate then gradually (2) ____ and reaches a maximum just before the (3) * * *. 18-33
esponse 18-38	In a fixed-interval schedule, a response contingency (1) * * * deliberately arranged; in a "superstition" experiment, a response contingency (2) * * * deliberately arranged. 18-39

avoid 33-3	Since stimuli from rapidly approaching objects often precede painful stimuli, visual stimuli from a rapidly approaching object become ____ ____ reinforcers. 33-4 ← To p. 224
reinforced 33-8	Certain behaviors are labeled "sinful," and many communities scorn "sinners." ____ associated with these behaviors become conditioned negative reinforcers. 33-9 ← To p. 224
anxiety 33-13	When we say that a man "seems to feel guilty" about doing something, we are describing a change in a pattern of behavior characteristic of ____. 33-14 ← To p. 224

(1) aversive
    stimulus
    (negative
    reinforcer)
(2) escape
    (terminate)
33-18
	When the holdup victim turns over his wallet, he (1) ____ a threat and (2) ____ physical injury.
	
	33-19
	← To p. 224

positive 33-23	Chopping wood because of criticism is hard work, in part, because the stimuli generated in the situation are paired with the aversive stimuli of criticism. The wood-chopping situation then provides ____ ____ stimuli. 33-24 ← To p. 224
$(S)\Delta$ 33-28	A pigeon reinforced with food for pecking a key in the presence of S^D but not during an occasional $S\Delta$, will peck a second key which delays the appearance of $S\Delta$. Pecking the second key is called ____ behavior because of the effects on $S\Delta$. 33-29 ← To p. 224

intermittently 18-3	Behavior must be not only acquired but also maintained in strength by reinforcement. Under continuous reinforcement, after reaching a maximal rate, an operant is _____ in maximal strength only if it continues to be reinforced. 18-4
intermittently 18-9	In throwing dice, winning is due to "chance." There is some average *ratio* of the number of throws to the number of wins. In technical terms, this is the average ratio of the number of (1) _____ (throws) to the number of (2) _____ (wins). 18-10
interval (variable- interval) 18-15	The availability of reinforcement depends on the number of preceding responses on (1) _____ schedules, and on the passage of time on (2) _____ schedules. 18-16
A, B, E (ANY ORDER) 18-21	On the recorder in these experiments, the paper moves very slowly, and the pen makes very small steps (1000 responses move the pen the width of the paper). It is often not possible to see the record made by a single _____. 18-22
no (few) 18-27	Experiment 1. The slope between B and C indicates a response rate nearly, or a little more than, _____ responses per second. 18-28
no increases next reinforcement 18-33	Experiment 1. On a fixed-interval schedule, the cumulative response curve is fairly smoothly accelerated during part of the interval. Since the rate is increasing, it is called _____ acceleration. 18-34
(1) is (2) is not 18-39	The "superstition" experiment * * * an example of a fixed-interval schedule of reinforcement. 18-40

negative reinforcement 33-2	The visual stimuli generated by rapidly approaching objects often precede painful stimuli. When we dodge such objects we _____ pain. 33-3
(1) avoids (2) escapes from (terminates) 33-7	A boy who hesitates to dive from the high board may be called a sissy. When he finally jumps, he escapes being called a sissy, and his dive is _____ by the termination of conditioned aversive stimuli. 33-8
anxiety 33-12	Stimuli generated by "sinful" behaviors may become aversive because they precede punishment. When the behavior is emitted (because of other variables), the conditioned aversive stimuli generate _____. 33-13
incompatible 33-17	The holdup man threatens his victim. He uses a(n) (1) * * * (TT) to control his victim's behavior. The victim can (2) * * * the threat by turning over his wallet. 33-18
negative 33-22	A camper may not find chopping wood aversive. Such behavior may be reinforced when a fire is built for cooking or warmth. Wood chopping in this case is reinforced by a(n) _____ reinforcer. 33-23
(1) $(S)^D$ (2) $(S)^\Delta$ 33-27	Loss of an opportunity to gain positive reinforcement is aversive. In other words, a(n) S_____ is an aversive stimulus. 33-28

maintained	An operant at maximal strength will be _____ if reinforcement continues. 18-4 18-5

An operant at maximal strength will be _____ if reinforcement continues.

maintained — 18-4

An operant at maximal strength will be _____ if reinforcement continues.
18-5
← To p. 118

---

1) responses
2) reinforcements — 18-10

A schedule of reinforcement in which the number of reinforcements obtained depends on the number of responses emitted is called a *ratio schedule.* Dice throwing may be reinforced on a(n) _____ schedule.
18-11
← To p. 118

---

(1) ratio
(2) interval — 18-16

READ DESCRIPTION OF EXPERIMENT 1. Experiment 1. A response is reinforced only after at least (1) _____ _____ have elapsed since the last (2) _____.
18-17
← To p. 118

---

response
(step of pen) — 18-22

The *scale* at the bottom of the exhibit shows several of the _____ which result from various rates of responding.
18-23
← To p. 118

---

zero — 18-28

Experiment 1. The hatch mark at B indicates that a response was (1) _____. Immediately (2) _____ B, the record indicates a period of no responding.
18-29
← To p. 118

---

positive — 18-34

Experiment 1. When the pigeon was *first* exposed to this schedule, it pecked at a high rate even just after reinforcement; but the responses which occur soon after reinforcement are never _____.
18-35
← To p. 118

(1) escapes (2) negative reinforcer (aversive stimulus) 33-1	A common practice is to whip a horse until it gallops. Galloping is conditioned through _____ _____. 33-2
(1) reinforced (2) conditioned negative 33-6	The person who runs from the dentist's office after merely hearing the drill (1) * * * the painful stimulation involved in drilling, and (2) * * * the sound of the drill. 33-7
conditioned 33-11	The emotional predisposition called anxiety is generated by conditioned aversive stimuli. A stimulus which regularly precedes pain generates _____. 33-12
reinforced 33-16	Severe punishment of sexual behavior may also condition stimuli which elicit the respondents seen in anxiety. These respondents may be _____ with adequate sexual behavior. 33-17
(1) reinforced (2) higher 33-21	The camper is criticized for not chopping wood in an effort to increase the rate of that behavior by using a(n) _____ reinforcer. 33-22
lower (reduce, decrease) 33-26	In a discriminative operant, (1) S_____ is the occasion upon which a response is followed by reinforcement. (2) S_____ is the occasion upon which no reinforcement follows a response. 33-27

Read only Experiment 2 now and wait until
instructed to read the rest of the exhibit.

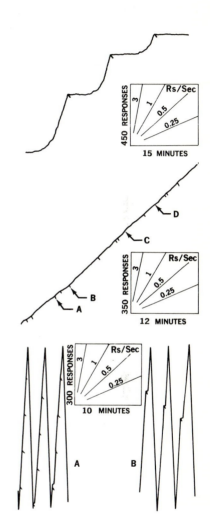

EXPERIMENT 1.

A fixed-interval schedule.

EXPERIMENT 2.

A variable-interval schedule.
The experimental equipment is
arranged so that a response is reinforced after an interval of time,
which may vary from a few seconds to 6 minutes, measured from
the previous reinforcement. The
average interval is 3 minutes.

EXPERIMENT 3.

A fixed-ratio schedule. Reinforcement occurs only at the 210th
(Record A) or the 900th response
(Record B) after the preceding
reinforcement. (Such large ratios
can be reached only by beginning
with smaller ratios and gradually
increasing them.)

EXPERIMENT 4.

Resistance to extinction varies with the type of schedule to which the
organism has been conditioned. Operants maintained by continuous reinforcement extinguish rapidly when reinforcement is discontinued (the organism seldom emits more than a few hundred unreinforced responses). Operants
maintained by *intermittent reinforcement* take considerably longer to extinguish. For example, in one experiment, after the response had been maintained on a fixed ratio of 900 and reinforcement was then discontinued, the
pigeon emitted 73,000 responses during the first 4½ hours of extinction.

A horse is whipped until it gallops. By galloping, the horse (1) _____ from the (2) _____ _____, whipping.

33-1

---

conditioned

33-5

After experience with the sound of the dentist's drill, behavior which terminates it will be (1) _____. The sound of the drill is a(n) (2) _____ _____ reinforcer.

33-6

---

activation syndrome

33-10

"Anxiety" is a common name for the "emotional" predisposition generated by a stimulus which frequently *precedes* an unconditioned aversive stimulus. Anxiety is thus generated by a(n) _____ aversive stimulus.

33-11

---

aversive stimuli (conditioned aversive stimuli)

33-15

When, as the result of punishment, stimuli involved in sexual behavior become conditioned aversive stimuli, then sexual behavior in marriage will suffer if responses are still _____ by the termination of these stimuli.

33-16

---

activation syndrome

33-20

A camper is criticized for not doing his share of wood chopping. Either wood chopping has *not* been (1) _____ in ways appropriate to his current deprivations or some incompatible behavior has a(n) (2) _____ probability.

33-21

---

decreased (lowered)

33-25

The teacher who uses strong aversive control to get students to study may _____ the probability that the students will study after graduation.

33-26

---

negative reinforcers (aversive stimuli)

33-30

End of Set

·ill occasionally
e (may be,
an be)

19-6

Experiment 2. The shortest interval in a variable-interval schedule may be very small. One reinforcement may therefore occur * * * another reinforcement.

19-7

0.5

19-13

Compared with rates observed on some schedules, the rate in Experiment 2 is moderate. We can say that variable-interval schedules generate a relatively _____ and fairly _____ rate.

19-14

---

(1) 210
(2) 900

19-20

A pigeon could not change abruptly from continuous reinforcement (every response reinforced) to a fixed ratio of 900 because the response would be _____ before the 900th response.

19-21

---

(1) variable
(2) variable

19-27

A pause sometimes occurs after reinforcement on a(n) (1) _____ -ratio schedule, but not on a(n) (2) _____ -ratio schedule.

19-28

---

(1) pause
(2) positive(-ly)
    accelerated

19-34

To generate a very high rate of responding without appreciable pausing, we should use a(n) _____ - _____ schedule.

19-35

---

more

19-41

The phrase *resistance to extinction* refers to the number of responses emitted after reinforcement is discontinued. When few unreinforced responses are required for extinction, we say there is low * * *.

19-42

---

conditioned
negative

33-4

The sound of the dentist's drill normally precedes painful stimulation of a tooth.   The sound of the drill becomes a(n) _____ aversive stimulus.

33-5

Stimuli

33-9

In addition to its role as a reinforcer, an aversive stimulus is an "emotional" variable. An aversive stimulus elicits the group of respondents called the * * *.

33-10

---

anxiety

33-14

A child is severely punished for sexual play. The stimuli involved in sexual behavior may become * * *.

33-15

---

(1) escapes
    (terminates)
(2) avoids

33-19

When threatened by a bandit, a man may engage in extensive respondent behavior (e.g., increased heart rate, sweating, pupil dilation, goose flesh, etc.). Collectively these are called the _____ _____.

33-20

---

conditioned
aversive

33-24

The conditioned aversive stimuli accompanying "wood chopping to escape criticism" may make that activity even more aversive and the probability that it will occur in the absence of criticism will be _____ even further.

33-25

---

avoidance

33-29

A pigeon continues to peck a key which postpones S^Δ. This demonstrates that S^Δs also can act as * * *.

33-30

In Experiment 2, the availability of a reinforcement for a particular response depends on the passage of * * *.

19-1

---

immediately after (soon after)

19-7

Experiment 2. In the figure, two consecutive, relatively long periods of unreinforced responding occur at _____ and _____.

19-8

---

moderate (and fairly) uniform (steady, constant)   19-14 (EITHER ORDER)

Experiment 2. If the average interval had been shorter (density of reinforcement higher), the rate would have been higher. The longer the average interval, in a variable-interval schedule, the _____ the rate of responding.

19-15

---

extinguished

19-21

Experiment 3. In record B there is a pause after _____.

19-22

---

(1) fixed
(2) variable

19-28

In comparing Experiment 2 and Experiment 3, would you conclude that interval or ratio schedules produce the highest over-all rates?

19-29

---

variable(-) ratio

19-35

Since a(n) (1) _____-ratio schedule produces no pause after reinforcement, the over-all curve is smoother than that produced by a(n) (2) _____-ratio which frequently produces a pause.

19-36

---

resistance to extinction

19-42

When an operant is "resistant to extinction," _____ unreinforced responses are emitted before extinction is complete.

19-43

increases **32-4**	A synonym for "negative reinforcer" is "aversive stimulus." An electric shock is a(n) (2) _____ reinforcer or a(n) (2) _____ stimulus. **32-5** ← To p. 218
termination (removal) **32-10**	Behavior reinforced by the termination of an aversive stimulus is called _____. **32-11** ← To p. 218
(1) is (can be) (2) is not (cannot be) **32-16**	When termination of a stimulus reinforces a response, the stimulus is a(n) (1) _____ _____. It (2) * * * defined scientifically as "unpleasant." **32-17** ← To p. 218
avoid **32-22**	Shock elicits the activation syndrome and predisposes the organism to emit escape behavior. Because it does this even without previous conditioning, shock is a(n) _____ aversive stimulus. **32-23** ← To p. 218
does not **32-28**	The immediate reinforcement for avoidance responses is the _____ of conditioned negative reinforcers (e.g., a light which regularly precedes shock). **32-29** ← To p. 218
paired **32-34**	The dog which jumps from compartment to compartment as soon as a light is presented avoids a shock, a(n) (1) _____ _____ stimulus, and escapes the light, a(n) (2) _____ _____ stimulus. **32-35** ← To p. 218

(variable intervals of) time 19-1	Experiment 2. When a response has been reinforced, a variable amount of time elapses before another response is reinforced. This is called a(n) _____ - _____ schedule. 19-2
C (and) D 19-8	Experiment 2. The curve has many small "bumps" or a "grainy" appearance. This means that there are slight moment-to-moment changes in the * * *. 19-9
lower (slower, less) 19-15	Experiment 2. If we changed the average interval from 3 minutes to 1 minute, we would expect the response rate to _____. 19-16
reinforcement 19-22	Experiment 3. In record A there are few (1) _____ after reinforcement. The rate is high and (2) _____. 19-23
ratio schedules 19-29	In comparing Experiment 2 and Experiment 3, we may conclude that a(n) (1) _____ - _____ schedule generates a higher rate than a(n) (2) _____ - _____ schedule. 19-30
(1) variable (2) fixed 19-36	READ EXPERIMENT 4. Under continuous reinforcement every response is reinforced. After such a schedule, when reinforcement is no longer provided, the time required for extinction is _____. 19-37
many 19-43	It requires many _____ unreinforced responses to extinguish a response after intermittent reinforcement than after continuous reinforcement. 19-44

escape	When a rat has once escaped from shock by pressing a lever, the probability that it will press the lever when shock is again administered ____.
32-3	32-4

elicits	Escape is a form of behavior reinforced by the ____ of an aversive stimulus.
32-9	32-10

increasing	A positive reinforcer (1) * * * defined in terms of its capacity to increase the rate of a response it follows. Such a reinforcer (2) * * * defined scientifically as "pleasant" or "satisfying."
32-15	32-16

(1) avoidance (2) avoided	In a two-compartment box, when a light precedes a shock, the dog is shocked in the presence of the light for the first few trials, because it has not yet acquired behavior which will ____ the shock.
32-21	32-22

escapes (terminates, eliminates)	Avoidance behavior might appear to be unreinforced, since the unconditioned aversive stimulus (e.g., shock) * * * occur after successful avoidance responses.
32-27	32-28

unconditioned	As extinction of avoidance behavior proceeds, the animal soon waits until the unconditioned aversive stimulus is again presented; then conditioned and unconditioned aversive stimuli are ____ once more and the behavior reestablished.
32-33	32-34

variable(-) interval 19-2	Experiment 2. On this schedule, the interval be- tween reinforcements varies from (1) * * * to (2) * * *. 19-3
rate [frequency (of responding)] 19-9	The rate of responding between C and D is ap- proximately * * * the rate of responding between A and B. 19-10
increase 19-16	Experiment 2. If we changed the average interval from 3 minutes to 4 minutes, we would expect the response rate to _____. 19-17

(1) pauses
    (breaks)
(2) constant
    (stable,
    uniform) 19-23
	Experiment 3 suggests that _____ after reinforce-
	ment are more likely, the larger the fixed ratio.
	
	19-24

(1) fixed(-)
    ratio
(2) variable(-)
    interval
 	
19-30
	A gradual positive acceleration between reinforce-
	ments is generated by a(n) _____ - _____ schedule
	of reinforcement.
	
	19-31

short (small, brief) 19-37	A response which is always reinforced is said to be maintained on _____ reinforcement. 19-38
more 19-44	A response continuously reinforced is less _____ to extinction than one intermittently reinforced. 19-45

negative (-ly) reinforced 32-2	Operant behavior which is reinforced by termination of a negative reinforcer is called *escape.* Pressing a lever which turns off shock is _____. 32-3
deprivation 32-8	In addition to its role as a negative reinforcer, shock _____ many responses which are part of the activation syndrome. 32-9
reinforcement 32-14	Negative reinforcement (termination of a negative reinforcer) and positive reinforcement (presentation of a positive reinforcer) both are defined exclusively in terms of their effect in _____ the rate of a new response. 32-15
avoids 32-20	After conditioning, a dog jumps out of a compartment when a light, usually followed by shock, appears. This is (1) _____ behavior since the shock is (2) _____ by the dog. 32-21
) avoids) unconditioned 32-26	By jumping after the light comes on but before the shock, the dog *avoids* shock but _____ (TT) the light. 32-27
extinguished 32-32	When a conditioned negative reinforcer becomes ineffective because the animal has consistently avoided the unconditioned reinforcer, the animal begins to wait too long, and the _____ aversive stimulus is again received. 32-33
terminated (escaped, eliminated) 32-38	Aggression against a tyrant who uses aversive control is _____ if it results in reduction of the aversive stimuli the tyrant uses. 32-39

(1) a few seconds (2) 6 minutes 19-3	Experiment 2. On this schedule, 3 minutes is the * * * between reinforced responses. 19-4
the same as 19-10	Experiment 2. Except for the fine grain, on a variable-interval schedule the rate of responding is fairly _____, in contrast with the rate on a fixed-interval schedule. 19-11
decrease 19-17	READ EXPERIMENT 3. Experiment 3. On a fixed-ratio schedule, reinforcements follow some (1) _____ number of (2) _____. 19-18
pauses 19-24	Experiment 3. Except for pauses, is the rate of responding close to 3, 1, 0.5, 0.25, or 0 response(s) per second on these fixed-ratio schedules? 19-25
fixed (–) interval 19-31	On a fixed-ratio schedule of reinforcement, the first response on a new ratio is followed by additional responses at a(n) _____ and also _____ rate. 19-32
continuous 19-38	There is little resistance to extinction for a response which has always been reinforced (i.e., _____ reinforcement). 19-39
resistant 19-45	A mother trying to stop temper tantrums may not always give in to them. Occasionally, when she is especially tired, she may. She is reinforcing temper tantrums _____. 19-46

(1) positive (2) negative reinforcer (aversive stimulus) 32-1	A rat on an electric grid presses a lever which turns off an electric current strong enough to stimulate painfully. The response is _____-ly _____. 32-2
reinforce 32-7	Presenting an aversive stimulus is analogous to a sudden increase in the _____ appropriate to a positive reinforcer. 32-8
(1) escape (terminate) (2) aversive 32-13	When a response terminates a negative reinforcer (aversive stimulus), its rate on such occasions in the future increases. The event is termed negative _____. 32-14
(1) avoidance (2) escape 32-19	A dog in one of two adjacent compartments learns to jump into the other compartment when a light comes on if a shock regularly follows the light. This is *avoidance* behavior because, by jumping before the shock, the dog _____ shock. 32-20
conditioned 32-25	The dog which jumps from the compartment when the light comes on but before the shock comes on (1) _____ shock (the (2) _____ aversive stimulus). 32-26
lose 32-31	With repeated, successful avoidance behavior, the conditioned and unconditioned negative reinforcers are no longer being paired and the conditioned reinforcer becomes less effective. The avoidance behavior then begins to be _____. 32-32
negative interfere (conflict, be incompatible) 32-37	The "bully" uses a dangerous method of control because the aversive stimuli he administers may be _____ by his victim in a kind of counteraggression. 32-38

erage interval ean time) <div align="right">19-4</div>	A response made immediately after reinforcement is never reinforced on a(n) (1) _____-interval schedule. A response immediately after reinforcement is sometimes reinforced on a(n) (2) _____-interval schedule.<div align="right">19-5</div>
constant (uniform, steady, even) <div align="right">19-11</div>	The record can be made smooth or "grainy" by slight changes in the particular intervals of the variable-interval schedule. The moment-to-moment rate * * * controlled by the component intervals.<div align="right">19-12</div>
(1) fixed (constant, definite) (2) responses <div align="right">19-18</div>	A *timer* or *clock* is used to program (1) fixed-_____ schedules, and a *counter* to program (2) fixed-_____ schedules.<div align="right">19-19</div>
3 <div align="right">19-25</div>	On a fixed-ratio schedule, reinforcements occur after a fixed number of responses. A variable-ratio schedule provides reinforcement after a(n) _____ number of responses.<div align="right">19-26</div>
high (and) uniform (EITHER ORDER) <div align="right">19-32</div>	Pauses sometimes occur after reinforcement on both fixed-ratio and fixed-interval schedules. In the case of _____ - _____ schedules, responding is abruptly resumed.<div align="right">19-33</div>
continuous <div align="right">19-39</div>	Experiment 4. After behavior had been maintained on a ratio of 900:1, reinforcement was discontinued. In the first 4 1/2 hours of extinction_____ responses were emitted.<div align="right">19-40</div>
intermittently (randomly, variably) <div align="right">19-46</div>	By intermittently reinforcing temper tantrums, the mother is making them very _____ to extinction.<div align="right">19-47</div>

When presentation of a stimulus reinforces the response it follows, the stimulus is called a(n) (1) _____ reinforcer. When termination of a stimulus reinforces the response it follows, the stimulus is a(n) (2) _____ _____.

32-1

---

(1) deprivation
(2) present
　　(give, turn on)

32-6

Presenting an aversive stimulus is like depriving an organism of food in that they both make it possible to _____ a response.

32-7

---

(1) negative
　　reinforcer
(2) aversive
　　stimulus
(EITHER ORDER)
32-12

When we close a window facing on a noisy street, we (1) * * * noise which is a(n) (2) _____ stimulus.

32-13

---

avoidance

32-18

A dog might jump from a compartment before a shock is delivered in the case of (1) _____ behavior, or it might jump after the shock is delivered in the case of (2) _____ behavior.

32-19

---

unconditioned
aversive
conditioned
aversive

32-24

When a light is frequently followed by shock, any response which then terminates the light is reinforced. The light becomes a(n) _____ negative reinforcer (aversive stimulus).

32-25

) conditioned
) unconditioned

32-30

If the dog continues, on trial after trial, to jump as soon as the light appears, the light is no longer paired with shock; thus, the light begins to _____ its property as a conditioned negative reinforcer through extinction.

32-31

---

respondents
(reflex
responses)

32-36

It is generally not convenient to shape skillful behavior with a(n) (1) _____ reinforcer because it elicits many respondents which may (2) _____ with the behavior to be shaped.

32-37

(1) fixed (2) variable 19-5	Experiment 2. Unlike a fixed-interval schedule, on a variable-interval schedule a response made soon after an earlier reinforced response * * * reinforced. 19-6 ← To p. 125
is 19-12	Experiment 2. On this variable-interval schedule (average interval of 3 minutes) the rate of responding (in responses per second) is closest to which of these: 0.0, 0.25, 0.5, 3? 19-13 ← To p. 125
(1) interval (2) ratio 19-19	Experiment 3. In record A, there are (1) ____ responses between reinforcements, and in record B, there are (2) ____ responses between reinforcements. 19-20 ← To p. 125
variable 19-26	A pause after reinforcement occurs under fixed-interval schedules but not under (1) ____-interval schedules. Similarly, we expect *no* consistent pauses after reinforcement with a(n) (2) ____-ratio schedule. 19-27 ← To p. 125
fixed(-) ratio 19-33	On a fixed-interval schedule of reinforcement, there is a(n) (1) ____ after reinforcement, responding then resumes and is (2) ____-ly ____ until it reaches a terminal steady rate before the next reinforcement. 19-34 ← To p. 125
73,000 19-40	Responses maintained by intermittent reinforcement are ____ resistant to extinction than responses maintained by continuous reinforcement. 19-41 ← To p. 125
resistant 19-47	**End of Set**

(1) negative (2) aversive 32-5	Before a positive reinforcer, such as food, can be used effectively, we must arrange an appropriate state of (1) _____. Similarly, before termination of a shock can reinforce a response, we must first (2) _____ the shock. 32-6
escape 32-11	A stimulus which reinforces behavior which terminates it, is called a(n) (1) _____ _____ or a(n)(2) _____ _____ . 32-12

(1) negative
  reinforcer
  (aversive
  stimulus)
(2) is not
  (cannot be)
32-17
	In avoidance behavior, a response is emitted before the aversive stimulus occurs and the response delays or prevents the stimulus. A dog which learns to jump out of an experimental compartment before shock is presented, shows _____ behavior.
	
	32-18

unconditioned 32-23	Shock is a(n) (1) _____ _____ stimulus. When a light is paired several times with shock, the light becomes a(n) (2) _____ _____ stimulus. 32-24
termination (elimination) 32-29	The reinforcement for an *avoidance* response is the termination of a(n) (1) _____ aversive stimulus. In successful avoidance, the (2) _____ aversive stimulus is not presented. 32-30

) unconditioned
  aversive
) conditioned
  aversive
32-35
	Presentation of an aversive stimulus not only provides an opportunity to reinforce by removing it but elicits the many _____ of the activation syndrome.
	
	32-36

Set 20

Schedules of Reinforcement:
Summary and Review

Estimated time: 11 minutes

Turn to next page and begin ▶

---

ratio

20-4

Generally, interval schedules generate a(n) ____ rate than ratio schedules.

20-5

---

resistant to
extinction

20-9

Once a response has been conditioned, it can be made very * * * by intermittent reinforcement.

20-10

---

slowly

20-14

A salesman may make a sale to one out of every 30 contacts *on the average*.   Sales occur on a(n)____ - ratio schedule.

20-15

---

c (variable-
ratio)

20-19

A moderate rate of responding *without* long pauses is produced by ____ -interval schedules.

20-20

---

pause

20-24

The student who finishes one term paper may find it difficult to start another assignment. "Difficulty in starting" seems analogous to the ____ after reinforcement when reinforcements are never close together.

20-25

---

resistance to
extinction
(persistence)

20-29

When a husband who has *always* been responsive to his wife's affectionate advances suddenly grows indifferent, his wife's efforts to be affectionate may ____ more quickly than if he had occasionally been indifferent in the past.

20-30

(1) reinforced (2) reinforced 31-3	Deprivation of food _____ the probability of emission of a whole class of operants which have in the past been reinforced with food. ← To p. 213 31-4
incompatible 31-8	The reflexes comprising the activation syndrome occur together in many different emotions, such as anger, fear, or rage. Therefore we * * * define any one specific emotion by listing the reflexes involved. ← To p. 213 31-9
are not 31-13	In most cases of fear and anger, any response which terminates the exciting condition will increase in frequency. Reinforcement by terminating a stimulus is called _____ _____. ← To p. 213 31-14
elicits 31-18	Physical restraint, an unconditioned emotional stimulus for an infant, elicits the _____ behavior of the activation syndrome, and provides for the reinforcement for any operant behavior which removes the restraint. ← To p. 213 31-19
adaptation 31-23	When a neutral stimulus is paired with an unconditioned emotional stimulus, the neutral stimulus becomes a(n) _____ _____ capable of eliciting the respondents. ← To p. 213 31-24
emotional 31-28	When we fail to receive an accustomed reinforcement, we say that we are *frustrated*. We are reporting an emotional state produced by * * * a usual reinforcement. ← To p. 213 31-29

A response is maintained by continuous reinforcement when _____ response is reinforced.

20-1

---

lower
(slower,
lesser)

20-5

The most rapid extinction occurs after _____ reinforcement.

20-6

---

resistant to
extinction
(persistent)

20-10

Affection, attention, and approval sometimes serve as generalized reinforcers. They furnish such subtle stimuli that they sometimes go unnoticed. When they are unnoticed, they * * * likely to serve as reinforcers.

20-11

---

variable

20-15

Salesmen are often on a variable-ratio schedule because sales often depend on the (1) _____ of contacts made and because it (2) * * * predictable that any given contact will result in a sale.

20-16

---

variable

20-20

A long pause after reinforcement, followed by a *gradual* acceleration, is generated by a(n) _____ - _____ schedule.

20-21

---

pause

20-25

A radar observer searching for unidentified planes must emit "looking behavior." This is reinforced by seeing a plane. Since planes appear at irregular *times,* his looking is on a(n) _____ - _____ schedule.

20-26

---

extinguish

20-30

When a cigarette lighter which has worked *very consistently* suddenly fails to light, we stop trying to light it after a few attempts. This is an example of rapid (1) _____ of a response maintained on (2) _____ reinforcement.

20-31

class (group, set of) 31-2	A *hungry* animal can be (1) _____ with food; a *frightened* animal can be (2) _____ by termination of the threatening condition. 31-3
reinforced 31-7	Even when deprived of food, an *anxious* person may not eat. The responses which increase in probability during *anxiety* are _____ with eating. 31-8
operant 31-12	The scientist must, in each case, discover the operations which change the frequency of a class of responses. The emotions, fear, anger, etc., * * * in themselves causes of behavior. 31-13
adaptation 31-17	Physical restraint is an unconditioned emotional stimulus for infants; thus it _____ the reflex responses of the activation syndrome. 31-18
adaptation 31-22	When a manufacturer designs an elevator to descend at a rate of acceleration which is not disturbing to most adults but frightens children or inexperienced adults, he is counting on the process of _____ to an unconditioned stimulus. 31-23
activation syndrome 31-27	Some conditions defined by their effects on operant behavior also have emotional effects. Taking candy, a reinforcer, from a baby has a(n) _____ effect (anger, rage, etc.). 31-28
emotional 31-32	**End of Set**

every (each) 20-1	Reinforcement continues to be important after behavior has been acquired. Certain schedules of reinforcement continue to have an effect in _____ behavior in strength. 20-2
continuous 20-6	To generate persistent and stable behavior, we shift from continuous to _____ reinforcement by gradually increasing the size of interval or ratio. 20-7
are not 20-11	Because affection, attention, and approval are often unnoticed by the recipient, behavior reinforced by them tends to be _____-ly reinforced. 20-12
(1) number (2) is not 20-16	The legendary perseverance of salesmen may illustrate the resistance to extinction created by _____ _____ schedules. 20-17
fixed (-) interval 20-21	Industrial piecework pay is an example of a(n) _____ - _____ schedule. 20-22
variable (-) interval 20-26	The radar observer may stop "looking" if the average time between planes is too great, that is, his looking behavior * * * if not occasionally reinforced. 20-27
(1) extinction (2) continuous 20-31	When an unreliable cigarette lighter lights after five tries *on the average*, the behavior of trying to light it is reinforced on a(n) _____ - _____ schedule. 20-32

predisposed 31-1	Deprivational conditions alter the probability of a whole class of responses. Similarly, emotional conditions alter the probability of a whole * * * of responses. 31-2
(1) more (2) less 31-6	We ourselves are _____ by reinforcing a person we are "in love with." 31-7
predisposed (more likely) 31-11	The layman can fairly accurately identify states of fear, anger, etc., not from reflex behavior but from changes which act upon the environment. Individual emotions are identified by _____ behavior. 31-12
unconditioned 31-16	A pigeon placed in an experimental box for the first time shows much conditioned or unconditioned emotional behavior. Before attempting to condition a response, we allow time for _____. 31-17
unconditioned stimulus 31-21	A jet pilot eventually reacts unemotionally to zero g. This illustrates that an *un*conditioned emotional reflex eventually undergoes _____. 31-22
conditioning 31-26	After words like "bad" and "wrong" have frequently accompanied punishment, they will elicit the group of respondents comprising the _____ _____. 31-27
(1) emotional (2) reinforced 31-31	When a response has been consistently reinforced in the past and reinforcement is then suddenly discontinued, *emotion* may result. Rapid pulling of the lever on a candy machine which is out of order may have one such _____ effect. 31-32

maintaining	Availability of reinforcement depends on the passage of time in _____ schedules.
20-2	20-3

intermittent	In the early conditioning of a response, reinforcement must be rather frequent (preferably continuous); if this is not the case, the response may be _____ before the next reinforcement is due.
20-7	20-8

intermittent(-ly)	Very persistent behavior is produced by intermittent reinforcement, i.e., considerable _____ to extinction is generated.
20-12	20-13

variable-ratio	Pathological gambling illustrates the high rate of responding produced by _____ _____ schedules.
20-17	20-18

fixed(-)ratio	Unless complicated by other working conditions, industrial piecework pay generates a _____ and uniform rate of working except perhaps for some pausing after completing a unit.
20-22	20-23

is extinguished	On a variable-interval schedule, the longer the average interval, the lower the rate. Thus, the radar observer in an area with many planes will show a(n) _____ rate of "looking" than one in an area with few planes.
20-27	20-28

variable(-)ratio	Which cigarette lighter do we stop trying to light after fewer trials: (a) one which has always worked to date, or (b) one which has generally worked after a few trials?
20-32	20-33

An animal deprived of food is predisposed to emit behavior previously reinforced with food. A *frightened* animal is _____ to emit behavior previously reinforced by terminating the *frightening* situation.

31-1

---

increases

31-5

When *angry,* we are (1) _____ likely to strike a person and (2) _____ likely to reinforce him positively.

31-6

---

can (do)

31-10

Predispositions characterize a particular emotion. An *angry* man may pound the table, slam the door, or pick a fight. The angry man is _____ to emit certain operants rather than others.

31-11

---

reinforced
(reinforcing)

31-15

Since "unfamiliar" implies no previous conditioning, we treat the resulting reflexes as _____ reflexes.

31-16

---

adapted

31-20

"Falling" is an emotional stimulus for the very young infant. A marked "reduction in gravity" (i.e., the value of *g*) is a(n) _____ _____ which elicits many reflex responses of the activation syndrome.

31-21

---

conditioning

31-25

Words like "bad" and "wrong" frequently accompany punishment. Therefore, through _____, the words came to elicit the respondents of the activation syndrome.

31-26

---

emotional

31-30

Finding no cigarettes in the house when the stores are closed can result in a(n) (1) _____ state because responses such as looking in pockets, cigarette boxes, etc., are not (2) _____ by the discovery of cigarettes.

31-31

interval	Availability of reinforcement depends on the number of responses in _____ schedules.
20-3	**20-4** ← To p. 132

extinguished	Intermittent reinforcement can make behavior very persistent, i.e., very _____ to _____. (TT)
20-8	**20-9** ← To p. 132

resistance	Responses reinforced by the generalized reinforcers of affection, approval, etc., often are extinguished very _____ because the subtlety of the stimuli has made the schedule intermittent.
20-13	**20-14** ← To p. 132

variable-ratio	The highest rate of responding is generated by which class of schedules? (a) variable-interval; (b) fixed-interval; (c) variable-ratio; (d) continuous reinforcement.
20-18	**20-19** ← To p. 132

high (rapid)	If the unit of work paid for on piece rate is large, there may be a(n) _____ after completing a unit.
20-23	**20-24** ← To p. 132

higher	When a husband is sometimes responsive but sometimes indifferent, his wife may continue to make affectionate advances during a long period when he is indifferent. Her behavior shows strong * * * because it is maintained by intermittent reinforcement.
20-28	**20-29** ← To p. 132

(a)	**End of Set**
20-33	

increases

31-4

Presenting a painful stimulus ____ the probability of emission of a whole class of operants which have been reinforced in the past by reduction of painful stimulation.

31-5

---

cannot
(do not)

31-9

Under different emotional conditions, different events serve as reinforcers, and different groups of operants increase in probability of emission. By these *predispositions* we * * * define a specific emotion.

31-10

---

negative
reinforcement

31-14

Highly unfamiliar surroundings may function as an emotional situation. Escape from these surroundings will be ____. (TT)

31-15

---

reflex
(respondent)

31-19

With time, the Indian papoose becomes ____ (TT) to physical restraint and no longer shows the unconditioned emotional behavior in response to it.

31-20

---

conditioned
stimulus

31-24

An unlimited range of stimuli can become "emotional" through the process of ____.

31-25

---

not receiving
(lacking, loss of)

31-29

Emotional states may occur when an accustomed reinforcer is not received. In the early stages of extinction after continuous reinforcement, we expect to find a(n) ____ effect.

31-30

PHASE 1.

A hungry pigeon was conditioned to peck the key in the usual way. The behavior was maintained in short daily sessions for four weeks by reinforcing every 25th response. During this time, the key was illuminated by a red or a green light. The key changed color after each reinforcement. Figure 1 is the cumulative record for the last session on the procedure. Hatch marks indicate reinforcement.

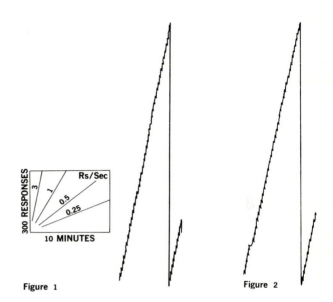

Figure 1

Figure 2

PHASE 2.

When the key was red, a reinforcement followed every 25th response as before. However, after each reinforcement the key turned green for 2 minutes during which *no* response was reinforced. After 2 minutes the key again turned red, and the 25th response was reinforced. The key then turned green, etc.

The behavior was recorded for alternate periods of red and green lights on two cumulative recorders. Figure 2 is the cumulative record of responses made to the red key. The paper moved only while the key was red. Hatch marks indicate reinforcements.

Figure 3 is the cumulative record of responses to the green key only during 2-minute periods alternating with the red periods of Figure 2. Responses to the green light were not reinforced; the hatch marks on this record indicate when the key was red (this recorder being stopped until the pigeon emitted 25 responses recorded in Figure 2).

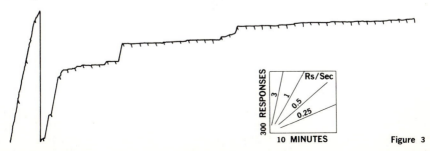

Figure 3

activation syndrome 30-3	Part of the activation syndrome supplies needed oxygen. Inhalation quickens, and the bronchioles in the lungs dilate. These reflexes * * * involved in the emotions of fear or anger. 30-4 ← To p. 208
(1) quickens (increases) (2) dilate (3) secreted 30-8	In the activation syndrome, certain reflexes increase the flow of oxygen and sugar to striate muscles. The heart rate _____. 30-9 ← To p. 208
lowers (decreases) 30-13	One way to detect the activation syndrome is to record the GSR. One of the reflexes in the activation syndrome (sweating) (1) _____ the electrical resistance of the skin. This response is called the (2) _____ _____ response. 30-14 ← To p. 208
(1) many (2) activation syndrome 30-18	In the activation syndrome, electrical skin resistances (1) _____, blood-sugar level (2) _____, oxygen in the blood (3) _____, and pupils (4) _____. 30-19 ← To p. 208
does not 30-23	The activation syndrome occurs in certain emotions, but it also occurs when there is great _____ without emotion. 30-24 ← To p. 208
harmful 30-28	Doctors often advise patients with heart trouble, high blood pressure, or stomach ulcers to avoid exertion and emotional situations. The visceral effects would be especially _____ in such cases. 30-29 ← To p. 208

Set 21

PART VI Stimulus Control

Stimulus Discrimination

See exhibit on preceding page

Estimated time: 35 minutes

Turn to next page and begin ▶

(1) red
(2) reinforced

21-10

In Phase 2, after a response has been reinforced, the key turns green and _____ responses are reinforced.

21-11

---

was (is)

21-21

Figure 3. After the first three S^Δ periods (6 minutes of S^Δ), responding became more irregular and, by the eighth period in S^Δ, the rate was much _____ than before.

21-22

---

extinguished

21-32

A conditioned operant may continue to be reinforced in the presence of a certain tone. Responding in the presence of that tone * * * maintained by the continued reinforcement.

21-33

---

multiple

21-43

Behavior comes under _____ _____ in a multiple schedule.

21-44

---

three

21-54

In conditioning a respondent, a response occurs but nothing is contingent upon it. One need only _____ a neutral stimulus with an unconditioned stimulus.

21-55

---

(1) $(S)^D$
(2) $(S)^\Delta$

21-65

When an employee wishes to leave work early, his employer, if smiling, is more likely to say "yes." The smile functions as a(n) (1) _____ since it is then that the response of asking to leave early may be (2) _____. (TT)

21-66

survival (acceptable: existence, safety) 30-2	The term *activation syndrome* describes the effect of a large group of responses which are elicited together by certain stimuli (e.g., painful stimuli). The ____ ____ is characteristic of the emotions of fear and anger. 30-3

(1) activation
   syndrome
(2) respondents
   (reflex
   responses)
30-7
	In the activation syndrome, inhalation (1) ____, bronchioles (2) ____, and adrenalin is (3) ____.
	
	30-8

(1) cease
   (decrease)
(2) cease
   (decrease)
30-12
	As part of the activation syndrome, a painful stimulus elicits perspiration which ____ the electrical resistance of the skin (the galvanic skin response or GSR).
	
	30-13

activation syndrome 30-17	In "emotional states," (1) ____ respondents occur together in what is technically called the (2) * * *. 30-18
activation syndrome 30-22	While the activation syndrome always occurs in fear, anger, anxiety, etc., it also occurs as the result of heavy work in the absence of emotion. Hence, the activation syndrome * * * necessarily imply emotion. 30-23

(1) useful
(2) useless
   (even
   harmful)
30-27
	Psychosomatic disorders are, in part, attributable to the activation syndrome in prolonged anxiety. The activation syndrome is not only often useless; in the case of psychosomatic disorders it is ____.
	
	30-28

During Phase 1, the behavior was maintained by a(n) * * * schedule of reinforcement.

21-1

---

no

21-11

When a certain stimulus is the occasion upon which responses are followed by reinforcement, the stimulus is called a *discriminative stimulus* (S^D). In Phase 2, the red light is a(n) * * * for pecking the key.

21-12

---

lower
(slower)

21-22

Responses are never reinforced in the presence of S$^\Delta$. Withholding reinforcement results in _____ of a response.

21-23

---

is (will be)

21-33

If a response is reinforced when a tone has a high pitch but not when the tone has a low pitch, the high pitch becomes an (1) S_____ and the low pitch an (2) S_____.

21-34

---

stimulus
control

21-44

In a "multiple variable-interval extinction schedule," responses are reinforced on a variable-interval schedule during one stimulus and * * * during another stimulus.

21-45

---

pair

21-55

In contrast with the development of stimulus control in respondent behavior, a discriminative operant requires a(n) _____ - _____ contingency.

21-56

---

(1) S^D
(2) reinforced

21-66

The girl whose facial expressions make her look "approachable" instead of "aloof" is more likely to be asked for a date. She may assume an "approachable" expression to exert stimulus _____ (TT) over a young man's behavior.

21-67

elicits 30-1	Most of the responses elicited in fear and anger activate the organism in the sense that they increase its capacity for physical exertion. This "activation syndrome" is important for an organism's _____ in a highly primitive environment. 30-2
adrenalin 30-6	In the so-called (1) _____ _____, the blood is richly supplied with both sugar and oxygen. The mechanisms responsible are members of a group of (2) _____ characteristic of some emotions. 30-7
cease (stop, decrease) 30-11	In the activation syndrome, activity of the smooth muscles of the intestines (1) _____; similarly, salivation and other gastric secretions (2) _____. 30-12
dilation 30-16	In certain emotions, many respondents are active together in what is called the * * *. 30-17
is not 30-21	A prominent characteristic of organisms in situations we call "emotional" is the presence of the _____ _____. 30-22
lacks (has no, is not of, has lost its) 30-26	For a person about to run a race, the activation syndrome would be biologically (1) _____ while for the executive working at a desk, the activation syndrome would be biologically (2) _____. 30-27
together (at once) 30-31	Many different emotions involve the activation syndrome. For this reason, early attempts to distinguish between emotions on the basis of the reflexes involved * * * successful. 30-32

fixed-ratio 21-1	Figure 1. Twenty-five responses per reinforcement is a relatively small ratio. Figure 1 shows a(n) (1) _____ (and relatively constant) rate of responding and few, if any, (2) _____ after reinforcement. 21-2
S^D (discriminative stimulus) 21-12	An S^Δ (S-delta) is a stimulus which is consistently present when responses are *not* reinforced. In Phase 2, the (1) _____ light is the S^Δ, and the (2) _____ light is the S^D. 21-13
extinction 21-23	In Figure 3, responding in the presence of the (1) _____ undergoes nearly complete (2) _____ before the end of the session under discrimination procedure. 21-24
(1) $(S)^D$ (2) $(S)^\Delta$ 21-34	If a response is frequently reinforced when a high-pitched tone is present but not when a low-pitched tone is present, a(n) _____-tion develops (in any organism capable of distinguishing pitches). 21-35
not reinforced (extinguished) 21-45	Discrimination is a special case of stimulus control. When a response has been extinguished in the presence of one stimulus and maintained in the presence of another, a(n) _____ has been developed. 21-46
three(-)term [three(-)number] 21-56	In operant discrimination, a response (1) _____ in the presence of (2) S_____ is likely to be reinforced, while a response (3) _____ in the presence of (4) S_____ will not be reinforced. 21-57
control 21-67	When an infant says "da-da," the response may be especially well-reinforced when the father is present. The visual pattern provided by the father becomes a(n) (1) _____; all other visual patterns become (2) S_____ for emitting "da-da." 21-68

A painful or *frightening* stimulus _____ many responses as part of the respondent behavior seen in the emotions of fear or anger.

30-1

---

adrenalin

30-5

In fear or anger, the quantity of sugar in the blood increases because _____ is secreted by the adrenal gland, which in turn acts upon the liver.

30-6

---

(1) sugar (and) oxygen
(2) higher (increased)

30-10

In the activation syndrome, there is cessation of activity of the smooth muscles of the viscera. Stomach contractions _____ .

30-11

---

more

30-15

The activation syndrome includes _____ of the pupil.

30-16

---

is

30-20

The activation syndrome * * * biologically useful when no unusual activity is required.

30-21

---

activation syndrome

30-25

In civilized cultures, persons seldom engage in physical attack when angry, or run when afraid. Although the activation syndrome is present, it probably * * * biological usefulness.

30-26

---

cease

30-30

The activation syndrome consists of a large number of reflex responses which are all elicited _____ in a single pattern.

30-31

<table>
<tr><td>

(1) high
(2) pauses

21-2

</td><td>

The experimental conditions in effect when the data in Figure 1 were collected differ from the ordinary fixed ratio in one respect, the color of the key (1) _____ after (2) _____ reinforcement.

21-3

</td></tr>
<tr><td>

(1) green
(2) red

21-13

</td><td>

In Phase 2, two recorders were used. The recorder producing Figure 2 operated only under S^D, and the other (producing Figure 3) only under S^Δ. While one recorder was running, the other * * *.

21-14

</td></tr>
<tr><td>

(1) S^Δ
   (green light)
(2) extinction

21-24

</td><td>

Phase 2. After each 2-minute period of S^Δ, there is a period of (1) S_____ during which the pigeon emits 25 responses, and the 25th response is (2) _____.

21-25

</td></tr>
<tr><td>

scrimina(-tion)

21-35

</td><td>

When an operant response is emitted in the presence of an S^D and not in the presence of an S^Δ, a(n) _____ has developed.

21-36

</td></tr>
<tr><td>

discrimination

21-46

</td><td>

When responses occur in the presence of one stimulus and not in the presence of another, a(n) (1) _____ has been formed; the response is under (2) _____ _____.

21-47

</td></tr>
<tr><td>

(1) emitted
(2) (S)^D
(3) emitted
(4) (S)$^\Delta$

21-57

</td><td>

The stimulus control of an operant differs from that of a respondent. The action of a stimulus in producing a response is called "elicitation" only in the case of _____ behavior.

21-58

</td></tr>
<tr><td>

(1) S^D
(2) (S)$^\Delta$s

21-68

</td><td>

In a discriminative operant, the S^D sets the occasion upon which a response may be _____ if emitted.

21-69

</td></tr>
</table>

are 30-4	In the activation syndrome, the hormone called *adrenalin* releases sugar into the blood from the liver. In fear or anger, secretion of _____ is elicited from the adrenal gland. 30-5
increases 30-9	In the activation syndrome, the blood is richly supplied with (1) _____ and _____ which are carried to muscle tissue more quickly by the (2) _____ pulse rate. 30-10

(1) decrease
    (lowers)
(2) galvanic
    skin
 	
30-14
	In strong emotion the eyes bulge slightly, and the pupils dilate (enlarge). These respondents allow _____ light to enter the eye.
	
	30-15

(1) decrease (2) increases (3) increases (4) dilate 30-19	The activation syndrome * * * biologically useful if great physical exertion is required (as in running or fighting). 30-20
exertion (work, energy expended) 30-24	In moments of crisis, people have been known to do herculean feats such as lifting the front of an automobile. Such extreme effort is possible, in part, because of the _____ _____. 30-25
harmful (dangerous) 30-29	Strong emotional responses after a heavy meal may be harmful because, in the activation syndrome, gastric secretions cease, and contractions of the stomach and intestines _____. 30-30

(1) changed (changes) (2) each (every) 21-3	In Phase 1 of the experiment, the color of the key alternated between (1) _____ and _____, changing after (2) * * *. 21-4
was not 21-14	In Phase 2, Figure 2 shows responses which occurred during those parts of the session in which the fixed ratio was in effect. Responses in the presence of S^D were recorded in Figure _____. 21-15
(1) $(S)^D$ (2) reinforced 21-25	Phase 2. Toward the end of the session, stimulus control has been established since responding during S^Δ occurs at a(n) (1) _____ rate while responding in S^D occurs at a(n) (2) _____ rate. 21-26
discrimination 21-36	Discrimination is a special case of stimulus control. When two different response rates occur in the presence of different stimuli, the response is under * * *. 21-37
(1) discrimination (2) stimulus control 21-47	Stimulus control is developed when some _____ schedule is in effect. 21-48
respondent 21-58	A respondent is (1) _____-ed by its stimulus, but in a discriminative operant the S^D is simply the occasion upon which a response will be reinforced if (2) _____-ed. 21-59
reinforced 21-69	The presence of the father, as a discriminative stimulus or S^D, is the (1) _____ upon which the child's saying "da-da" is (2) _____ if emitted. 21-70

(1) interval (2) ratio Set 18 **29-3**	The frequency with which a normal organism eats, given free access to food, changes in _____. **29-4** ← To p. 203
(1) lower (2) higher Set 22 **29-8**	A response occurring immediately after a reinforcement is never reinforced on a(n) (1) _____-interval schedule. A response immediately after reinforcement is sometimes reinforced on a(n) (2) _____-interval schedule. **29-9** ← To p. 203
cyclic (periodic, cyclical) Set 28 **29-13**	Objects at two adjacent points in space usually control reaching responses of only slightly different _____. **29-14** ← To p. 203

(1) reinforce
(2) extinguish
    (do not
    reinforce)
 	
Set 24   **29-18**
	When a response is under the control of a single property of a stimulus (which cannot exist alone), we call it a(n) * * *.
	
	29-19
	← To p. 203

less probable (less frequent) Set 26 **29-23**	In drawing a copy of a picture, only those movements which produce a likeness are reinforced; thus reinforcement is _____. **29-24** ← To p. 203
reinforced (maintained) not reinforced (extinguished) (EITHER ORDER) Set 21 **29-28**	**End of Set**

) red (and) green) each reinforcement (25 responses) 21-4	In Figure 1, the hatch marks, or pips, indicate responses which were _____. 21-5
2 21-15	The rates of responding are nearly the same in Figure 1 and Figure 2. Responding continues to be maintained at full strength in the presence of the _____ stimulus. (TT) 21-16
(1) low (perhaps zero) (2) high 21-26	By the end of the first session in Phase 2, key pecking is under stimulus control since changing the key-color from green (S^Δ) to red (S^D) immediately _____ the rate of responding. 21-27
stimulus control 21-37	A key is illuminated by a yellow light during fixed-interval reinforcement and a blue light during variable-interval reinforcement, and a pigeon performs appropriately under each schedule. This is an example of * * *. 21-38
multiple 21-48	A discrimination procedure is essentially a(n) _____ _____ in which one schedule is extinction. 21-49
(1) elicit(-ed) (2) emitt(-ed) 21-59	An S^D is the *occasion* upon which a given operant may be reinforced. The dinner bell, as an S^D, is the _____ upon which going to the table will be reinforced. 21-60
(1) occasion (2) reinforced 21-70	When we read aloud, our vocalizations are under the control of a series of visual stimuli on the page. The printed characters are discriminative (1) _____, whereas the vocalizations are discriminative (2) _____. 21-71

continuous Set 25 29-2	Availability of reinforcement depends on the passage of time in (1) _____ schedules, and on the number of responses in (2) _____ schedules. 29-3
(1) reinforcing (2) S^D (stimulus) Set 23 29-7	If a bright white light is often present when a response is reinforced, a light of medium intensity should produce a rate of responding (1) _____ than that of the bright light and (2) _____ than that of a very faint light. 29-8
slowly intermittently Set 20 29-12	Eating, drinking, sexual behavior, sleeping, and general activity all show _____ changes when the various conditions of deprivation are not manipulated experimentally. 29-13
(1) deprivation (2) generalized Set 27 29-17	In teaching a child to copy a line, we do not wait for a perfect drawing. We (1) * * * movements which produce lines fairly similar to the copy, but (2) * * * movements which produce lines very different from the copy. 29-18
(1) a (2) d (3) b (4) c 29-22 Sets 18 and 19	The more food an animal has just eaten, the _____ _____ its ingestive behavior. 29-23
differential Set 24 29-27	In establishing a discrimination, a response is * * * in the presence of one stimulus and * * * in the presence of another stimulus. 29-28

reinforced 21-5	If the red and green key-colors controlled different rates of responding, the _____ of the record would change after each reinforcement. 21-6
discriminative 21-16	Phase 2, Figure 3 shows responses which occurred while the key was green and no responses were reinforced. Responses in the presence of S_____ are recorded in Figure 3. 21-17
increases (raises) (acceptable: changes) 21-27	At the end of the period shown in Figures 2 and 3, response rates are quite different for S^D and S^Δ. This is a form of stimulus _____ called discrimination. 21-28
stimulus control 21-38	Immediately after reinforcement, a yellow key-light is turned on for 10 minutes, and a 10-minute fixed-interval schedule is then in effect. A pigeon so reinforced will first (1) _____, then emit responses at a(n) (2) _____ _____ rate. 21-39
multiple schedule 21-49	A very common case of discrimination is continuous reinforcement in the presence of one stimulus, and no reinforcement in the presence of another. The two components of this multiple schedule are (1) _____ reinforcement and (2) _____. 21-50
occasion 21-60	A whispered word of warning may be the occasion on which a man will run vigorously. In operant discrimination, the magnitude of a response is *not* necessarily dependent upon the _____ of the S^D. 21-61
(1) stimuli (2) responses (operants) 21-71	A child learning to read is told he is "right" when the correct vocal pattern occurs in the presence of a certain visual pattern. In describing the development of his (1) _____-tive response, we must specify (2) _____ terms. (HOW MANY?) 21-72

1) discriminations
2) generalization

Set 22   29-1

Properly steering an automobile requires that the organism have a(n) _____ repertoire.

29-2

---

1) class (set, group, category, range)
2) class (set, group, category, range)
Set 26   29-6

Each stimulus in a chain has the dual function of (1) _____ the response it follows and being a(n) (2) _____ for the response it precedes.

29-7

---

is not

Set 27   29-11

Responses reinforced by the generalized reinforcers of affection, approval, etc., are often extinguished very (1) _____ because reinforcement has occurred (2) _____ due to the subtlety of the stimuli.

29-12

---

generalization (stimulus generalization)

Set 22   29-16

When paired with several unconditioned reinforcers appropriate to various deprivations, a conditioned reinforcer will be effective under several types of (1) _____. Such a reinforcer is called a(n) (2) _____ reinforcer.

29-17

---

resistant

Set 20   29-21

(1) _____ fixed-interval
(2) _____ variable-interval
(3) _____ fixed-ratio
(4) _____ variable-ratio

a   b   c   d

29-22

---

food deprivation

Set 28   29-26

Skill in "drawing from copy" will continue to be shaped without help from other persons once "likeness" has become a reinforcer, since this will automatically provide the _____ reinforcement needed for shaping.

29-27

---

slope 21-6	When the rate or form of a response is different under different stimuli, the behavior is said to be under stimulus control. Figure 1 presents *no* evidence for _____ _____ by either the red or green light. 21-7
$(S)^\Delta$ [(S) delta] 21-17	Figure 3 uses hatch marks to indicate when the S_____ ended and the recorder stopped. 21-18
control 21-28	An organism is said to have developed a discrimination when responding is maintained in the presence of (1) _____ (TT), and has undergone some degree of extinction in the presence of (2) _____. (TT) 21-29
(1) pause (2) positively accelerated 21-39	Immediately after reinforcement, the key-light changes to blue and a *short* fixed ratio is in effect. The experienced pigeon will respond at a(n) _____ rate (perhaps without an initial pause). 21-40
(1) continuous (2) extinction 21-50	An operant discrimination is established with a *three-term* contingency. Reinforcement is arranged in this order: (a) present an S^D, (b) wait for the response to be emitted, and (c) provide _____. 21-51
intensity (magnitude) 21-61	Response magnitude depends upon the stimulus intensity in the case of (1) _____ behavior, but much less so in the case of (2) _____ behavior. 21-62
) discrimina(-tive)) three 21-72	In operant discrimination, a response is likely to be reinforced when the (1) _____ is present, but not when the (2) _____ is present. 21-73

The professional winetaster can make very fine (1) _____ . He shows little (2) _____ among various wines.

29-1

---

generalized

For most states of deprivation, there are alternative procedures which belong to the same (1) _____ since they have similar effects on a whole (2) _____ of responses.

Set 27   29-5

29-6

---

chain

A high rate of responding * * * in itself evidence for inferring a high level of deprivation without knowledge of other factors such as the reinforcement schedule.

Set 23   29-10

29-11

---

(1) respondent
　　(reflex)
(2) operant

An organism may emit the same response to two fairly similar stimuli when only one of them has been present during reinforcement. The term for this phenomenon is * * *.

Set 21   29-15

29-16

---

(1) water
　　deprivation
(2) reinforced

Intermittently reinforcing temper tantrums makes them very _____ to extinction.

Set 26   29-20

29-21

---

(1) S^D (stimulus)
(2) response
(3) reinforce

In the laboratory, an animal's weight expressed as a percentage of its normal weight is used as a measure of its history of _____ _____ .

Set 21   29-25

29-26

---

stimulus control 21-7	In Phase 1, Figure 1, there is no evidence for stimulus control because the rate of responding is * * * for the red and green key-colors. 21-8
(S)Δ 21-18	Responses in the presence of SΔ are never (1) _____. The responses recorded in Figure 3 (2) * * * rein-forced. 21-19
(1) S^D (2) SΔ 21-29	The exhibit experiment demonstrates a procedure for creating a form of *stimulus control* called _____-tion. 21-30
high 21-40	When the key-light is sometimes yellow and some-times blue (and the schedule sometimes fixed-interval and sometimes fixed-ratio respectively), responding by an experienced pigeon * * * appro-priate to the schedule in effect at any moment. 21-41
reinforcement 21-51	The S^D is the occasion upon which a response, if _____, is likely to be reinforced. 21-52
(1) respondent (2) operant 21-62	A whispered warning may be quickly followed by running. In operant discrimination, the time be-tween stimulus and response is not necessarily dependent upon the _____ of the S^D. 21-63
(1) S^D (2) SΔ 21-73	Bringing an operant under stimulus control involves three events: a(n) (1) _____ which is the occasion upon which a(n) (2) _____ will be followed by (3) _____. 21-74

cycles

Set 28   29-4

Independent of the specific deprivation state present at the moment, a(n) _____ reinforcer can be used to condition a new response.

29-5

(1) fixed
    (-interval)
(2) variable
    (-interval)
Set 19   29-9

The operant called "pressing a lever for food" is composed of many stages or parts integrated as a(n) _____ of stimuli and responses.

29-10

forms
(topographies)

Set 25   29-14

Response magnitude varies closely with stimulus intensity in the case of (1) _____ behavior, but much less so in the case of (2) _____ behavior.

29-15

abstraction

Set 22   29-19

Excessive sweating due to heavy work or emotion is similar to (1) _____ _____ in its effect on the class of responses which have been (2) _____ by water.

29-20

differential

Set 24   29-24

In operant discrimination we speak of a *three-term* contingency. Events are arranged in this order: (a) present the (1) _____, (b) wait for the (2) _____, and (c) (3) _____.

29-25

(approximately)
the same

21-8

In Phase 2, a response is no longer reinforced when the key-light is (1) _____, but continues to be reinforced on a fixed ratio of 25 when the key-light is (2) _____.

21-9

(1) reinforced
(2) were not
   (are not)

21-19

In Figure 3, each hatch mark occurs _____ minutes apart.

21-20

discrimina(-tion)

21-30

In establishing a discrimination, a response is (1) * * * in the presence of one stimulus and (2) * * * in the presence of another stimulus.

21-31

.s (will be)

21-41

When a performance is appropriate to one schedule during one stimulus and another schedule during a second stimulus, it is an example of _____ _____.

21-42

emitted

21-52

In operant discrimination, a(n) (1) _____ stimulus must precede the response, and a reinforcing stimulus must (2) _____ the response at least occasionally.

21-53

ntensity
acceptable:
magnitude)

21-63

Latency varies as a function of stimulus intensity in (1) _____ behavior but only slightly so, if at all, in (2) _____ behavior.

21-64

1) S^D (stimulus)
2) response
3) reinforcement

21-74

In respondent behavior, the conditioned stimulus is said to (1) _____ the conditioned response. But in a discriminative operant, the S^D is merely the (2) _____ upon which a response may be reinforced.

21-75

C (and) E
(EITHER ORDER)

28-3

The two mice (C and E) taking the longest times to obtain 720 pellets * * * normal in weight.

28-4

← To p. 198

(1) 1
(2) slower (less)

28-8

The normal mice's repetitive pattern of high and low rates of eating is called a *feeding* cycle. Each ____ lasts 24 hours.

28-9

← To p. 198

cycles

28-13

If an experimenter were not careful to control deprivation, the results of experiments on operant conditioning using a food reinforcer * * * confused by cyclical changes in rate as shown in C.

28-14

← To p. 198

(1) increase
(2) cycles

28-18

The female of many species shows an oestrous cycle affecting sexual behavior. The probability of sexual behavior is ____ in some parts and ____ in other parts of the cycle.

28-19

← To p. 198

(1) C
(2) A

28-23

Records A and B reach the 720 pellet level in much (1) ____ time than Records C and E although the rates at **a** and **b** are slightly (2) ____ than those found in Records A and B.

28-24

← To p. 198

(1) A (and) B
(2) D

28-28

Of the three obese mice (A, B, and D), the one(s) providing Record(s) (1) * * * eat(s) rather steadily while the one(s) providing Record(s) (2) * * * eat(s) very frequent "meals" with short pauses between.

28-29

← To p. 198

(1) green (2) red 21-9	In Phase 2, the green and red lights still alternate; when the key turns (1) _____, the 25th response thereafter will be (2) _____. 21-10 ← To p. 138
2 21-20	Figure 3. During the first 6 minutes of Phase 2, responding during S^Δ occurred at a rate which * * * close to the rate shown on the previous day in Figure 1. 21-21 ← To p. 138
) not reinforced (extinguished) :) reinforced (conditioned, maintained) EITHER ORDER)21-31	If responses are not reinforced when a tone of a certain pitch is presented, responding in the presence of that tone is _____. 21-32 ← To p. 138
stimulus control 21-42	In a *multiple* schedule, two or more schedules are in effect and a different stimulus is present during each. A fixed-interval during a yellow light and a fixed-ratio during a blue light is a(n) _____ fixed-interval fixed-ratio schedule. 21-43 ← To p. 138
) discriminative :) follow 21-53	The necessary conditions for establishing an operant discrimination are: a discriminative stimulus, a response, and a reinforcing stimulus. The contingency contains _____ (HOW MANY?) terms. 21-54 ← To p. 138
(1) respondent (2) operant 21-64	Nature provides many S^Ds. In an orchard where only red apples are sweet, the "redness" of a ripe apple is an (1) S_____; the color of an unripe apple is an (2) S_____ for the response of picking and eating. 21-65 ← To p. 138

25 **28-2**	The mice taking the longest times to obtain 720 pellets are shown in Records ____ and ____. **28-3**
5 **28-7**	Each day the mice of normal weight have (1) ____ period(s) of rapid continuous eating followed by a period of sporadic and, in general, much (2) * * * eating. **28-8**
(1) less (2) fewer (3) increases **28-12**	We conclude that when an organism is always able to obtain food, its frequency of eating goes through ____. **28-13**
constant (stable, level) **28-17**	Passage of time since the last period of sleep serves to (1) ____ the probability that the organism will sleep. Sleeping, like eating, goes through (2) ____. **28-18**
deprivation (acceptable: satiation) **28-22**	Records A and C differ. (1) ____ shows large-scale cycles whereas (2) ____ shows a nearly constant, high rate of responding for food. **28-23**
(1) D (2) obese (overweight) **28-27**	Of the three obese mice, Records (1) ____ and ____ look alike. A different kind of record for an obese mouse is shown in (2) ____. **28-28**

A stimulus present when a response is emitted and reinforced becomes a *discriminative stimulus* (S^D). In the future, the response is relatively likely to be emitted when this stimulus is present. Other stimuli having something in common with S^D are also effective, but produce a lower response frequency. The spread of controlling power to other stimuli is called stimulus *generalization*.

EXPERIMENT

Phase 1. A pigeon is placed in a standard experimental box. A yellowish-green light with a wavelength of 550 millimicrons is constantly projected on the key. The key-pecking response, shaped in the usual way, is reinforced on a variable-interval schedule, the average interval between reinforcements being 1 minute. This schedule generates a steady rate of responding and, more important here, a considerable resistance to extinction.

Phase 2. Reinforcement is discontinued, and during extinction the color of the light projected on the key is changed at short, regular intervals. Each of sixteen colors, 10 millimicrons apart, is presented many times in random order and for the same total time per color. The responses emitted by the pigeon in the presence of each wavelength (color) are counted and plotted in the figure on the right. The resulting function is called *stimulus generalization gradient*.

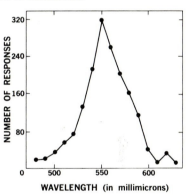

WAVELENGTH (in millimicrons)

(1) 25 (2) fixed-ratio **28-1**	The vertical scale gives the number of pellets obtained. If we were interested in the number of bar presses at any point on the scale, we would multiply by _____. **28-2**
high (highest) **28-6**	Record C covers about five days and shows _____ (HOW MANY?) periods of sustained high rate. **28-7**
(1) satiated (2) lower (more gradual) **28-11**	As the normal mouse becomes satiated with food, it responds (1) * * * frequently and obtains (2) * * * pellets. As additional time passes, food deprivation (3) _____. The *cycle* then repeats. **28-12**
(1) deprived (2) food deprivation **28-16**	In experiments which use food reinforcement for pigeons, the birds are fed at a particular time of day and fed just enough to keep weight constant (e.g., 80 per cent of normal). In this way, the deprivation level is held approximately _____. **28-17**
cycles **28-21**	The class of responses previously reinforced with food shows periodic changes in rate which resemble changes in the level of _____. **28-22**
cycles (periods) **28-26**	Extremely high rates alternating with short (1- or 2-hour) pauses are shown in Record (1) _____ which is a record made by a(n) (2) _____ mouse. **28-27**
two **28-31**	**End of Set**

no 22-10	If all wavelengths had acquired equal control as a result of Phase 1, then in Phase 2 each new color would have produced approximately * * * number of responses as 550 millimicrons. 22-11
(1) was not (2) does (can, will) 22-21	As the wavelength changes in either direction from the wavelength present during reinforcement, the number of responses _____ . 22-22
common 22-32	The Morse code signal for the letter C (– • – •) and the letter Y (– • – –) are often confused by the learner. The two stimulus patterns (1) * * * common elements and therefore show (2) _____ . 22-33
s^D 22-43	In the behavioral development of a child, smiles mark occasions for reinforcement. The extent of the _____ (TT) among smiling and other facial expressions decreases as discriminations are developed. 22-44
control 22-54	Verbal discriminative stimuli are commonly established in formal education. "Columbus discovered America in . . ." is the S^D after which the response "1492." is _____ if emitted. 22-55
do not occur (cannot exist) 22-65	In developing an abstraction, we must use many different stimulus objects as "S^Ds"; each must have the property in question, but among them there must be a range of other _____ . 22-66

The mice emit (1) _____ responses for each pellet of food. This is a(n) (2) * * * schedule of reinforcement.

28-1

---

(1) less
(2) slope

28-5

The mice of normal weight (C and E) show cyclic changes in the rate of responding for (and eating) food. In the portions labeled **a** and **b** (in C), the rate is _____ and, for a time, relatively uniform.

28-6

---

cycles

28-10

In portions of Record C, as at **a** and **b**, the normal mouse obtains many pellets in a few hours. The mouse becomes (1) _____ with food, and this explains intervening portions of the curve having (2) _____ slopes.

28-11

---

deprived
(of food)

28-15

An animal loses weight when (1) _____ of food. The animal's resulting weight, expressed as a percentage of its normal weight, is a measure of its current level of (2) _____ _____.

28-16

---

cycle

28-20

The frequency of emission of food-getting responses by a normal organism which can always obtain food goes through _____.

28-21

---

lack
(do not have,
fail to exhibit)

28-25

The steplike character of Record D represents relatively short _____ of eating and not eating.

28-26

---

one

28-30

Because mice A and B have similar records, we can say that in terms of the behavioral data in the exhibit, _____ types of obesity are clearly distinguishable.

28-31

Page 199

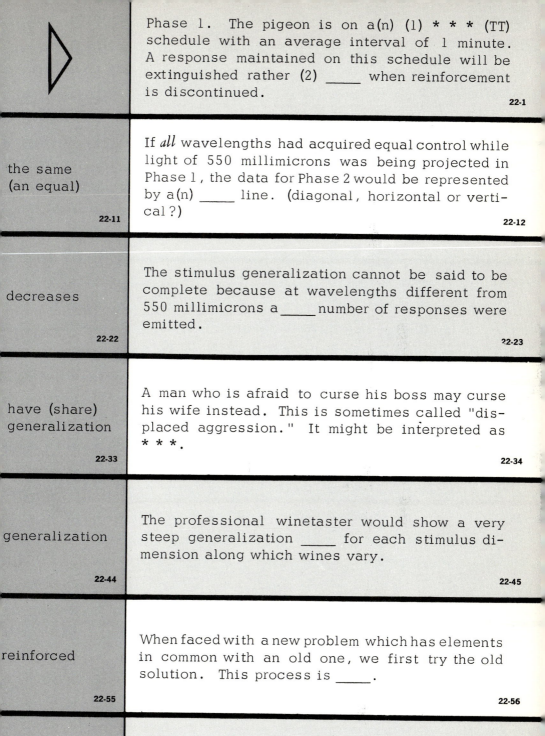

Phase 1. The pigeon is on a(n) (1) * * * (TT) schedule with an average interval of 1 minute. A response maintained on this schedule will be extinguished rather (2) _____ when reinforcement is discontinued.

22-1

---

the same
(an equal)

22-11

If *all* wavelengths had acquired equal control while light of 550 millimicrons was being projected in Phase 1, the data for Phase 2 would be represented by a(n) _____ line. (diagonal, horizontal or vertical?)

22-12

---

decreases

22-22

The stimulus generalization cannot be said to be complete because at wavelengths different from 550 millimicrons a _____ number of responses were emitted.

22-23

---

have (share)
generalization

22-33

A man who is afraid to curse his boss may curse his wife instead. This is sometimes called "displaced aggression." It might be interpreted as * * *.

22-34

---

generalization

22-44

The professional winetaster would show a very steep generalization _____ for each stimulus dimension along which wines vary.

22-45

---

reinforced

22-55

When faced with a new problem which has elements in common with an old one, we first try the old solution. This process is _____.

22-56

---

properties
(elements)

22-66

Since isolated properties of objects do not occur in nature, an abstraction * * * be developed if only one object is used to provide the S^D.

22-67

were (are) 28-4	The fact that the obese mice ate 720 pellets in (1) _____ time than normal mice is shown by the steeper over-all (2) _____ of the records for the obese mice. 28-5
cycle 28-9	The rhythmic changes in ingestive behavior represented by Records C and E are called _____ of ingestive behavior. 28-10
would be (might be) 28-14	When food is used as a reinforcer in the usual experiment, the organism is * * * before each experimental session. 28-15
high, low (EITHER ORDER) 28-19	A rat confined in a small cage with continuous access to a running wheel alternated between active and inactive phases with considerable regularity. The rate shows an activity _____. 28-20
(1) less (shorter) (2) higher 28-24	The mice which produced records A and B overeat. Although they do *not* eat at an especially high rate, they * * * the cycles of fast and slow eating shown by the normal mice. 28-25
(1) A and B (2) D 28-29	The three obese mice look alike and cannot be distinguished by weight. Lacking the behavioral evidence, we might have concluded (erroneously) that only _____ type of obesity was involved. 28-30

(1) variable- interval (2) slowly 22-1	Phase 1. A light having a wavelength of 550 milli- microns is (1) * * * in color. During Phase 1, such a light is projected on the key at (2) ____ times. 22-2
horizontal , 22-12	The wavelength which was present during condi- tioning was (1) ____ millimicrons. In Phase 2, the greatest number of responses was emitted when the light had a wavelength of (2) ____ millimicrons. 22-13
smaller 22-23	The gradual decline in number of responses as a function of distance from the stimulus present at reinforcement is called a *stimulus generalization gradient.* The figure shows the stimulus ____ ____ as a function of wavelengths. 22-24
generalization (stimulus generalization) 22-34	Generalization and discrimination are reciprocal processes. The professional winetaster can make very fine (1) ____. He shows little (2) ____ among various wines. 22-35
gradient 22-45	The sergeant says "Squad halt!" and all the men halt. Their behavior is under the ____ of a verbal stimulus. 22-46
generalization 22-56	The child reinforced for saying "red" when looking at a red book may call all books "red." This is an example of (1) ____. In part, it is due to the common (2) ____ of shape shared by books differing in color. 22-57
cannot (22-67	An abstract response is acquired only when some single stimulus property which cannot "stand alone" comes to control the response, and other ____ of the stimulus, which normally accompany the single property, have no control. 22-68

A mouse was kept in a standard experimental box continuously for several days. After every 25th response (pressing a bar), a mechanism delivered a small pellet of food. (Water was continuously available.) The experiment was repeated with five different kinds of mice, as follows: (Letters refer to their cumulative records.)

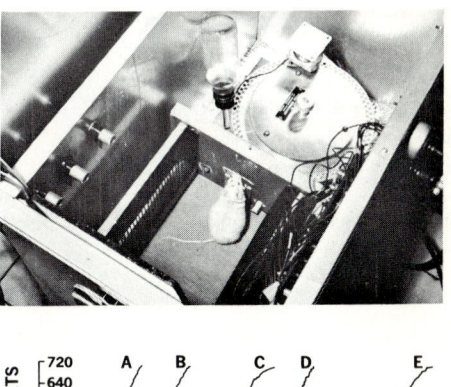

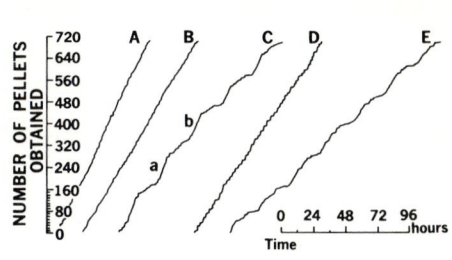

(A) A mouse poisoned by goldthioglucose which damages part of the brain called the hypothalamus causing overeating and obesity.

(B) A mouse with surgical damage to the hypothalamus, with the same effects as mouse A.

(C) A normal mouse from a normal strain.

(D) An obese mouse from a strain some members of which suffer from hereditary obesity.

(E) A normal mouse from the same strain (mice E and D were litter mates).

(1) yellow- green (2) all 22-2	In Phase 2, the light with a wavelength of 550 millimicrons was not projected on the key at _____ times. 22-3
(1) 550 (2) 550 22-13	Phase 2. In the figure, the wavelength at which most responses were emitted is that which was present when the response was _____. 22-14
generalization gradient 22-24	A steeper gradient would indicate a less extensive (1) _____ _____, while a relatively flat gradient would indicate a (2) _____ extensive stimulus generalization. 22-25
) discriminations) generalization 22-35	When a child calls all furry animals "dog," it is a case of * * *. 22-36
control 22-46	The sergeant says "Squad halt!" and all the men halt. This verbal stimulus is a(n) _____ for halting. 22-47
) generalization) element 22-57	A child reinforced for saying "red" when looking at a red book might say "red" when shown a black book. This is, in part, due to the control acquired by the _____ _____ of shape. 22-58
properties (aspects, elements) 22-68	Nature seldom makes a single stimulus property the occasion for reinforcing a response; hence, an _____ is seldom developed unless a second organism arranges the appropriate contingencies for reinforcement. 22-69

chain 27-3	Pressing the bar is a part of a(n) (1) _____ of behavior which ends with ingestion of food. Food deprivation (2) _____ the rate of emission of the whole chain. 27-4 ← To p. 192

(1) likely
    (more likely)
(2) likely
    (more likely)
27-8
	After conditioning, a pigeon pecks a key and the food magazine operates with an audible click which is a(n) _____ _____ for pecking the key.
	
	27-9
	← To p. 192

deprivation 27-13	In the usual pigeon experiment, the click of the food magazine has been followed only by food. The click of the food magazine * * * a generalized reinforcer. 27-14 ← To p. 192
are 27-18	The frequency of responses conditioned by a generalized reinforcer is relatively independent of the nature of the deprivation at the moment. The frequency of responses reinforced by money is usually * * * of any specific deprivation. 27-19 ← To p. 192
dependent upon (not independent of) 27-23	A variable-ratio schedule, as in a gambling device, produces a steady and _____ rate of responding. This is true even when the level of deprivation is relatively low. 27-24 ← To p. 192
satiating (decreasing the deprivation of) 27-28	The widespread existence of waterfront brothels catering to sailors is a result of _____ _____ involved in life at sea. 27-29 ← To p. 192
deprivation 27-33	**End of Set**

all 22-3	In Phase 2, reinforcement _____ occurs. 22-4
reinforced (conditioned) 22-14	At wavelengths other than 550 millimicrons, the number of responses in a constant period of time is _____ than at 550 millimicrons. 22-15
) stimulus generalization) more 22-25	The control exerted by a continuous series of stimuli, similar in some respect to a stimulus present during reinforcement, is shown by a stimulus _____ _____, such as that in the figure. 22-26
neralization timulus neralization) 22-36	When a child emits the word "dog" only in response to dogs, a(n) _____ has been formed. 22-37
S^D 22-47	The verbal stimulus "9 times 9" is a(n) _____ controlling the verbal response "81." 22-48
common element 22-58	The child who first calls all books "red" soon calls only red books "red." When he is not reinforced for saying "red" to books of other colors, books of other colors come to provide S_____ for the response of saying "red." 22-59
abstraction 22-69	The verbal community * * * which single stimulus property will be the occasion for reinforcing a child's abstract verbal response. 22-70

(1) conditioned (secondary) (2) deprived (of) food 27-2	A food-deprived rat presses a bar, a feeding mechanism clicks, the rat bends down, seizes food, and eats it. This sequence of stimuli and responses forms a(n) _____ from pressing to eating. 27-3
chain 27-7	When we have gone without water for some time, we are (1) * * * to drink water, and we are (2) * * * to walk to a water fountain. 27-8
generalized (conditioned generalized) 27-12	When paired with several unconditioned reinforcers appropriate to various deprivations, a conditioned reinforcer will be effective under several types of _____. 27-13
more than one (several, many) 27-17	There are not many cases of primary reinforcers which are effective under more than one state of deprivation. Therefore, most generalized reinforcers * * * conditioned reinforcers. 27-18
independent of (unaffected by) 27-22	When a response has been reinforced by a stimulus previously paired only with a single unconditioned reinforcer, the response is * * * a particular deprivation. 27-23
deprivation 27-27	In order to serve small portions without complaint, a table d'hôte restaurant may serve a large supply of delicious bread while the meal is being prepared. The restaurant is * * * the customers inexpensively. 27-28
water deprivation 27-32	"You can lead a horse to water, but you can't make him drink." This saying overlooks the possibility of controlling behavior through _____. 27-33

never (no longer)	In Phase 2, since reinforcement no longer occurs, if the key-color were not changed, responses would be emitted at a gradually _____ rate for many hours because the response had been maintained on a variable-interval schedule.
22-4	22-5

smaller (lower, less)	The experiment demonstrates that colors which are not actually present when the response is reinforced nevertheless acquire some _____ over the response.
22-15	22-16

generalization gradient	If a high-pitched tone is often present when a response is reinforced, a tone of medium pitch should exert some _____ over the response.
22-26	22-27

discrimination	A young child may be reinforced when approaching a smiling parent but not reinforced when approaching a frowning parent. Under these conditions a(n) _____ will develop.
22-37	22-38

s^D	The patient may come to love or hate his psychoanalyst in ways which resemble his emotional reaction to one of his parents. The analyst might call this "transference." It involves _____.
22-48	22-49

$(s)^\Delta s$	The child who calls only red books "red" may show some likelihood of saying "red" on seeing a red car. This is (1) _____ (TT); but the probability may be (2) _____ because red books and red cars are very different.
22-59	22-60

determines (sets, decides)	In the laboratory, when the experimenter arranges contingencies under which a single stimulus property is the occasion upon which a response is to be reinforced, even animals develop _____.
22-70	22-71

) conditioned
  (secondary)
) unconditioned
  (primary)

27-1

A stimulus which is frequently paired with food becomes a(n) (1) _____ reinforcer. Such a stimulus will be effective in conditioning a response only if the animal is (2) _____ of _____.

27-2

---

unconditioned
reinforcer
(primary
reinforcer)

27-6

Satiating a rat with food lowers the probability of pressing a bar if this behavior is a part of a(n) _____ of behavior which ends with ingestion of food.

27-7

---

is not

27-11

A stimulus which has been paired with unconditioned reinforcers appropriate to *many different* deprivations becomes a(n) _____ reinforcer.

27-12

---

unconditioned
generalized

27-16

Although generalized reinforcers are usually conditioned reinforcers, there are cases (e.g., a thin soup or a malted milk) of unconditioned reinforcers appropriate to * * * condition(s) of deprivation.

27-17

---

without

27-21

The probability of a response previously reinforced by the phrase "that's correct" is largely * * * food deprivation.

27-22

---

(1) rate
    (frequency)
(2) are not

27-26

When we make a child more likely to drink milk by restricting his water intake, we employ _____ in the control of behavior.

27-27

---

conditioned
generalized

27-31

Cocktail lounges often serve free pretzels or potato chips. Since they are salty, they have an effect similar to _____ _____ and increase the sale of drinks.

declining (decreasing)	At regular intervals in Phase 2, the color, or wavelength, of the light projected on the key is _____.
22-5	22-6

control	Stimuli not present at reinforcement may acquire control over a response due to the _____ of the response in the presence of a similar stimulus.
22-16	22-17

control	If a high-pitched tone is often present when a response is reinforced, a tone of medium pitch should produce a rate of responding (1) _____ than that of a high-pitched tone and (2) _____ than that of a very low-pitched tone.
22-27	22-28

discrimination	A very young child may approach his parents in more or less the same way regardless of whether they are frowning or smiling. A smile has not yet become an (1) S_____ nor a frown an (2) S_____.
22-38	22-39

generalization (stimulus generalization)	A young child may pick up and listen to a telephone receiver at any time, but eventually the ring becomes a(n) (1) _____ (TT) for this response, and no ring a(n) (2) _____. (TT)
22-49	22-50

1) generalization 2) low (small, decreased)	To bring the response "red" under control of redness, a single property, we reinforce the response in the presence of red objects of different shapes, sizes, etc. The *single* property, redness, acquires _____ over the response.
22-60	22-61

abstractions	**End of Set**
22-71	

| | In the usual experiment, pressing the bar is immediately reinforced by the click of the feeding mechanism, a(n) (1) _____ reinforcer. Pressing the bar for food is part of a *chain* of behavior ending, as the food is eaten, in a(n) (2) _____ reinforcer.

27-1 |

| (1) will not (doesn't)
(2) will not be (is not often)   27-5 | Bar pressing is immediately reinforced by the magazine click, a conditioned reinforcer. Behavior reinforced by a conditioned reinforcer varies with the deprivation appropriate to the _____ _____ used to establish the conditioned reinforcer.   27-6 |

| deprivation

27-10 | A generalized reinforcer * * * dependent upon one particular condition of deprivation.

27-11 |

| unconditioned

27-15 | A thin soup or a malted milk may reinforce either a food-deprived or a water-deprived organism, therefore, they are to some extent _____ _____ reinforcers.

27-16 |

| generalized reinforcer

27-20 | A generalized reinforcer can be used to condition a new response _____ (with or without?) many restrictions on which specific deprivation is present at the moment.

27-21 |

| is not

27-25 | Popular explanations of behavior frequently employ words like "want," "desire," or "need." The observable referent for these words is usually a high (1) _____ of responding. In such cases they (2) * * * really causes of the response rate.   27-26 |

| (1) decrease (prevent)
(2) satiation

27-30 | A government which gives money as a bonus to a family each time a baby is born is using a(n) _____ _____ reinforcer to increase procreation instead of relying on a single deprivation.   27-31 |

changed (varied) 22-6	Phase 2. Lights of many different (1) * * * are projected on the (2) _____ . 22-7
reinforcement 22-17	In *stimulus generalization*, a stimulus acquires control of a response due to reinforcement in the presence of a similar but different stimulus. The control exerted in Phase 2 by a 570-millimicron light demonstrates _____ _____ . (TT) 22-18
(1) lower (2) higher 22-28	The numbers of responses made to two monochromatic lights only 10 millimicrons apart are shown to be nearly the same on the _____ _____ . 22-29
(1) $(S)^D$ (2) $(S)\Delta$ 22-39	The traveler who says "all the inhabitants of this country look alike" is essentially reporting the flatness of his own _____ _____ . 22-40
(1) S^D (2) $S\Delta$ 22-50	The linguist distinguishes between two speech sounds which seem identical to many people. The two sounds normally control a single response in what is called (1) _____ , but the linguist has acquired a(n) (2) _____ . 22-51
control 22-61	When a single property of an object controls a response, we call the relation an *abstraction*. "Redness" is such a property. It never occurs alone. When a response is controlled by the isolated property of redness, we call it a(n) _____ . 22-62

(1) chain
  (acceptable:
  unit)
(2) increases
27-4
	A rat thoroughly satiated with food (1) * * * ingest food. A lever which in the past has operated only a feeding mechanism (2) * * * pressed by a rat satiated with food.
	27-5

conditioned reinforcer 27-9	Although the immediate reinforcement for pecking the key is a conditioned reinforcer (the click), the rate of pecking is higher for greater degrees of food _____. 27-10
is not 27-14	A thin soup or a malted milk is a(n) _____ reinforcer because its capacity to reinforce is largely independent of previous conditioning. 27-15
independent 27-19	Depriving an organism of food or water does not greatly change the rate of a response conditioned by a(n) _____ _____. 27-20
high 27-24	A high response rate * * * sufficient evidence for inferring a high level of deprivation because rate is influenced by other variables, such as the schedule of reinforcement. 27-25
sexual deprivation 27-29	Legalized prostitution is sometimes recommended on the grounds that it may (1) _____ sexual attacks on innocent women by providing another means of (2) _____. 27-30

) wavelengths
   (colors)
:) key

22-7

Plotted in the figure are the average (1) _____ of _____ during comparable periods of time at each (2) _____ used.

22-8

---

stimulus
generalization

22-18

With a minor exception, the greater the difference in wavelength, the _____ the difference in number of responses emitted during equal intervals of time.

22-19

---

generalization
gradient

22-29

Two stimuli which we describe as "similar" are likely to show _____ (TT) in their control over behavior.

22-30

---

generalization
gradient

22-40

The traveler who says "all the inhabitants look alike" has had too little contact to develop adequate _____ among the inhabitants.

22-41

) generalization
) discrimination
   (acceptable: S^D)

22-51

When a distant doorbell rings, you may "make a mistake" and go to the phone. The doorbell exerts some (1) _____ over going to the phone. This phenomenon is called (2) _____.

22-52

---

abstraction

22-62

When a response is under the control of a single stimulus property which cannot occur or exist alone, we call it a(n) * * *.

22-63

---

low (reduced)	In general, after the ingestion of a considerable amount of food, the probability of all operant behavior previously reinforced with food is _____.
26-8	26-9 ← To p. 182
higher rate (higher frequency)	Vigorous activity on a hot day causes sweating. The resulting loss of water increases the frequency of behavior previously reinforced by _____.
26-18	26-19 ← To p. 182
probability	When we see an individual drinking a large quantity of water, we usually infer a recent history of _____.
26-28	26-29 ← To p. 182
decreases (declines)	The experiment demonstrates that as deprivation (1) _____, the rate of an operant reinforced with food (2) _____.
26-38	26-39 ← To p. 182
(1) class (set, group) (2) water deprivation	If several different operants have been previously reinforced with water, then water *satiation* will (1) _____ the frequency of this whole (2) _____ of responses.
26-48	26-49 ← To p. 182
similar (the same)	Administration of salt, induction of sweating, and deprivation of water are members of a class of procedures. Responses reinforced by water are increased by _____ of these.
26-58	26-59 ← To p. 182

(1) number (of) responses (2) wavelength 22-8	The only wavelength which had ever been present when the response was reinforced was * * * millimicrons. 22-9
greater 22-19	Phase 2. The stimulus control exhibited by any given color is measured by the * * * which occur when that color is projected on the key. 22-20
generalization 22-30	When an abstract sculpture generates emotional responses resembling those generated by the human body, the effect is sometimes attributed to "symbolism." It is an example of _____ _____. 22-31
iscrimination(s) 22-41	An organism may emit the same response to two similar stimuli when only one of them has been present during reinforcement. The term for this phenomenon is _____ _____. 22-42
) control ?) generalization 22-52	Bells, whistles, and traffic signals, as S^Ds, are all occasions upon which appropriate responses will be _____ if emitted. 22-53
abstraction 22-63	In an abstraction, a response is under the control of a _____ property of a stimulus (or set of stimuli). 22-64

is not 26-7	After a heavy meal, the probability of immediately ingesting more food is _____. 26-8
increases 26-17	A soldier who is both incapacitated by wounds and dehydrated by loss of blood emits the verbal operant "Water!" at a(n)_____ _____ than normally. 26-18
satiation 26-27	The common phrase "an animal gradually grows more thirsty" crudely describes an increased_____ of drinking behavior caused by water deprivation. 26-28
decreases (declines) 26-37	As the session progresses, the total amount eaten gradually increases so that the rat's deprivation gradually _____. 26-38
food 26-47	Reaching for a water pitcher, asking for a glass of water, and walking to a drinking fountain, are all responses belonging to the (1) _____ of responses whose probability increases with (2) _____ _____. 26-48
is 26-57	Water deprivation, salt ingestion, and sweating are a class of operations or processes which increase the rate of emission of responses reinforced by water. Several procedures may have * * * effects on behavior reinforced by water. 26-58
activity satiation 26-67	For each state of deprivation, there are usually many alternative procedures which have the same effect on a whole _____ of responses. 26-68

550 22-9	If the 550 millimicron light were the only one which acquired control as a result of Phase 1, then _____ responses would have been emitted to the other lights presented in Phase 2. 22-10 ← To p. 150
number of responses [rate (since time is constant)] 22-20	Light of 560 millimicrons (1) * * * present when the response was reinforced; but the figure reveals that light of this wavelength (2) * * * exert considerable control over the rate of responding. 22-21 ← To p. 150
stimulus generalization 22-31	Generalization often depends on common elements in two or more stimuli. The control exercised by a black triangular form generalizes to a white triangular form because they have a given shape in _____ . 22-32 ← To p. 150
stimulus generalization 22-42	A stimulus which closely *precedes* or accompanies a reinforced response acquires control over that response. The stimulus becomes a(n) _____ for the response. 22-43 ← To p. 150
reinforced 22-53	"Red, white, and . . ." If you tend to say "blue," you show the _____ which this chain of verbal stimuli exerts over the verbal response "blue." 22-54 ← To p. 150
single (isolated) 22-64	Every red object has a specific shape, size, etc. Isolated properties of stimuli * * * alone in nature. 22-65 ← To p. 150

necessary (essential, vital) 26-6	Ingestive behavior * * * biologically useful to a man with a *full* stomach. 26-7
depriv(-ing) 26-16	An excessive amount of salt taken in food must be excreted in solution. Salty food therefore _____ the frequency of the operant behavior called "getting a drink of water." 26-17
deprivation 26-26	Saying "a man is *not* hungry" refers to a level of probability of his ingestive behavior which is most commonly brought about by the procedure termed _____. 26-27
58 26-36	The figure shows that, as the session progresses, the rate of responding gradually _____. 26-37
all (each of) 26-46	When a response is reinforced with *food*, it becomes a member of a class of responses whose rate increases with deprivation of _____. 26-47
(1) increase (2) class (3) water 26-56	Excessive sweating due to heavy work or emotion * * * similar to water deprivation in its effect on the class of responses previously reinforced by water. 26-57
deprivation 26-66	Drugs which decrease activity are similar in effect to _____ _____. 26-67

iscriminative
imulus)

23-5

At the same time that sight of food is an S^D for seizing food, it is a(n) * * * for bending down to the food magazine and looking in.

23-6

---

precedes
(produces)

23-11

A reinforcing stimulus (1)_____ a response which it reinforces. A discriminative stimulus (2)____ a response which it controls. (TEMPORAL ANSWERS)

23-12

---

chain

23-17

Each stimulus in a chain has the dual function of reinforcing the response it (1) _____ and being an S^D for the response it (2)____. (TEMPORAL ANSWERS)

23-18

---

chain

23-23

When the red key-light, as an S^D, is controlling the key-pecking response, any response which "produces" the red key-light is _____.

23-24

S^D

23-29

When the pigeon "looks at" a key, which is sometimes red (S^D for pecking), the behavior of orienting its eyes toward the key is (1)_____ by the red key, and the behavior of looking is added to the beginning of the (2) _____.

23-30

---

does not
(should not)

23-35

A billboard which "catches our attention" is one at which we are likely to look. We look at other billboards if earlier ones contained stimuli which _____ "looking" behavior.

23-36

(1) respondent (reflex) (2) conditioned operant 26-5	Behavior reinforced by intake of water is * * * to the survival of the organism. 26-6
more probable (more frequent) 26-15	Causing an animal to lose water through the excretion of sweat or urine has the same effect on drinking as ____-ing it of water. 26-16
has (is of) 26-25	A parent who complains that a child is a "fussy" eater is advised to forbid between-meal snacks. The operation appealed to in such a case is ____. 26-26
continuous 26-35	During the first 30 minutes, the rat pressed the bar 58 times and received (and ingested) ____ pellets. 26-36
increases the probability (increases the rate) 26-45	In most animals, many different responses have been reinforced with food. Food deprivation will increase the probability of ____ these responses. 26-46
decline (fall, drop) 26-55	Eating heavily salted food and being deprived of water both (1) ____ the probability of the entire (2) ____ of responses which have been reinforced with (3) ____. 26-56
satiation 26-65	Drugs (such as benzedrine) which increase activity are similar in effect to activity ____. 26-66

In the usual pigeon experiment, the sight of food sets the occasion upon which seizing food is _____ (TT) by food in the mouth.

23-1

---

reinforcing
stimulus
(reinforcer)

23-6

This sequence forms a chain: bending down, seeing food, seizing food. Sight of food is a(n) (1) * * * for bending down to food and a(n) (2) * * * for seizing food.

23-7

---

(1) follows
(2) precedes

23-12

In the usual experiment, when closure of a key operates a feeding mechanism, the noise of the feeding mechanism follows and _____ (TT) the response of pecking the key.

23-13

---

(1) follows
(2) precedes

23-18

The sequence of stimuli and responses between pecking the key and food in the mouth is called a(n) _____.

23-19

---

reinforced

23-24

If the apparatus is so designed that a red key-light flashes on automatically when the pigeon stretches its neck, neck stretching is (1) _____ by the red light (the S^D for pecking), and neck stretching is added to the (2) _____.

23-25

---

(1) reinforced
(2) chain

23-30

The pigeon is more likely to "see" the key turn red if it orients its eyes toward ("looks at") the key. This behavior of orienting the eyes is intermittently reinforced by the view of a(n) _____. (TT)

23-31

---

reinforced

23-36

The radar operator searches the radarscope for small luminous blips; if none appear, the behavior of scanning the scope with eye and head movements is _____.

23-37

unconditioned respondent 26-4	Swallowing water which is already in the mouth is mainly unconditioned (1) _____ (TT) behavior. Finding water and putting it into the mouth is mainly (2) _____ _____ behavior. 26-5
less probable (less frequent) 26-14	The longer an organism goes without water, the _____ _____ becomes any behavior previously reinforced by water. 26-15
would 26-24	Animals which do not eat or drink sufficient quantities when severely deprived of food or water will die. Increased ingestive behavior in deprived animals * * * survival value. 26-25
24 hours 26-34	In this experiment every response is reinforced. Thereby, bar pressing is said to be under _____ reinforcement. 26-35
seven (all these) 26-44	When many different responses have successfully produced food, then food deprivation * * * of all these responses. 26-45
satiating 26-54	On some intermittent schedules, the animal may receive very little food as reinforcement. Thus, level of deprivation does not _____ as quickly under intermittent reinforcement as under continuous reinforcement. 26-55
deprivation 26-64	Forcing an animal to keep moving, as on a motor-driven treadmill, produces a reduction in activity when the animal is released. Forced activity is a form of _____ since it reduces subsequent activity. 26-65

reinforced 23-1	The sight of food is a(n) _____ stimulus for seizing food. 23-2

(1) reinforcing
    stimulus
    (reinforcer)
(2) S^D
 	
23-7
	In the simple chain (bending down, seeing food, seizing food), the two responses are "linked together" in that bending down produces (and is reinforced by) a stimulus which is the S^D for * * *.
	
	23-8

reinforces 23-13	In the usual experiment, when a key operates the feeding mechanism which makes a noise, the pigeon bends down to the feeding mechanism. The noise is a(n) _____ for bending down. 23-14
chain 23-19	If the chain of behavior is seldom broken, all of it is treated as a unit. The phrase "the operant behavior of pecking a key for food" describes a well-integrated chain as though it were a(n) _____ of behavior. 23-20
(1) reinforced (2) chain 23-25	A key was raised and shielded so that the pigeon had to raise its head to see it. Raising the head was (1) _____ by any color on the key which served as a(n) (2) _____ for pecking the key. 23-26
S^D 23-31	Responses described as "looking," "searching," "attending," etc., which generally produce stimuli, frequently occur early in a(n) _____. 23-32

water (liquids) 26-3	Ingestive behavior (e.g., eating) which is important for survival may involve respondent, conditioned or unconditioned, and operant behavior. Swallowing water which is already in the mouth is mainly _____ _____ behavior. 26-4
decreases (drops) 26-13	In general, the more food an animal has just eaten, the _____ _____ its ingestive behavior. 26-14
decreases (reduces, lowers) 26-23	If satiation *did not* make food-getting and eating behavior less frequent, biologically use*less* behavior * * * occupy much of an animal's time. 26-24
immediately (rapidly) 26-33	The rat has ingested no food for * * * before being placed in the box. 26-34
decreases (lowers, reduces) 26-43	If seven different operants have been reinforced with food, then food deprivation will increase the probability of _____ operants. 26-44
(1) satiated (2) one 26-53	By using very small bits of food, the experimenter can reinforce a response many times without_____ the animal. 26-54
class 26-63	Confining an animal in a limited space produces an increase in activity above the normal level when the animal is released. Confinement is a form of _____ since it increases subsequent activity. 26-64

discriminative **23-2**	Bending down to the food magazine makes the food visible. The *sight* of food (a conditioned reinforcer) _____ bending down to the magazine. **23-3**
seizing food (next response in chain) **23-8**	In a chain of behavior, the same stimulus is both a(n) (1) * * * and a(n) (2) * * *. **23-9**
S^D (occasion) **23-14**	The noise from the operation of the feeding mechanism is a(n) (1) _____ stimulus for key pecking and a(n) (2) _____ stimulus for bending down to the feeding mechanism. **23-15**
unit **23-20**	An operant is rather arbitrarily designated as "key pecking," "walking," etc. It is implied that a well-integrated chain is functioning as a(n) _____ of operant behavior. **23-21**
(1) reinforced (2) S^D **23-26**	The pigeon raises its head to the level of a shielded key and "looks at the color." Because the color is a(n) _____ for pecking, the pigeon pecks and is reinforced with food. **23-27**
chain **23-32**	When the pigeon raises its head and "looks at" or "attends to" a shielded key, the behavior *produces* or *clarifies* the S^D in that it brings the S^D clearly into view. What is colloquially called "attending" is a response which _____ an S^D. **23-33**

individual (organism, member) 26-2	Biological processes cannot go on in dry tissue. The drying out of the body of an organism (such as man) is prevented if responses are emitted which result in the intake of _____ . 26-3
(1) increase (2) depriving 26-12	The probability that an animal will engage in behavior previously reinforced with food _____ as it ingests a large quantity of food. 26-13
deprivation (food deprivation) 26-22	Satiation is an operation which in general _____ the probability of responding. 26-23
conditioned (reinforced) 26-32	In the exhibit experiment, it is clear that bar pressing has already been conditioned because the rat begins responding _____ . 26-33
declines 26-42	A pigeon has been reinforced with food for pecking a key, stretching its neck, and walking in a circle. Satiation with food _____ the frequency of *all* these responses. 26-43
(1) reinforces (2) deprivation 26-52	It would be inefficient to train your dog by giving it a full day's ration after a single response because the dog would be substantially (1) _____ after only (2) _____ reinforcement. 26-53
deprivation 26-62	Sexual deprivation and the use of drugs and hormones which increase the frequency of sexual behavior belong to a single _____ of procedures. 26-63

reinforces **23-3**	We have been using the term "reinforcer" for "re-inforcing stimulus." Since reinforcers are certain stimuli which follow responses, a synonym for re-inforcer is _____ _____. **23-4**
(1) discriminative 　　stimulus (S^D) (2) reinforcing 　　stimulus 　　(reinforcer) (EITHER ORDER) **23-9**	A stimulus will become an S^D when a(n) (1) _____ which regularly follows it is reinforced. An S^D will become a conditioned reinforcer when (2) _____ regularly follows it closely in time. **23-10**
(1) reinforcing (2) discriminative 　　(S^D) **23-15**	Bending down to the magazine makes food visible, and the pigeon seizes food with its beak. With respect to seizing food, the sight of food is a(n) (1) _____. With respect to bending down, sight of food is a(n) (2) _____. **23-16**
unit **23-21**	If pecking is reinforced when a red key-light is on, but not when other key-lights are on, the red key-light becomes a(n) _____ for "key pecking." **23-22**
S^D **23-27**	The pigeon raises its head and looks at the color of a shielded key. If the color on the key is an S^D, looking at the key is _____. **23-28**
produces (clarifies) **23-33**	We might say that an S^D is effective only if the organism "attends to" it. "Attending" is not a mental event; it is a general name for behavior which produces or clarifies a(n) _____. **23-34**

species 26-1	Operants reinforced by food are involved in the survival of each _____ of the species. 26-2
more probable (more frequent) 26-11	We can (1) _____ the probability of drinking by depriving an organism of water. We can increase the probability that an organism will eat by (2) _____ it of food. 26-12
deprived 26-21	From a practical point of view, to get an individual to eat we may use the operation called _____. 26-22
(1) deprived (2) reinforcer 26-31	READ EXHIBIT ON PAGE 181 AND REFER TO IT AS NEEDED. Prior to the experimental session during which the record shown in the exhibit was obtained, the response (bar pressing) had already been _____. 26-32
lower 26-41	The figure shows that the rate of responding declines as the degree of deprivation _____. 26-42

(1) reinforces
(2) decreases
    (reduces,
    lowers)
 	
26-51
	Ingested food (1) _____ a response which it follows; it also reduces food (2) _____.
	
	26-52

(1) lowered (decreased) (2) increases 26-61	If the probability of sexual behavior is increased by administration of certain hormones or of "aphrodisiacs," the effect is similar to that of sexual _____. 26-62

reinforcing stimulus 23-4	The same stimulus may be both a reinforcing stimulus and an S^D. The sight of food is a(n) * * * for seizing food but a reinforcing stimulus (i.e., reinforcer) for bending and looking into the magazine. 23-5 ← To p. 161
(1) response (2) reinforcement 23-10	When a stimulus has become an S^D for one response, it is also a reinforcer for any other response which _____ it. 23-11 ← To p. 161
(1) S^D (2) reinforcer 23-16	When a response produces an S^D for another response, the two form a chain. The sequence of events, beginning with pecking the key and ending with food in the mouth, forms a(n) _____ of responses. 23-17 ← To p. 161
S^D 23-22	When a red key-light has become an S^D for pecking, the red light has been added to the beginning of a(n) _____ of responses. 23-23 ← To p. 161
reinforced 23-28	In the pigeon experiments, looking at the key is reinforced by the _____ for pecking the key. 23-29 ← To p. 161
S^D (stimulus) 23-34	"Attending" * * * imply a mental event but rather a kind of behavior. 23-3 ← To p. 161

	Operant behavior often has biological significance for survival of the individual or the species. Responses reinforced by sexual contact have an obvious bearing on the survival of the _____.
	26-1
more (highly) 26-10	When an organism has been without water for a period of time, behavior previously reinforced by water becomes _____ _____. 26-11
(1) increases (raises) (2) deprivation 26-20	A hungry man is generally one who has been _____ of food. 26-21
satiation 26-30	In many experiments discussed earlier in the course, organisms were (1) _____ of food before being placed in the experimental box. This was done whenever food was to be used as a(n) (2) _____. 26-31
negatively 26-40	If the rat had been given some food before the session began, the initial rate of responding would have been _____. 26-41
(1) reinforced (conditioned) (2) class of (all) 26-50	In the exhibit experiment, after each response the rat receives food which (1) _____ the response. The food also (2) _____ the deprivation level. 26-51
class (set, group) 26-60	Immediately after orgasm, the probability of further sexual behavior is (1) _____; as time passes (i.e., as sexual deprivation increases), the probability of this behavior (2) _____. 26-61

Many highly skilled forms of behavior, e.g., drawing pictures, singing, etc., require a *continuous repertoire* — a set of responses differing from one another only very slightly (when the response field is said to be continuous) and under the control of discriminative stimuli also differing from one another only very slightly (when the stimulus field is said to be continuous). In *drawing* a straight line with a given slope, the response field is composed of all the movements which produce an indefinitely large family of lines:

In *copying* a straight line with a given slope, the stimuli are a similar family of lines. With an adequate repertoire, the subject can draw a line with a slope close to any slope given to him to be copied. Differences between slopes can be as small as desired. In the same way, a good singer can sing a pitch which corresponds to a pitch he hears, where both stimulus and response fields are also practically continuous.

Many such skills are shaped quite gradually during the individual's life. The contingencies may be arranged in formal training (as in art or music instruction, driver training, etc.) or left to the vicissitudes of the environment. Once a child has acquired the ability to be reinforced when the "produced stimulus" matches the "stimulus to be copied," shaping may proceed without the frequent intervention of another person. Learning includes (1) discriminating subtle differences among stimuli to be imitated (in the *continuous stimulus field*) and (2) discriminating among those stimuli produced and (3) executing movements showing subtle differences of the *continuous response field*.

Set 26

PART VII Deprivation

Basic Concepts

Estimated time: 26 minutes

See exhibit on preceding page
Turn to next page and begin ▶

---

low (reduced)

26-9

When an animal has been without food, its conditioned and unconditioned ingestive behavior becomes _____ probable when food is again available.

26-10

---

water

26-19

Deprivation is a procedure which in general (1) _____ the probability of a group of responses. The probability of food-related behavior occurring is increased by food (2) _____.

26-20

---

deprivation

26-29

When a horse led to water does not drink, we can infer a recent history of _____.

26-30

---

(1) decreases
(2) decreases

26-39

Since the rate of responding is declining, the curve is _____ (positively or negatively?) accelerated.

26-40

---

(1) decrease
　　(reduce)
(2) class (set,
　　group) of

26-49

Food deprivation increases the probability of the whole class of responses which have been (1) _____ with food. Water deprivation increases the probability of the (2) * * * responses which have been reinforced with water.

26-50

---

each (all)

26-59

Responses reinforced by a given reinforcer will be increased in probability by a whole _____ of deprivation-like procedures.

26-60

Set 24

PART VI Stimulus Control

Shaping Continuous Repertoires

See exhibit on preceding page

Estimated time: 20 minutes

Turn to next page and begin ▶

(1) be no
(2) would not

24-6

A parent may reinforce a child for making a particular drawing movement (as by saying "Good!" or "How pretty!"). The relative frequency of such movements will then _____.

24-7

---

differential

24-13

A particular "produced" visual pattern * * * closely related to the hand movements which produced it.

24-14

---

(1) reinforce
(2) extinguish
(do not
reinforce,
not)   24-20

In teaching a child to draw a more complex picture, we may show him a picture and reinforce any drawing made by the child which _____ it in some respect.

24-21

S^D (stimulus)

24-27

When the property of likeness in the child's drawing has become an S^D for showing us the drawing, the property of likeness will also _____ the drawing movements which produce the likeness.

24-28

---

is not (is no
longer, will
no longer be)

24-34

When a child cannot discriminate between a perfect reproduction of a picture and a fair reproduction, the automatic reinforcement is as great for a(n) _____ reproduction as for a perfect one.

24-35

---

sound
("s," sound
produced)

24-41

The adage "practice makes perfect" is probably true only if some product of one's behavior provides _____ _____.

24-42

Exhibit for

Set 26   Do not read exhibit yet. Wait until instructed
to do so.

A white rat is placed in a standard experimental space having a horizontal bar protruding from one wall. The rat has been deprived of food for 24 hours. Pressing the bar operates a food magazine which drops a small ($\frac{1}{15}$ grain) pellet of food into a tray.

The rat has previously been adapted to the box and to the sound of the magazine and has been reinforced many times for pressing the bar.

As an experimental session progresses, the rat ingests more and more pellets, becomes less food *deprived* or closer to being *satiated* with food. The cumulative record of bar presses is presented below.

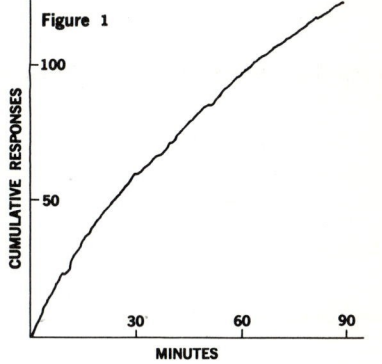

Figure 1

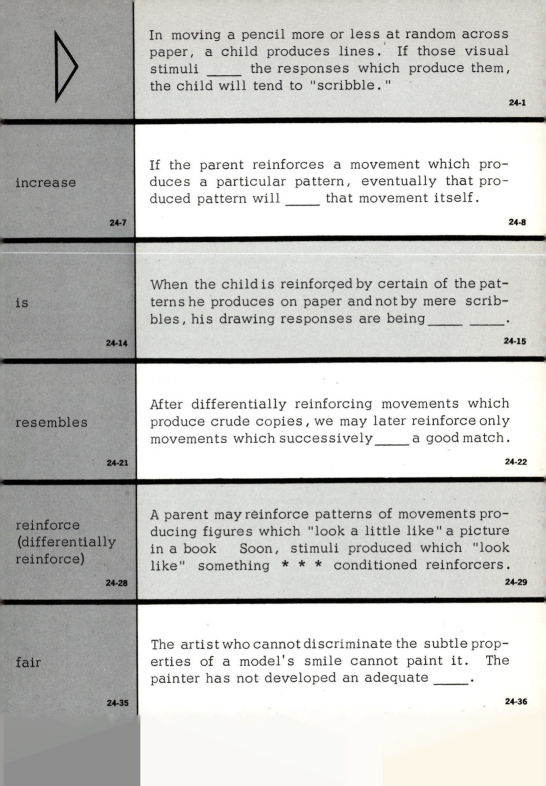

In moving a pencil more or less at random across paper, a child produces lines. If those visual stimuli _____ the responses which produce them, the child will tend to "scribble."

24-1

increase

24-7

If the parent reinforces a movement which produces a particular pattern, eventually that produced pattern will _____ that movement itself.

24-8

is

24-14

When the child is reinforced by certain of the patterns he produces on paper and not by mere scribbles, his drawing responses are being _____ _____.

24-15

resembles

24-21

After differentially reinforcing movements which produce crude copies, we may later reinforce only movements which successively _____ a good match.

24-22

reinforce (differentially reinforce)

24-28

A parent may reinforce patterns of movements producing figures which "look a little like" a picture in a book Soon, stimuli produced which "look like" something * * * conditioned reinforcers.

24-29

fair

24-35

The artist who cannot discriminate the subtle properties of a model's smile cannot paint it. The painter has not developed an adequate _____.

24-36

can (might) **25-4**	The positions of reachable objects constitute a continuous field in the sense that any position has adjacent positions on all sides. In other words, there * * * gaps, holes, or breaks in the field. **25-5** ← To p. 175
greater (larger) **25-10**	"Reaching for an object" refers to a movement made in a particular direction which is reinforced by (1) _____ with an object which is in a particular (2) _____. **25-11** ← To p. 175
topographies (forms) **25-16**	All reaching movements need not be separately conditioned. After being reinforced for touching two points which are fairly close together, it is likely that a person * * * efficiently touch a point between them. **25-17** ← To p. 175
is similar to (is like, resembles) **25-22**	A person who can "make a good copy of any line" must possess a repertoire consisting of a(n) _____ number of drawing responses which produce an indefinite number of possible lines. **25-23** ← To p. 175
is (requires, constitutes) **25-28**	Skillfully drawing from copy requires a(n) _____ _____. **25-29** ← To p. 175
(1) can (2) cannot (may not be able to) **25-34**	With a continuous repertoire, a person * * * able to respond to discrete points in a stimulus field. **25-35** ← To p. 175

reinforce 24-1	Lines drawn in scribbling are not wholly random. They reveal the natural lever-like movements of hand and arm. Therefore, all forms of responses * * * occur with equal frequency even prior to differential reinforcement. 24-2
reinforce 24-8	When a child has been reinforced for drawing a particular pattern, that pattern, having been paired with a reinforcer, can itself become a ____ ____. 24-9
differentially reinforced 24-15	After certain produced visual patterns have become reinforcing, in the future the patterns of movements which produce them are reinforced by the * * *. 24-16
approximate 24-22	In gradually raising our standards, first reinforcing crude copies and later better and better copies, we are shaping "drawing from copy" in ____ ____. 24-23
will be (become) 24-29	When "drawing from copy" has been well conditioned, a drawn line which resembles a line being copied ____ the movement of drawing it, even if the parent occasionally provides no reinforcement. 24-30
discrimination 24-36	An artist working without a model cannot paint the subtle properties of a smile unless he can discriminate those properties because the painting movements will not receive precise ____ ____. (TT) 24-37

movement (reaching) 25-3	The positions taken by objects within our reach comprise a continuous three-dimensional field. An object can be in any position in that field, and two positions * * * differ by as small a distance as we can specify. 25-4
(1) position (point) (2) continuous 25-9	The finer the differences in the positions of objects within reach (i.e., the greater the number of possible positions), the _____ the number of different reaching movements. 25-10
stimuli (S^{D}s) 25-15	A continuous response field is one having many responses of only slightly different _____. 25-16
discrete 25-21	To copy a line, the artist must first look at a stimulus and then respond in a manner which produces a drawing which * * * the pattern being copied. 25-22
discrete repertoire 25-27	A movement producing a specific line can differ from another movement by as small an amount as we can distinguish. Therefore, the behavior of drawing lines skillfully * * * a continuous repertoire. 25-28
(1) discrete repertoire (2) continuous repertoire 25-33	One who can copy all sorts of lines and patterns (1) * * * copy the alphabet, but one who has only the discrete repertoire of copying 26 block letters (2) * * * copy a drawing or even letters of an unfamiliar style. 25-34

do not	It is useless to ask a child to copy a picture until he has acquired a(n) _____ repertoire of drawing responses.
24-2	24-3

conditioned reinforcer	The scribbling child may produce a line which looks to him like a pattern which has already been reinforced. The scribbled line, therefore, to some extent automatically _____ the movement which produces it.
24-9	24-10

produced visual pattern (drawn copy)	When a child is learning to "draw from copy," the picture to be copied consists of visual (1) _____ which act upon the child (2) _____ (TEMPORAL ANSWER) he has made the first drawing movement.
24-16	24-17

successive approximations	If we raise our standard for reinforcing a child's drawings too rapidly, even the best of his responses will not be reinforced. His drawing behavior will * * *.
24-23	24-24

reinforces	Producing a pattern like a pattern to be copied is said to be _____ reinforced because only successful movements are reinforced while movements producing unlike patterns are not.
24-30	24-31

differential reinforcement	A so-called tone-deaf person often has perfectly adequate sensory mechanisms. Such a person has not acquired adequate _____ of tones.
24-37	24-38

continuous field 25-2	In reaching for an object, the direction of _____ of the arm and hand is controlled by the position of the object in the field of vision. 25-3
position (object) 25-8	A man who is very skillful in reaching and touching objects has a "continuous" repertoire of reaching movements which brings him into contact with objects at any (1) _____ in a(n) (2) _____ field. 25-9
topographies 25-14	Each reaching response has its own topography and is under the control of appropriate _____ supplied by an object in a position in space. 25-15
discrete 25-20	A response which brings the hunt-and-peck typist's finger tip *between* two keys is not reinforced. Typing behavior is not continuous; rather it is a set of _____ responses. 25-21
continuous 25-26	Discrete movements under the control of stimuli forming a discrete field comprise a(n) _____ _____. 25-27
26 (discrete) 25-32	The ability to copy the alphabet in block letters involves a(n) (1) _____ _____ while the ability to copy any line involves a(n) (2) _____ _____. 25-33

| continuous | A child who simply "likes to scribble" is said to be _____ by the lines he produces regardless of direction, change of direction, or length. |
| 24-3 | 24-4 |

| reinforces | Only a few of the stimuli produced by scribbling movements will resemble special reinforcing patterns. Hence, such patterns will reinforce only a few of the _____ in scribbling. |
| 24-10 | 24-11 |

| (1) stimuli (patterns) (2) before | Two visual stimuli are present when a line has been copied. The line to be copied occurred first; it was followed by the line * * *. |
| 24-17 | 24-18 |

| be extinguished | A child can be conditioned to call two visual patterns "like" or "unlike," quite apart from learning to draw. We present two patterns and reinforce "like" if they are (1) _____ and extinguish "like" if they are (2) _____. |
| 24-24 | 24-25 |

| differentially | Skill in "drawing from copy" will continue to be shaped in the parent's absence once "likeness" has been established as a(n) _____ for the drawing movements. |
| 24-31 | 24-32 |

| discrimination | A so-called tone-deaf person cannot sing because he cannot (1) _____ differences in tones he is to match. The sounds he produces do not provide automatic reinforcement which (2) _____ good as opposed to poor pitch. |
| 24-38 | 24-39 |

continuous repertoire 25-1	An adult can usually reach for and touch either of two objects which lie very close together in the field of vision. Most adults have a(n) ____ ____ of reaching movements. 25-2
continuous field 25-7	The movements with which we touch objects within reach may also comprise a continuous field in the sense that for any movement there is another movement which will reach an adjacent ____. 25-8
topography 25-13	Differences between two movements are described as differences in the topographies of the responses. Objects at two adjacent points usually control reaching responses of only slightly different ____. 25-14
do not 25-19	Some collections of stimuli have discrete, as opposed to continuous, differences among them. The keys on a typewriter occupy ____ positions. 25-20
continuous 25-25	A repertoire of a continuous-response field under control of stimuli forming a continuous field is a(n) ____ repertoire. 25-26
discrete 25-31	If we call the behavior of printing a letter one response, then the behavior of copying the 26 letters of the alphabet in block letters comprises a repertoire of ____ responses. 25-32
discrete 25-37	**End of Set**

reinforced 24-4	A child who "likes to scribble" gets more (1) _____ the more he (2) _____. 24-5
movements (responses) 24-11	When only certain produced patterns are reinforcing, movements which produced ordinary *scribbled* lines * * * reinforced. 24-12
drawn (copied) 24-18	In teaching a child to draw from copy, we reinforce a given movement only if it results in a(n) _____ resembling the line he was asked to copy. 24-19
(1) alike (2) unlike 24-25	If a child calls two visual patterns "like" when they are alike, the stimulus which controls this verbal response must show the "property of likeness." Since this property never occurs in isolation, the response is an example of _____. 24-26
reinforcer (conditioned differential reinforcer) 24-32	The better a child can discriminate "like" patterns, the _____ precise the automatic differential reinforcement of his drawing behavior. 24-33
(1) discriminate (2) differentiate 24-39	Many children articulate the "s" sound and yet say "Thammy Thnake" for "Sammy Snake." Usually these children cannot yet tell which of these sounds another person is saying; they cannot _____ between the "s" and the "th" sounds. 24-40

In a continuous repertoire, two responses may differ by only a very slight amount. Reaching for objects around you is a(n) ____ ____.

25-1

---

position

25-6

A continuum of stimuli comprises a continuous field when we can discriminate very fine differences between adjacent stimuli on the continuum. Points in space are in a(n) ____ ____.

25-7

---

indefinite

25-12

Two movements in a continuous field of movements may have only slightly different forms or *topographies*. Thus, another name for form of response is response ____.

25-13

---

forty

25-18

The keys on a typewriter, as "objects within reach," occupy *discrete* positions. There are in-between positions not occupied by keys. The keys * * * comprise a continuous field.

25-19

---

differs

25-24

Lines on a surface comprise a(n) ____ two-dimensional field.

25-25

---

discrete repertoire

25-30

One letter differs from another by considerably more than a barely distinguishable amount; thus copying the alphabet requires a(n) ____ repertoire.

25-31

---

is not

25-36

Someone just learning to drive turns the wheel in large jerky movements. The novice still has a(n) ____ repertoire.

25-37

← To p. 168

reinforcement scribbles

24-5

If all scribbled marks were equally reinforcing, there would (1) * * * differential reinforcement of scribbling behavior (and the child's scribbling (2) * * * "improve").

24-6
← To p. 168

---

are not

24-12

When certain drawing movements are reinforced and other drawing movements are not, reinforcement is _____.

24-13
← To p. 168

**line
(mark, pattern)**

24-19

In teaching a child to copy a line, we do not wait for a perfect match. We (1) _____ all movements producing lines which are fairly similar to the copy, but (2) _____ movements producing lines which are very different from the copy.

24-20
← To p. 168

---

abstraction

24-26

If we repeatedly reinforce a child only when the picture he draws is much like the picture to be copied, the "property of likeness" becomes a(n) _____ for his behavior of showing us his successful drawings.

24-27
← To p. 168

---

more

24-33

After the property of likeness in a drawing has been established as a reinforcer, the presence of the parent * * * required for further differential reinforcement.

24-34
← To p. 168

---

discriminate

24-40

After the child has learned to discriminate between "s" and "th," his correct production of "s" will be differentially reinforced automatically by the * * *.

24-41
← To p. 168

are no	For each _____ that an object within reach may occupy in our field of vision, there corresponds a particular movement of arm and hand which will produce tactual contact with the object.
25-5	25-6

(1) contact (2) position	There are an indefinite number of reaching responses and a corresponding _____ number of possible positions in a continuous field.
25-11	25-12

can	A hunt-and-peck typist must reach for about forty keys on the typewriter. Efficient typing requires at least _____ different discrete responses.
25-17	25-18

indefinite (large)	A line can always be drawn which _____ from another line by as small an amount as we can distinguish.
25-23	25-24

continuous repertoire	The behavior of typewriting requires a(n) _____ _____ .
25-29	25-30

is	With a discrete repertoire, the person * * * able to respond to all points of a continuous stimulus field.
25-35	25-36

Turn book over and invert for start of Set 25

Holland-Skinner

alysis of Behavior

Second half of program; do not start here
until you have completed Sets 1 through 24.